PORTFO

GLOBALIZATION BEFORE ITS TIME

DR CHHAYA GOSWAMI, Honorary University Fellow, University of Exeter, UK, specializes in western Indian Ocean maritime history. She has authored a previous book on Kachchhi traders. Her current research explores maritime trade and piracy in the gulfs of Kachchh and Persia in the eighteenth century. Her book, *The Call of the Sea: Kachchhi Traders in Muscat and Zanzibar c.1800–80* (Orient BlackSwan, 2011) was selected for the Hiralal Gupta Prize by the Indian History Congress as the best book by a woman historian on any period of Indian history.

JAITHIRTH (JERRY) RAO is an author, columnist, banker, IT entrepreneur and the founder of two companies.

GURCHARAN DAS is a world-renowned author, commentator and public intellectual. His bestselling books include *India Unbound*, *The Difficulty of Being Good* and *India Grows at Night*. His other literary works consist of a novel, *A Fine Family*, a book of essays, *The Elephant Paradigm*, and an anthology, *Three Plays*. A graduate of Harvard University, Das was CEO of Procter & Gamble, India, before he took early retirement to become a full-time writer. He lives in Delhi.

THE STORY OF INDIAN BUSINESS
Series Editor: Gurcharan Das

THE STORY OF INDIAN BUSINESS

GLOBALIZATION
BEFORE ITS TIME

*The Gujarati Merchants
from Kachchh*

CHHAYA GOSWAMI

Edited by
Jaithirth Rao

Introduction by
Gurcharan Das

PORTFOLIO
PENGUIN

An imprint of Penguin Random House

PORTFOLIO

USA | Canada | UK | Ireland | Australia
New Zealand | India | South Africa | China

Portfolio is part of the Penguin Random House group of companies
whose addresses can be found at global.penguinrandomhouse.com

Published by Penguin Random House India Pvt. Ltd
7th Floor, Infinity Tower C, DLF Cyber City,
Gurgaon 122 002, Haryana, India

Penguin
Random House
India

First published in Portfolio by Penguin Books India 2016

ISBN 9780143425120

Typeset in Aldine401 BT by Manipal Digital Systems, Manipal
Printed at Repro Knowledgecast Limited, India

www.penguin.co.in

MIX
Paper from
responsible sources
FSC® C047271

CONTENTS

CONTENTS

ACKNOWLEDGEMENTS

This book had its own journey and I just followed it. After a first one on Kachchhi traders in Muscat and Zanzibar, I naively felt that there was little left out on this subject. However, with time, when the understanding of the subject becomes deeper and clearer, it is realized that it is simply difficult to encompass in one volume multifaceted research work such as this, and that is why we get new editions and sequels. In that sense, my second book, I believe, is a combination of being a sequel cum new edition. There were many aspects related to the exclusive business practices of Kachchhis—the system of apprenticeship, the role of the state, the money-spinning commodity trading in textile, pearls, dates, gum copal and arms, the existing material culture and consumption patterns and its impact on the high-value ivory trade, the shipbuilding industry and marine insurance and intricate details on the family firms and their trading partnerships with the Euro-American mercantile firms among others—on which I did not write much in my first book. And thus, the challenge was posed to weave those intriguing aspects together in my second book. This challenge then became the integral part of the journey of writing the new manuscript.

However, this piece of the journey was not undertaken alone. In fact, it was initiated and shaped by Gurcharan Das, who envisioned and nurtured the concept of a business-history series. Once the concept note was designed, Gurcharan Das, on recommendation of Professor Mariam Dossal, made me part of the mega journey of writing 'the story of Indian businesses'. I am deeply indebted to both of them because of whom journeying the Indian Ocean once again became possible. I must not forget to mention that Gurcharan Das, from the beginning, took great interest in my work and his valuable comments and questioning helped me to considerably change the viewpoint of my research work. His faith in the work certainly made the difference. A similar role was played by Professor Lakshmi Subramanian, who provided a crisp perceptive to my subject. She explained to me how to overhaul the entire argument of the work and make it cohesive in nature. I truly appreciate the efforts of all three, and express my heartfelt gratitude to them.

Jerry Rao and Vijay Rao entered the second phase of the journey when my manuscript was ready, but not without the puzzling problem of the word limit. The apt editorial support of Jerry Rao in reducing the size of the manuscript, and his insightful introduction, has truly raised the importance of this book. His son, Vijay Rao also took a keen interest in understanding the nature of my work. I am sincerely thankful to both of them.

I am truly and greatly thankful to the patrons of this journey, i.e. Penguin Random House and especially, to Udayan Mitra for all his help and patience.

My advance research work, from where I had left off, wouldn't have been successfully completed if I would have not received first-hand information and original documents of the Ratanshi Purshottam firm from Muscat-based Vimal Purecha and Professor Allen Calvin. I am truly indebted to them for their unconditional help and support.

Though the reason of the journey was changed, one thing that remained unchanged was my visits to the Maharashtra State Archives and Asiatic Society of Mumbai. The efficient staff of the Archives and Society gave me all the required documents without any impediments.

My understanding of the working conditions of weavers and other artisans, and their equation with the traders and local and global markets, became more comprehensive while working on the European Research Council (ERC) sponsored oral history project. For that, I am grateful to its principal investigator Professor Maxine Berg, University of Warwick. During the course of the project, several field trips and interviews helped broaden my outlook on the subject. It also gave me another opportunity to visit the DnyanGiri Nirmalgiri monastery (math) of the Goswamis. This time around, Darshan Rajeshgiri Goswami helped me get hold of the pictures of the *math*'s documents. I am thankful to him for his warm hospitality and help. From Mandvi I could then go to Mundra, where the descendents of Jairam Shivji and Tulsidas Swaly made available the photos of Jairam Shivji, Ibji Shivji and Laddha Damji. I extend my heartfelt thanks to Tulsidas Swaly family for all their help.

The story of my journey will sound incomplete, if I do not mention my family and their role. When I wrote a book proposal to Orient Black Swan, I had conceived, so the entire writing of the book was coupled with the additional challenge of pregnancy and motherhood. That roller coaster ride gave me as many jolts as possible, and yet, with the grace of God and the unconditional support of my parents and in-laws, I could look after both the baby and the book. At this stage, my nephew, Jugal, too helped me out with his point of view. When I commenced writing the book for Penguin, the early phase of motherhood challenges continued, as did the plights. Imagine the web of time and destiny I was entangled in! It made me resilient in nature, but of course at a great cost. My daughter, Priyal, is that extra dear to me because she is the one who coped with not-so-normal circumstances ever since she was born. Along with her, my husband, Kaushal Bhatt, too made many compromises. Any words will fall short to express my gratitude to both of them and that is why I dedicate this book to both Priyal and Kaushal.

FOREWORD

The first thing to contend with is our general level of ignorance about Kachchh, starting with its spelling— it is Kachchh, not Kutch. One remembers vaguely from school geography texts that there is a Gulf of Kutch. One also remembers that there is something known as the Rann of Kutch, where we clashed with the Pakistanis in 1965. The results of that encounter were a tad less than desirable from the Indian point of view. The region again came into the limelight in a very tragic way in 2001, when a big earthquake ravaged it, and the town of Bhuj was all over the press. From a non-incident perspective, Kachchh gets attention from the glossy wildlife magazines that carry photographs of the flamingo and the wild ass, and from the glossier crafts magazines, which feature lavish pictures of the embroidery and mirror work from the region. And there ends our knowledge of Kachchh.

This book by Chhaya Goswami, herself a Kachchhi, and an academic at Mumbai University, is an attempt to take us down some important, if less-known, bylanes of Indian history and to introduce us to some fascinating vignettes regarding the role of Kachchhi traders and capitalists in the wave of globalization that preceded what we see today. This book focuses on the doings and wanderings of Kachchhi merchants in the eighteenth and nineteenth centuries. It restores balance to several assumptions that many of us have implicitly internalized. It establishes that there was a vibrant, market-based capitalist tradition in remote Kachchh well before Max Weber was even born. It emphasizes that religious or caste traditions among Indian Hindus and Muslims by no means inhibited the development of sophisticated markets and financial systems, including international banking and insurance. In fact, these traditions may have played a constructive role in market development. It also speaks eloquently of the fact that there was little of the classical Ruler-versus-Merchant conflict in India in the past. Mutually beneficial, symbiotic relations did exist. The book categorically demolishes the view that somehow, imperial Mughal decline led to a dark age all over India. It demonstrates that Indians were not always losers or the exploited in their encounters with colonizers, whether with the Portuguese first, with the Dutch later, or with the British finally. In fact, Indian mercantile traditions were robust enough to challenge European interests and seek advantages in the interstices of intra-European competition. The book also throws light on the fact that Hindu–Muslim contradictions did not in any way prevent the growth of trade and prosperity in the Kachchhi community. In fact, intelligent cooperation and sensitive division of labour marked their endeavours.

Let us start with the Kings of Kachchh—or the Raos, as they were known. In Mughal times, a clan of Rajputs—which deserves more attention than it has received—called the Jadejas took control of Kachchh. They had a loose group of feudal followers among the nobles known as Bhayats. The important fact is that the Jadejas figured out very early in their history that revenue from land and agriculture was going to be limited. As a result, they had none of the disdain for trade that we have been told was a Rajput trait. The Jadejas positively encouraged trade. They even participated in it. They understood the importance of a low rate of taxation combined with a predictable tax administration. The Jadejas were almost early believers in the Laffer curve. They were committed to increasing their revenues, not by increasing their rates of duty but by ensuring that the total volume of trade increased. The Jadejas were also acutely aware of the political economy of their fiscal measures. In the nineteenth century, when the Rajputana–Bombay railway started hurting the inland trade in Kachchh, the Raos sharply reduced duties in order to make Kachchhi trade competitive. The Raos were also committed to infrastructure. Some four hundred years ago, the then ruler invited a specialist from Sind (now Sindh) to plan and supervise the construction of Mandvi port, which served the people of his state for several centuries. The state of Kachchh had intelligent commercial laws. One law required that registered brokers should not participate as principals in the same trades or activities where they operated as brokers. The state clearly had a very good understanding of conflict of interest as it went about drafting its laws. The state encouraged commercial institutions like the Mahajan and the Nagarsheth to practise self-regulation and arbitration of disputes without resort to acrimonious lawsuits, while at the same time providing for state officials to adjudicate where appropriate. The rulers of Kachchh did not view merchants as antagonistic agents who should be milked for whatever could be extracted from them. They viewed traders and financiers as collaborators. Most of their diwans and other senior ministers and officials were not just Sanskrit scholars or Rajput kinsmen but reputed merchants themselves.

The caste system or religious identities were not handicaps in the development of the Kachchhi version of modern capitalism. While many prominent traders of Kachchh came from the traditional Bania caste of Bhatias, there were quite a few from the Rajput, peasant and artisan castes, as well as from among the Brahmins too, who in this case went well beyond their traditional caste vocations to embrace trade and finance. The Goswami monks made for an almost unique Kachchhi institution. They had forty monasteries that functioned simultaneously as temples and banks. The main monastery in Mandvi acted literally as a central bank for Kachchhis everywhere. Borrowing the *hundi* from the Multanis, who, according to tradition, were its creators, the merchants of Kachchh were successful innovators since they created *hundi*s embedded with marine insurance. One might be tempted to hazard a guess that they were pioneers of what we today refer to as credit-linked insurance.

Money transfers, bill discounting, long- and short-term credit and foreign-exchange trading were all part of the sophisticated trans-oceanic banking network that the Kachchhis set up. They stood up for the sanctity of the market when they had to. At one time, French currency was illiquid and in low demand, and was trading at a discount in Zanzibar. The French Consul tried to get the Sultan to change this by fiat. The Kachchhis resisted this, and successfully so. They were also active participants in the market in Ujiji in East Africa, where beads (which had acquired the status of quasi-money) of different types were exchanged. Traditional Hindu restrictions were somehow overcome when profitable commerce was at stake. Kachchhi merchants pretty much ignored ritual prohibitions on overseas travel. Some made up for their 'sins' by indulging in extravagant charities. The so-called quasi-Protestant religious movements like Vaishnavism did play their part in the emergence of nascent capitalism, but they cannot be seen as critical, causal factors. Traditional Hindus too had no problems with overseas travel,

and leaving their womenfolk behind in India was
probably one convenient patriarchal solution to satisfy
ritual restrictions. There is no evidence of conflicts
between Kachchhi Hindu merchants and their Muslim
counterparts. The Kachchhi Muslims, who were mainly
Khojas (Ismailis), Bohras and Memons, kept their pre-
conversion caste memories alive and were very much
part of the overall Kachchhi Mahajan. One reason
that these Muslims might not have resented successes
scored by Hindu merchants was simply that Hindus
vacated certain businesses which were then under
Muslim monopoly. Hindu merchants stayed away from
trades that went against their vegetarian traditions, such
as the fish trade, the meat trade, or trade in livestock
or in cowries, which involved the killing of molluscs.
So, one witnesses a coexistence that usually involved
physical separation by way of separate neighbourhoods,
division of some businesses and overall commercial
cooperation. Curiously, Kachchhi Hindus either
ignored the violence behind the ivory trade, which
involved cruelty to elephants, or pretended that ivory
was procured not from elephants that were deliberately
killed for it but from those that had died naturally.
Kachchhis were also pretty much without doubt
financiers—if not active participants—in the slave
trade. The related ethical conundrum has been elided
rather cleverly from the popular community history.
Kachchhi business systems—accounting, record-
keeping, forecasting, inventory management, orderly

tackling of bankruptcies, and training (including the finely tuned apprenticeship) systems—all reveal themselves as precursors of modern systems that we take for granted. Theirs was no incipient capitalism, but rather a fairly well-developed one.

It was providential that the Kachchhi merchants' first halt in their overseas expansion was Oman, which, under Yarriba rule, turned out to be very similar to Kachchh under Jadeja rule. The Sultans of Oman by and large ignored strict Islamic principles. They stood for a level of religious tolerance that was considerably ahead of the times. Kachchhi Hindus were allowed to practise their religion freely, to build and run their temples in Oman, and conduct musical activities that were part of their religious rituals. Omani Sultans, like the Raos of Kachchh, derived very little revenue from agriculture. They understood the importance of trade and the symbiotic mutuality between Kachchhi merchants and themselves. Like the Jadeja Raos, the Yarriba Sultans too, by and large, believed in low and consistent duties and in revenue growth from volumes rather than from high rates. Fortuitously again for the Kachchhis, the Oman–Zanzibar connection developed, and the Kachchhi diaspora moved to that important tropical island, virtually as companions of the Omani Sultans who had moved there. A Kachchhi business infrastructure was very quickly established, and for decades this infrastructure of credit, legal agreements, mortgages, futures contracts and money transfers supported not only Kachchhis, but all the Europeans and Americans who became active in Zanzibar.

The proper chronicling of the romance and vigour of the mercantile cultures and commerce in the Indian Ocean littorals calls for an incarnation of a historian like Braudel. Kachchhis were part of this extraordinary tapestry, whose weaving started in the seventeenth century and went on to the early part of the twentieth century. Due credit must be given to many other communities: the Gujaratis, Arabs, Sindhis, Swahilis, Parsis, Malabaris, Portuguese, Dutch, British, French, Germans and Americans. The Portuguese deserve special mention. In many cases, they were the ones who started it all, and if they did not, they certainly transformed Indian Ocean trade. Their traditional image as religious fanatics harassing peaceful sailors by insisting on payment for the much-hated and much-valued *cartaz* could do with some more mellow appreciation. The history of Indian Ocean commerce is also about the fall and rise of ports—the decline of Surat, the unexpected rise of Mandvi, the inexorable rise of Bombay, the decline of Bandar Abbas, the solid positioning of Muscat and the fortuitous growth of Zanzibar. The extraordinarily contemporary approach of the Sultans of Oman and Zanzibar, who anticipated the needs of free and fair trade and the global nature of markets, reminds one of contemporary Singapore or Dubai. The American involvement in the region in the eighteenth and nineteenth centuries has not received much attention. Luckily, Goswami has done some very interesting research based on original sources and documents that tells us a lot about the Americans, who were the biggest buyers of Omani dates. Goswami has some intriguing material on the attempts at cartelizing the American market for Omani dates. The Americans were also the biggest buyers of east African ivory that was routed through Zanzibar. Till an artificial substitute was developed, ivory was indispensable for making piano keys, and nineteenth-century America had a very fast-growing piano industry. Probably the most important item that the Americans brought to the Indian Ocean was cotton cloth from the mills of New England. This cloth displaced British textiles almost completely. Curiously, the textiles of Kachchh held a reasonable market share throughout. And once modern textile mills came up in India, they began to dominate the market. But for decades prior to the American Civil War, cloth shipped from Salem ruled the roost. It became so ubiquitous that it became a substitute currency in east Africa, where it was known as *merikani*.

Goswami's book has a meandering tone, which lends a certain charming authenticity to the text. No attempt has been made to convert values, whether they are recorded in rupees or in dollars, to contemporary levels. The penumbra of ambiguity invites the reader to make her own assessment—which can be exciting—when dealing with values of exports, imports or customs duties.

The book is in four chapters. The first focuses on Kachchh and its port of Mandvi, in many ways the source of what, over the decades and centuries, became the veritable Ganga of Kachchhi commerce. Shipbuilding, an important Kachchhi activity in the days before the steamship displaced the sailing ship, gets covered in depth, as also the relatively understudied mystique of the Kachchhi trade in horses. The life and times of the inveterate gambler-turned-honest horse trader Sunderji are well-covered, and should hopefully encourage someone to attempt a biography of this lovable, prodigal, merchant prince. Muscat is about three items of trade: pearls, dates and guns. Details of the pearl trade in the age when the Persian Gulf was known not for petroleum but for pearls, make for fascinating reading; as well as how the otherwise lowly *Fard* date attained prominence because Americans liked to have it during the Thanksgiving holidays—a piece of anecdotal history that is not to be missed. The role of Kachchhi financing in pearling expeditions and in date plantations was the thread that held the businesses together. The arms trade of Muscat also has such a contemporary ring to it! For years, the unhappy British kept trying to suppress it, only to find that British manufacturers and even British workers were hell bent on continuing with it. The French gave legal cover to Kachchhi-financed Arab ships by allowing them to fly the French flag, adding to British frustration. And so the story goes on! Zanzibar was first about slaves. Then about ivory. Then about cloves. And lastly, there is a treasure of information about copal, a resin that not many have heard of.

The period covered by the book coincides with the British ban on the slave trade. Perhaps that is why there is not much on this grim commerce in the book. Or perhaps, Kachchhi sources have avoided this subject for reasons that we can guess. The book does cover ivory in detail. A case can be made that in financing ivory caravans, Kachchhis were not lending money against security. There was no boat or plantation pledged as collateral. They were, in fact, behaving like modern venture capitalists. And their risks and returns were both high, just as in the case of a VC of today. The ivory trade had begun the process of the near annihilation of the African elephant. Fortunately, as artificial ivory substitutes came on the market, this trade declined. But while it lasted, ivory dominated Zanzibar and Kachchhi traders controlled the market for it. The cloves of Zanzibar, and later of Pemba, were of course part of the fabled spice trade of antiquity. The Sultans loved and supported clove plantations. Arabs owned the plantations, on which the workers were African slaves and, subsequently, freedmen. Kachchhis financed the plantations and exported cloves around the world. Copal was a resin imported from east Africa and sold by the Kachchhis of Zanzibar to the emerging factories of America and Germany—another instance of globalization long before the word was conceived.

The very landscape of Kachchh highlights adversity. It has no fertile soil, verdant plains or life-giving rivers. But the silver lining was its long coastline and some wonderful harbours. The sea became the life-giving river of Kachchh, nourishing its trade, and invigorating its people. The fact that Kachchh was not part of British India but a semi-independent princely state meant that lucrative opportunities like the China trade were not available. By accident or by intent, Oman, a nondescript, independent sultanate in the Persian Gulf becomes the second silver lining. Oman becomes an extension of Kachchh, and Muscat an extension of Mandvi. The Omanis, again, more or less by serendipity, become rulers of Zanzibar, and the Kachchhis tag along. The disincentives of access and taxation in the face of the colossal edifice of the British Raj were just too many. Instead of trying to beat them, why not join them? So the Kachchhi diaspora, including its baggage of monks and monasteries, moves to Bombay, the commercial capital of British India. The conversion of adversity to opportunity is a repetitive theme in the history of the Kachchhis. And all along, their responses to their challenges and opportunities are characterized by the extraordinary sophistication of their systems and processes and a level of pragmatism that gives them the Midas touch converting ships, horses, pearls, dates, guns, ivory, cloves, copal and even the humble sesame seed into quantities of gold, or more appropriately, paper gold buried in the accounting entries of the Bhatias and Goswami monasteries. The story of Kachchhi capitalism and its impact on early globalization trends, despite some warts, is on balance one that is worthy of celebration.

Jaithirth Rao   March 2015
                                                    Mumbai

INTRODUCTION

When no one was looking, the maritime entrepreneurs of Kachchh quietly linked three great masses of land—India, Arabia and Africa—in a 'golden triangle' of trade during the dying days of the Mughal Empire. The business flourished over the next two hundred years, over the eighteenth and nineteenth centuries, on the high seas of the Arabian Sea, almost unnoticed by the colonial powers. How did this happen? Like a good detective, Chhaya Goswami investigates this mystery in the eighth volume of Penguin's *Story of Indian Business*. The book grew out of her innovative PhD thesis for Bombay University. It was the notable Jaithirth Rao who helped her breathe life into her tale, as only a talented and generous editor can. What we have as a result is an exciting, untold story, and a fine example of what makes this history series special. Instead of going over that story, I shall provide here some background, situating Goswami's tale in the broad historical context of maritime trade in the Indian Ocean.

The conditions for the phenomenal success of the Kachchhis in the Arabian Sea are universal: shipbuilding and navigational techniques; the ability to exploit patterns of wind, ocean currents and the stars above; entrepreneurs who know how to grow capital, seek markets, and, where they don't exist, create them; an appetite for negotiating the risks of long-distance voyages in primitive ships with utter lack of information and communications; and most importantly, business-friendly rulers of port cities who understood the power of trade to create a prosperous citizenry and a tax base, and who gave their citizens economic freedom, which encouraged them to risk their hard-earned capital and make something of their lives. The Kachchhis had these in plenty; plus, they had the 'Gujarat advantage'.

The Gujarat Advantage

On the western flank of the Indian subcontinent is the state of Gujarat, which for millennia has been busy creating precisely these conditions and continues to do so even today in the twenty-first century. With a long coastline extending from the Gulf of Kachchh (Kutch) to the Gulf of Khambat (Cambay), it has forty-six small ports and one larger one at Kandla, which together contribute almost half of India's shipping volume today. Right down history, the ports have tended to shift geographically because of the silting mouths of rivers and changes in inland supply routes. The most dramatic of these changes was the disappearance of the great port at Broach, which in ancient times connected maritime merchants to the great food and textile producing areas of north India and further through the 'silk road' to central Asia. Almost as spectacular was the decline and fall of the great Mughal port of Surat. This book is concerned, however, with the rise and fall of another forgotten port, Mandvi, situated near the mouth of the Gulf of Kachchh—the latter a word that literally means 'intermittently wet and dry'. The Gulf of Kachchh gets its name from the shallow wetland known as the Rann of Kachchh that is submerged in water during the monsoons but is dry the rest of the year.

Cambay in Gujarat was undoubtedly the greatest commercial city on the western coast of India when Europeans discovered the Indian Ocean. Tome Pires, an apothecary who accompanied the founders of the Portuguese *Estado da India,* wrote that the merchants of Gujarat were exceptionally skilled in business and that the people of Cambay excelled in minimizing transaction costs. He also felt that Gujaratis were better navigators and seamen than others, which is why Vasco da Gama employed a Gujarati pilot on his first voyage to 'discover' India.

Fifteen hundred years earlier, *Periplus of the Erythraean Sea,* a first-century text of the Greco-Roman period, describes 'fully manned long ships' from Gujarat, called *trappaga* and *kotumba,* similar to the modern two-masted *kotia* that competitors referred to as 'oceanic tramps of Indian craft'. Gujarati sailors had also understood early on the cycles of the Indian monsoon, which delivered the basic rhythms of long-distance voyages across the Indian Ocean. These winds broke the limitations of travel for merchants and sailors, giving regular and swift passage across great distances of the Indian Ocean, which separated east Africa, the Middle East, south Asia and further, South East Asia. The monsoon cycles were seasonal, and this imposed a tyranny of time, setting sailing seasons, imposing months of dormancy at ports and dictating timetables for the movement of commodities. Eventually, the steam engine broke this tyranny, but until its advent, voyages, business decisions and customs collections were a function of the rhythms of the monsoons.

The irony is that the land-focused kings and emperors of Hindustan were almost oblivious of these advantages. Deriving their main income from agriculture, they regarded the sea as only worthy of sightseeing and picnics. The fourth Mughal emperor Jahangir (1605–27) displayed this aristocratic attitude towards the sea when he happened to visit his maritime province of Gujarat. He had visited to hunt wild elephants and 'look on the salt sea', he said. He enjoyed watching the rising and ebbing of tides as well as getting on a Portuguese ship in the port of Cambay.

Benign neglect by the politically powerful might have been a good thing for Kachchh. It left governance in the hands of local rulers such as the enlightened

Jadejas, who actively encouraged trade in order to bolster their tax base. Gujarat and other coastal provinces of India managed to have mostly business-friendly local powers. The Rajput Jadejas were exceptional even in this class, as Goswami explains in her book. They had a 'modern' port constructed at Mandvi, which served international trade for several centuries. They made good rules, kept taxes low, and encouraged self-regulation and arbitration through the Mahajans and Nagarsheths in order to resolve commercial disputes quickly. Good rules attract good traders, who in turn insist on better rules.

Pre-modern Free Trade in the Indian Ocean

The merchants of Kachchh in Goswami's story were building upon a rich legacy of vigorous free trade in pre-modern times between the ports of Gujarat, the Malabar coast, the Middle East, and South East Asia. Down the centuries from ancient times, the Indian Ocean has been a centre of global-maritime trade, linking the world of the Mediterranean in the west to the South China Sea in the east. The Indian Ocean trading region extended from the west coast of Africa to South East Asia, comprising a myriad communities, religions and cultures.

The ports on the east and the west coasts of India were strategically located about halfway down the stretch of this trading region. As a result, they became entrepôts of commercial exchange as merchant ships from the west rarely sailed beyond the Bay of Bengal while ships from the east, especially from China, did not venture further west than the ports of Kerala. Goods from the west were unloaded here and re-exported to the Far East; in the same way, goods from China were dropped here for delivery to the west. With this vigorous trade, the bazaars of Asia were laden with Indian textiles, Indonesian spices and Chinese silks and porcelains.

At these entrepôts there was, more or less, a separation of market and state; tariffs were modest and there were legal structures to adjudicate trade disputes. Local rulers were generally tolerant. Most pre-modern rulers may not have appreciated the wealth-creating function of these traders, but they instinctively valued their ready cash in financing their own unending military adventures. Ill-paid, mutinous soldiers were a constant threat to their power, and they were happy to grant the most powerful merchants special privileges in exchange for cash.

The pattern of monsoon winds, as noted, imposed limitations on voyages. Merchants and sailors had to spend long periods residing in foreign ports until the winds changed. Coastal towns thus acquired a cosmopolitan flavour where Jews, Nestorian Christians, Arabs, Persians and Hindus acquired their own distinct quarters. Gradually, they became immigrant communities, living in enclaves in different ports. Cultural diffusion was the result. This is in evidence today in the strong presence of Islam on the southwest coasts of India and Indonesia; the Chinese communities in the ports of South East Asia; the Hindu temples of Angkor in Cambodia; the popularity of the epics Ramayana and Mahabharata in Indonesia; the pervasiveness of Sanskrit names right across South East Asia; and the attraction to Buddhism in the Asian continent.

A Violent Mercantile Age Replaces the Free Trade Era

The coming of an Arab-Islamic empire, extending from the Atlantic to the Arabian Sea in the seventh and eighth centuries, and a parallel rise of the reinvigorated Chinese empire stretching from central Asia to the Pacific under the T'ang and Song dynasties (619–1279), added further dynamism to the Indian Ocean trade. However, they did not change the free character of trade in the Indian Ocean. By 1550, the southern part of the Indian Ocean carried more trade than did the north Atlantic, as Razeen Sally points out in a fine essay, 'Economic Freedom and the Asian Century'.

The Europeans had for long lusted after the riches of the Indies, and were envious of Asia's free trade. Their own great voyages of discovery to the Americas had given them experience of seaborne travel and a new confidence. The first initiative came from the

Portuguese, who barged into Asia on large ocean-going ships carrying guns. Suddenly, the free trade of an earlier era was under threat from an aggressive new mantra 'in search of Christians and spices'. Trade was now accompanied by violence and plunder. The Dutch and the British followed the Portuguese. By 1700, the Europeans had triumphed. Their brutal, nationalistic trading model now ruled the world's seas. They had dealt a mortal blow to Muslim supremacy in the western Indian Ocean and woken up the slumbering giants of India and China, says Sally.

Colonial expansion ended the pre-modern system of free trade in the Indian Ocean. The Europeans sought monopoly control of the seas and the coastal entrepôts. They imposed mercantilism, which became the ruling ideology of nationalistic European nation-states from the sixteenth to the eighteenth century. Mercantilism promoted state power by economic means, and governments began to intervene vigorously in their economies. They placed high-tariff barriers on foreign goods, subsidized exports, created overseas colonies, forbade the colonies to trade with other nations, banned exports of gold and silver even for payments, and even insisted that trade be carried on their own ships. Thus, free trade in the Indian Ocean came to an end.

It was only in the second half of the nineteenth century when Britain had become the preeminent world power that the destructive mercantilist restrictions lifted. With that, multilateral commerce began to flourish once again. Chinese and Indian diasporas fanned out across the British Empire, creating new trading networks. Alas, this brief liberal period came to an end very soon with World War I. Mercantilist ideology ruled during the years between the wars. Relatively freer trade and sanity only returned to the world after World War II.

The Story of Indian Business

We are accustomed to approaching history by looking at political maps that are divided into land-based nation-states. There is an alternative history, however, where the action took place on the high seas and in cities that faced the sea. The story of Kachchhi merchants is one such story. There are other stories that have engaged the authors of our unique, multi-volume history of Indian business. The series as a whole is attempting to mine great ideas in business and economics that have shaped commerce in the bazaars of the Indian subcontinent as well as on the high seas of the Indian Ocean.

Leading contemporary scholars closely examine historical texts, inscriptions and records, and interpret them in a lively, sharp and authoritative manner for the intelligent reader, who may have no prior background in the field. Each slender volume offers an enduring perspective on business enterprise in the past, avoiding the pitfall of simplistic cataloguing of a set of lessons for today. The value of the exercise is to promote a longer-term sensibility in the reader in order that he or she understands the material bases of our present human condition, and is able to think sensibly about our economic future. Taken together, the series celebrates the ideal captured in the Sanskrit word *artha*.

The series began with Tom Trautmann's interpretation for our times of the renowned treatise on the science of wealth, *Arthashastra*, which was authored almost 2000 years ago and is considered the world's first manual in political economy. Kanakalatha Mukund took us south in the next volume, *Merchants of Tamilakam*, to a beguiling world when at least one ship from Rome used to touch a port of south India daily. Mukund has reconstructed this world by drawing on the epics *Silappadikaram*, *Manimekalai* and other historical materials pertaining to the period up to the end of the Chola empire. Next, we jumped centuries to Tirthankar Roy's radiant account of the East India Company, which taught us, among other things, how much the modern multinational corporation is a child of a company that is reviled even today in India.

Our fourth volume hopped to the late eighteenth century during the time of decline of the port of Surat and the rise of Bombay. In the book *Three Merchants of Bombay*, Lakshmi Subramanian recounted vividly the ups and downs in the adventurous lives of Trawadi Arjunji Nathji, Jamsetjee Jeejeebhoy and Premchand Roychand. Arshia Sattar narrated in the fifth volume *The Mouse Merchant* some brilliant adventures and tales based on *Kathasaritsagara,* the *Panchatantra* and other sources. In the next volume, Tom Timberg's *Marwaris* revisited the bold, risk-taking world of India's most famous business community, quickly becoming a bestseller. In the seventh volume, Scott Levi took us back to the early modern period and recounted the saga of Punjabi khatri traders from Multan who took caravans on the 'silk road', across the Himalayas to central Asia and beyond, to Russia, from 1500 to 1850. This volume by Chayya Goswami on another business community, the Kachchhis, is the eighth in our series.

In the future lies a veritable feast. Three more books will cover the ancient and early medieval periods: Gregory Schopen will present the *Business Model of Early Buddhist Monasticism* based on the *Mulasarvastivada Vinaya.* Donald Davis will raise contemporary issues in the area of commercial and business law, based on medieval commentaries by authors such as Vacaspati Mishra and Chandeshvara on the voluminous Dharmasastras. The celebrated Sanjay Subrahmanyam and Muzaffar Alam will transport us into the world of sultans, shopkeepers and portfolio capitalists in Mughal India. Omkar Goswami will describe a new organizational structure—the managing agency— which came into existence with British private traders at the death of the East India Company; Bibek Debroy will narrate the exciting story of the building of railways in nineteenth- and twentieth-century India; Raman Mahadevan will describe the Nattukottai Chettiars' search for fortune, and his work will be followed by volumes on the Parsis and the Sindhis. Finally, Medha Kudaisiya will round out the series, recording a story of betrayal in the historic 'Bombay Plan' drawn by eminent industrialists in 1944–45, on the future shape of independent India's economy.

Gurcharan Das

I

KACHCHH: LAND OF ENTREPRENEURS

The tongue-land of Kachchh is distinctively marked by its natural boundaries on all our maps.

The Polity and Trade

The early modern history of Kachchh begins with the establishment of a centralized administration by the Jadeja dynasty in the mid-sixteenth century. In contemporary terms, the Jadejas can be described as pro-trade, pro-entrepreneur. The durbar (court/state) recognized that revenues from agriculture, which were significant in other parts of India, would never amount to much in Kachchh. Active promotion of trade, ports and shipbuilding became an obsession with the rulers.

Rao Khengarji I (1548) accepted the suzerainty of the Mughals and obtained peace on the landward side. He could now devote himself to exploiting the advantages of the long coastline of his kingdom. He invited the talented Topan Sheth of Nagar Thatta in Sindh to move to Kachchh and supervise the design and construction of the port at Mandvi. Khengarji's achievements were so considerable that a hundred years later, in the seventeenth century, his descendant Bharmalji I remained a beneficiary of Mandvi port and its revenues. The popular adage *Khatyo Kehngar Ane Bhogvayo Bhare* captured the fact that what was earned by Khengarji was used by Bharmalji I. Bharmalji turned out to be more than a passive inheritor. He spotted the immense potential associated with the Hajj pilgrims' need to make a sea voyage to Mecca from India. Bharmalji facilitated the shipping service from Mandvi. Being under obligation to Bharmalji, the Mughal emperor Jahangir exempted Kachchh from its tribute, thus further contributing to the state's financial well-being. Under Bharmalji, encouragement of trade became a state policy. Economic progress was the hallmark of Kachchh during the reign of Maharao Desalji I (1719–52). State revenues increased considerably after 1720. The proverbial Rajput disdain for trade did not apply to the Jadeja Rajputs of Kachchh. Sometimes, they—and even their officials—participated in trade themselves. As Professor Barendse says, 'Their to be sure rudimentary bureaucracy also did so.' The rulers of

Kachchh also co-opted prominent financiers into their durbar. Rao Desalji entrusted the control of the state's finances to a prominent financier, Devkaran Sheth of the Lohana caste. Under Devkaran's prudent management, the revenues of Kachchh were said to have amounted to nearly Rs 2 million grossly. Devkaran himself is reputed to have earned Rs 1 million for himself. The partnership between Devkaran and Desalji paid off handsomely for the state. Devkaran had built a fort called Kachchhigarh in Okhamandal, specifically in order to protect trading activities there. Devkaran also helped the Jadejas in 1730, when they rebuffed an attempt by the Subedar of Gujarat to subjugate them. The rather vague tributary status of Bhuj, the capital of Kachchh, within the Mughal Empire, was converted to one of almost complete autonomy. The alliance between the Rajput kings and the trading and financing castes was the foundation of the prosperity of the state. The diwan of the state was usually an important merchant.

The king was willing to grant powers to the diwan, not only to collect revenues, but also in some military matters. Apart from Devkaran Sheth, the merchants Askaran Sheth and Hansraj Shah also became diwans. The members of the Bania caste and those of the Nagar Brahmins too, who engaged in trade, were known for their wealth, and significantly for their proximity to the royal court. The Dutch VOC recorded, '. . . there are many who are very rich and who commonly reside at the court of the Maharaja and the princes.'

Rao Desalji was deposed by his son Lakho—or Lakha, or Lakhpatji. Under Lakhpatji, contacts with Dutch traders blossomed. The prosaic Dutch regarded Lakhpatji as 'quite civilized'. They went on to add: 'He often wears European dress and is a lover of all kinds of art, also of shipbuilding and of gifts which have however to be out of the ordinary for he has no interest in trifles.' The growing Dutch presence in Kachchh and Kathiawar is evident from local narratives about how Ramsinghji Malam, a sailor who faced a shipwreck, was saved by a Dutch ship, which took him to the Netherlands. During his stay of eighteen years in the Netherlands, he learnt the art of tile-making, glass-blowing, clock-making, and basic foundry-techniques. Back home, under the patronage of Rao Lakhpatji, Ramsinghji introduced European skills in Kachchh and established *karkhanas* (plants), acquired a glass factory near Mandvi and a tile factory turning out imitation Dutch *Delftsblauw*—perhaps partly intended for export to east Africa. Ramsinghji, along with his team of apprentices, visited the Mestre glassworks and workshops in Venice. Seemingly impressed and influenced by the industrial revolution of Europe, Ramsinghji endeavoured to introduce many different factories based on Dutch models and techniques. Ramsinghji also designed a sumptuous palace of mirrors for the king. The Dutch, on their part, were clearly impressed by Kachchh. Kroonenberg, a Dutch officer, wrote that Mandvi was a place of 'no minor trade'. The importance of Mandvi is confirmed by an analysis of the Portuguese *cartazes* handed out in Diu. Mandvi accounted for up to a third of all ships departing from Kathiawar. The adage was that 'the flags of eighty-four countries fluttered in Mandvi port'. The Portuguese ports '*Registro das Caratazes de State*' refers to Rao Lakhpatji as a '*mercador de Mandoi*'. Johannes Peacock, a Dutch officer, specifically stated that Lakhpatji had a particular interest in shipbuilding. Like many successful princes, Lakhpatji was a patron of the arts and education. He encouraged the opening of a school in Bhuj for study of *Vrij Bhasa*. He was interested in music and wrote several treaties on it. And, as if to underscore the burgeoning prosperity of his kingdom, Rao Lakhpatji was the first Rao ever to issue gold coins in the state of Kachchh. But the very success of commerce and manufacturing in his reign seem to have resulted in excesses. The *Kachchh Gazetteer* notes that the *durbar* began to lose its efficacy. Lakhpatji frequently changed his ministers and there was rampant extortion of money to fill up the coffers; tyrannical actions were followed by revolt and violence. The increasing state revenues were rapidly squandered, partly to fund industrialization and partly to fund the extravagant life of the Rao.

Rao Godji II, the next ruler, combined autocratic policies with support for commerce. He was often quarrelling with his feudal kinsmen, the Bhayats. He also precipitated an invasion by the Sindhis, resulting in a wasteful war (1762). The mercantile side of

Godji's personality asserted itself in his keen interest in shipbuilding. Being influenced by Dutch techniques, Rao Godji erected a model of a Dutch factory. This was meant to help merchants and seamen. Regrettably, it was destroyed in the earthquake of 1864. Mandvi port benefited greatly during the period when Surat went into gradual decline and Bombay had yet to gain complete ascendancy. Many migrant Surat shipwrights, who had learnt advanced skills from the Dutch and the English, relocated to Kachchh. The autocratic Godji, despite several missteps, had managed to keep in balance his feudal aristocracy, the Bhayats, and his mercantile interests. With his death, disintegration set in. Multiple fiefs under different Bhayats gained in strength as fragmentation set in. In 1803, David Seton saw the state studded with military fortresses—sixty-six in number, collectively called *Chahset Killah*—maintained by the Bhayats for their defence. Pragmalji I's coming to power (1667–1715) seems to have upset the allegiance that kept the Bhayats and fief-holders loyal to the durbar. His efforts to buy favours left Kachchh in a shaky state. Luckily, Rao Godji I (1715–1718) quickly resumed certain crown grants to heal the ruptures created by Pragmalji's politics of favour. The stability of Kachchh depended on the maintenance of a delicate balance between the ruler (Rao) and the Bhayat aristocracy. This balance got disturbed in 1778 during the reign of Rao Raidhanji. Raidhanji's dominion had fallen into anarchy, and his own authority sunk into contempt, in part due to 'his own reputed insanity'. Rao Raidhanji converted to Islam. He is alleged to have resorted to violent means to seek the conversion of his largely Hindu subjects to Islam. He was framed as 'insane' and imprisoned twice by his political associates. This caused a lot of confusion, with the Jadeja chieftains of the Rao's own lineage as well as other Bhayats assuming independence to varying degrees. The Rao's nominal authority was taken over by two rival chiefs. The first was Fateh Mohamed, a Muslim, whose influence was most extensive in Bhuj. The second was Hansraj Shah, a Hindu Vania merchant, who remained in possession of the principal port of Mandvi. A disputed succession to the estate of a rich Shroff who died at Mandvi was the reason for the first quarrel between Fateh Mohammed and Hansraj. Pretending that he needed funds for a war with Sindh, Fateh Mohammed demanded from Hansraj substantial arrears of revenue. The dispute, though apparently economic in nature, was political too. At one point, Hansraj and his compatriot Sunderji Shivji wished to aid two battalions of soldiers with guns, ammunition and stores for the professed purpose of overcoming what was represented to be the rebellious conduct of Fateh Mohammed. The attempt was expected to lead to restoration of the authority of the Rao's government. Some Jadeja Bhayats stayed neutral and remained in their forts; others served contending parties for money. These chiefs, apparently, did not wish to incur the wrath of either of the rival parties. Fateh Mohammed was opposed to the British East India Company. He encouraged Tipu to be active in Kachchh. Hansraj invited the British to intervene. Kachchh was lucky not to be annexed outright by the British. But it could not avoid an imposed treaty in 1809. After the death of Rao Raidhanji (1813) and under the new Rao, a new treaty came into effect in 1816. Things did improve, but not in the way the people of Kachchh had expected them to. To consolidate and centralize power, Rao Bharmalji II began to reduce Bhayati privileges, and seized the villages of some of the leading Bhayats. The British did not mind this development, but what they did mind was Bharmalji's desire for independence. Having tasted autonomy and power during the chaotic reign of Raidhanji, several prominent Jadeja nobles asked for protection against the Rao. Grabbing this inviting opportunity, the British invaded Kachchh in 1819 and quickly deposed Bharmalji to settle the matter in such a way that their influence in Kachchh remained dominant and unchallenged. The Bhayats secured vital positions in the complex structure of Kachchh's polity by gaining land and land rights by 'British Guarantee' through the treaty of 1819. This arrangement left the ruler a mere figurehead. Kachchh faced difficulties, as many Bhayats were not concerned about the progress of their *giras*. They seemed to be constantly searching for a pretext to fight with their neighbouring *giras*. The Rao's rule over the entire province was at best nominal, as a considerable portion of the territory and one half of the revenues were alienated from him, benefiting other Jadeja chiefs. Some of these chiefs, who were collectively known as the Bhayat—or kinsmen of the Rao—had almost independent jurisdiction, and the question of their relations with each other and with the head of the state gave rise to many complications throughout the nineteenth century. Kachchh, unofficially divided between the Rao and the Bhayats, could not live up to its full mercantile potential.

The political crisis was aggravated by a series of natural disasters—the plague, epidemics, locust attacks, and failed rains. The stability and prosperity of Kachchh, based on two-and-a-half centuries of central rule, were under assault. But the turbulent times did not completely impede trade, and their effects were mixed. Many military outposts were established in the Gulf of Kachchh by the state to provide protection to traders and common men. Among them, the military depot at Mandvi earned the highest income. The fort at Okhamandal (in the northern extremity of Kathiawar), Kachchhigadh, was reinforced time and again for the protection of traders in the Gulf of Kachchh. In eastern Kachchh, the energetic Fateh Mohammed built the fort of Fatehgadh. This encouraged many traders to settle there. Though Fateh Mohammed had endeavoured to protect the traders, he was not able to win the hearts of the Mandvi merchants, who feared his aggression and were scared of him as he had extorted money from Ashkaran

Sheth in order to build Tuna port. However, he was praised by his contemporaries and was able to secure a high, if controversial, place in the history of Kachchh. In tough times, we see that both Fateh Mohammed and Hansraj tried to provide protection to traders. This is evident from the fact that when Hansraj controlled Bhuj (c.1802), he frequently visited Mandvi. Hansraj's prime interest always remained in protecting Mandvi's seaborne trade, and for that purpose he fortified the castle at Narayan Sarovar facing the Arabian Sea. Most of his forces were engaged in providing protection to the Mandvi trade. Hansraj's political interests were quite secondary. His energies were mainly invested in the expansion of trade. As a result, he was better regarded in the trading world than was Fateh Mohammed.

The mixed fallout of the 'turbulent times' included the migration of many Kachchhi merchants to Bombay, Muscat and Zanzibar. But Mandvi was never completely abandoned, and its merchants continued to do business in the existing markets. This is evident through the ever-increasing customs income of the state. Kachchh trade assumed a dual character. The first axis revolved around Mandvi and Bombay. The second axis covered overland trade from Mandvi to Gujarat, Rajputana and Sindh. Once again, Kachchh lived up to its reputation of resilience in quickly reviving trade even while recovering from natural and man-made calamities, as it had in the preceding century after the dreadful war of Jhara's against Sindh (1762). When Punja Sheth,

Son of Devkaran Sheth, did not get the Diwan's post, he went over to the Sindh ruler and instigated him to invade Kachchh. Consequently, Ghulam Shah Kalhora invaded Kachchh in 1762. This war is known as the war of Jhara, which was too violent in nature.

The Mercantile Communities and the Mahajan

Amongst the mercantile communities, the noteworthy were the Hindu Bhatias, the Shaivaite Goswamis, the Bhanushalis and Lohanas, and the Muslim Khojas, Bohras and Memons. Rigid, text-based occupational distinctions did not bother the Hindu traders of Kachchh. Technically, the Bhatias, Goswamis and Lohanas were not trading castes. The Bhatias claimed a Rajput origin. The Lohanas claimed to be of Kshatriya Raghuvansh origin. Before taking to trade, they were primarily involved in agriculture. They held an ambiguous position in society, being considered neither a high nor low caste. The Bhanushalis, who claimed Suryvanshi descent, were engaged in agriculture before they shifted to trading. The Goswamis were temple priests who were Shiva worshippers. They too moved into trading quite easily.

Most of the Muslim traders were Hindus of different castes who had converted to Islam. The Memons were said to have been Lohanas, the Khojas believed to have been Lohanas or Bhatias before conversion, and the Bohras Brahmin converts to

Islam. The process of conversion was probably initiated in Sindh c.958, when an Ismaili principality was established. Multan became the nodal point where many Hindus were converted and brought into the Ismaili fold. When Ismaili rule ended in Sindh in 1005, the sect continued to flourish under the protective rule of the Sumras. From Sindh, the sect filtered down to other adjacent regions of Gujarat, especially in 1067 when missionaries from Yemen founded a new Ismaili community. Large-scale conversions happened in the thirteenth and fourteenth centuries. The converts retained the mercantile and trading traditions of the Hindu castes to which they had originally belonged.

The merchants of Kachchh acquired a reputation for honesty and integrity. The admiration of eighteenth-century Dutch officials extended to the Banias, Bhanushalis and Nagar Brahmins of Kachchh. 'They were incredibly honourable and kept their word, whatever happens. If goods are weighed there (Mandvi), the custom-official will chalk the weight on the bag; and even three years later the merchant will accept these and will not require them to be weighed again,' remarks Professor Barendse, in his seminal study on the Arabian Sea. He further elaborates: 'The Rajput code of honour in which the Kathiawari merchants were raised, gave the capitalists of Kathiawar unbeatable advantages over the competitors with which Armenians could vie.'

The Bhatias of Kachchh, who claimed Rajput descent, were known for their adventurous voyages.

According to General Cunningham, the term Bhatia comes from *Bhat,* a warrior. A poetic narrative, written by Kulgor Jassabhatt, encapsulates the history of the eighty-four endogamous divisions of the Bhatias. In Kachchh, the Bhatia community was influential in Mandvi and Mundra. They participated in the Gulf and east African trade. They were recognized as significant commodity traders. But they had strong positions in the money markets too. Over the centuries, scattered settlements of Bhatias grew in places far from Kachchh—in places like Bombay, Muscat and Zanzibar. They were particular about retaining their common identity, which was reflected in their dietary habits, dressing style, the dialect they spoke and the profession they followed. In their settled territories, the community had reconsolidated and had started expanding within a few generations. Most businessmen in Mandvi and Mundra were Vaishnavas. Vaishnavism was a manifestation of Hinduism that was originally probably a protest movement against the narrowness and exclusiveness of Brahminism. Vaishnavism introduced new gods not associated with the Vedas, and emphasized an exuberant affirmation of life and good works rather than escapist asceticism. Vaishnavas maintained a hereditary priesthood. The appeal of Vaishnavism was limited to a small number of devoted adherents, largely merchants and town dwellers. As these merchants interacted with many groups for trading purposes, they were less rigid about traditional Hindu social taboos. Their growing affluence fostered in them a desire to emulate the elite and ultimately be part of it. Merchants who strove to become more socially mobile sometimes found themselves blocked by the caste system. Being restless, they often preferred to follow new religious movements or sects that conferred upon them greater social value. They frequently opted for Jainism or Vaishnavism. These movements were compatible with mercantile needs and traditions. Vaishnavism had a preference for lay followers and did not favour monasticism. Vaishnavas spent lavishly on rituals in honour of Vishnu (Krishna). This provided them justification for seeking wealth, in order that they may pamper their Lord. This sect favoured the rational pursuit of economic gain and gave worldly activities a positive spiritual and moral meaning. Nathdwara Vaishnavism, like Buddhism and Jainism, was influenced by the heavy representation of merchants among its supporters. The egalitarian nature of Vaishnavism, which bypassed the compartmentalized caste system, supported market relations.

While religious movements like Vaishnavism did help propel many successful merchant groups, the aspiring merchant was able to succeed under the so-called traditional Hindu system as well. Communities like the Lohanas and Bhanushalis, as well as the Goswamis who adhered to traditional Brahmanical ways, were extremely successful in trade and commerce.

The Shaivaite Atit Gosains, or Goswamis, carved out an impressive position in the trading and banking world of Kachchh. Their *maths* (monasteries) emerged as more than merely important religious centres. In Kachchh, they became significant commercial and financial centres as well. Goswamis, according to Sampat, had migrated from Marwar to Kachchh. The Goswamis settled all over Kachchh, wherever there was a Shiva temple, where they served as priests. Monasteries were sometimes attached to these temples. By the end of the eighteenth century, most of the monasteries had turned into banks too. Each *math* had a chief (mahant). The mahant and his nominated successors were unmarried men. James Tod observed that a Gosain, in his orange-coloured robe, looked 'half priest and half merchant, a blend of Hindu "Banian".' He saw that they were wealthy and that they united commerce and religion. The monasteries acted as banks and managed and issued credit notes through the medium of *hundi*s.

Muslim Khojas were another group of successful merchants. The very name Khoja, or *Khwajah*, meant a rich and respectable gentleman, an opulent merchant. Under the Aga Khani and the Ithanasheri sects, Khojas emerged as a complex organization dedicated to mutual services. Khojas were members of their *jamatkhana*. *Jamat* stands for the Arabic *jamna'a*, i.e. a community or congregation; *Jamati* means pertaining to the *jamat*; *jamatkhana* means the *jamat's* place of worship. Khojas tended to remain within the well-knit structure of the *jamat* to protect their identity. Most Bohras, like Khojas, belonged to the Shia sect of Islam. The popular etymology derives the word from *vyawahar*, i.e. to trade, transact or deal. Another explanation goes that the word Bohra, also spelled Bohara or Vohra, is derived from the Gujarati word *vohorvu* meaning 'trade' and records the occupation of the first converters to Islam. The head of the Bohra community is the *Da'i Mutlaq*, who is regarded as the highest socio-religious authority of the Bohras. The five divisions of the Bohras are Daudi, Alia, Jaffari, Nagoshi and Sulaimani. Daudi Bohras form the majority. They were, and remain, a rich, well-organized and widely spread group of Gujarati Muslims, who developed deep interests in trade in hardware, silk, hide, horns and live cattle. Bohras, like the Khojas, were protective of their privacy and their identity. The Memons, who trace their roots largely to Sindh, Kachchh and Kathiawar, are primarily a mercantile community. They are known as *maumins* or believers. The word *maumin* was distorted to Memon. Kachchhi Memons migrated from Sindh to Kachchh after their conversion to Islam in 1422. Both Kachchhi and the Halari Memons flourished in business. Memons are mainly Sunni Muslims. They patronized specific shrines. The Shia groups had distinct clerical power structures and legal frameworks.

The common people of Kachchh collectively revered Hindu saints as well as Muslim pirs. The ideologies and practices of both religions were often peculiarly mixed. Both Hindu and Muslim merchants practised similar rituals before a voyage in order to acquire *barakat* (profusion). Vardhrajan writes that their rituals are intimately connected with their professional life, and that all the communities would gather together to participate as a group in public celebrations. Festivals and fairs were characterized by cross-community involvement. A blend of religious pluralism was a feature of Kachchhi culture. Lohanas, for instance, have imbibed the collective values of different Hindu traditions—Brahminical, Vaishnava, Dariyalal and those derived from the saint Jalaram Bapu.

The conglomerate of merchants, i.e. the *vepari* Mahajan, protected the collective interests of member merchants. It was considered to be prestigious to be part of the Mahajan. According to Professor Omprakash, the Mahajan seems to have exercised authority over its members, including the right to tax them in order to run an organization like the *panjrapole,* designed to aid animal protection. Such professional institutions as the Mahajan had their existence in Gujarat during the Mughal period and in Marwar during the eighteenth century.

Other than the wider *vepari* Mahajan, each caste had its Mahajan to administer caste affairs. The *vepari* Mahajan served as an informal link between the merchants and the state. They were approached both by merchants and by the royal authorities to resolve disputes. The Mahajans also sometimes acted as a religious pressure group. The dominant Hindu traders affiliated to the

Mahajan managed to forbid the consumption of meat by the Muslim population in the town of Mandvi. Alexander Burnes, a British official, was amused as he remarked, 'To even eat an egg is a crime'. The most striking effect of the Mahajans' influence on the state was the inclusion of a clause in the treaties of 1809 and 1819, which forbade animal slaughter in Mandvi. Pressure from the Mahajans sometimes served to deter trade in commodities that were considered ritually impure. For instance, trade in cowries and bullocks was forbidden among the community. The Mahajans were called upon to adjudicate commercial disputes among its members. Disputes usually involved interest payments, breach of contract, marine insurance claims and counter claims, bankruptcy and various other property matters. Enforceability of the decisions made by the panel was purely based on the reputation and mutual recognition of the jury's judicial powers. The conventional codes of the Mahajan managed to pressure the state effectively. One such example related to the issue of Bohra processions. Failure to abide by Mahajan decisions frequently resulted in social and economic sanctions, which were highly effective. For instance, the big business concern of Jairam Shivji's at Zanzibar was forced to revoke a deal with Messers Fraser, as it included a contract for trading in beef. Discreetly, the firm decided to stay away from the beef controversy, giving up the opportunity of partnering a profitable enterprise.

Offshore merchants, who could not fall back on the support of a state of their own, needed their Mahajans. Edward Alpers writes: 'Gujarati merchants successfully exploited the entrance of both the English and Dutch East Indies Companies into Indian Ocean trade by acting as their brokers and agents. Through all of this they successfully protected their interests through the agency of their Mahajans.' He also refers to the election of the Nagarsheth by the commercial communities of Diu as their collective representative to the civil authority. He points out the presence of a city 'commercial Mahajan' at Diu that influenced east African trade with Gujarat in the seventeenth century. In most of the cities and ports of Gujarat, the wealthiest and most influential businessmen acted as leaders of the Mahajan. Virji Vora was the undisputed head, without any formal portfolio, of the trading fraternity of Surat. Kachchhi merchants had their collective representatives, not only in Mandvi, but also in Muscat and Zanzibar. The most influential and rich merchants were selected for the function. Gopaldas Bhimani and Bhimji Gopaldas in Muscat, and Jairam Shivji and Laddha Damji in Zanzibar secured these privileged positions. The Mahajan leaders were 'recognized' by the British when they were invited as assessors during trials in slave trade cases involving Kachchhis at the consular courts. The Mahajan represented a type of social cohesiveness, which transcended caste and community boundaries, its voice prevailing in all judicial matters.

Merchants, Migration and Status

Migration was inextricably woven into the history of nineteenth-century Kachchh. While drought, shortfall in rain, crop failure, earthquakes, epidemics and locust attacks were the negative factors that forced outward migration, the search for wealth and commercial opportunities represented a positive set of incentives for migration. All sections of society were subject to migratory pressures. Even some of the Jadeja Rajputs left Kachchh temporarily. Herdsmen and cultivators usually left in drought years and returned when the rainfall improved. Craftsmen sought opportunities in other provinces, including those in British India. Several Kachchhi merchants relocated to British Indian ports like Bombay. Others ventured to the distant littorals like Muscat and Zanzibar. Hindu merchants who emigrated usually maintained a connection with Kachchh. Most of the Ismailis became emigrants who did not return. But they did leave behind imprints of their settlements—opulent monuments, cemeteries and religious buildings. The points of departure from Kachchh tended to vary. Jain merchants migrated from the internal hubs of Bhuj and Anjar. The original bases of the Bhatias were Mandvi and Mundra, while the main base of the Bohras was Mandvi, since it is a pilgrimage site in their religious tradition. Khojas came from villages like Kera and Baladia, in the vicinity of Bhuj.

In their towns of origin, as well as in their new locations, Kachchhi merchants were bounteous in donating to charitable works, which was seen as contributing to their prestige. The preponderance of merchants' names among the donors' lists inscribed on the walls of *dharmashalas*, *musafirkhanas*, temples, schools and hospitals reinforces this impression gained from literature. Giving to charity was in keeping with the tradition of *dharmada* i.e. donation in the name of religion. Sheth Narsi Natha, Jivraj Balu, Velji Malu, Keshavji Naik, Gokuldas Tejpal and Khimji Ramdas were and are still known for their magnanimous endowments. Muslim merchants too were driven by religious motivations in donating to charity. A merchant who regularly donated a part of the profits from his businesses for the construction of community halls, hospitals and schools, gained in reputation in the eyes of the local people.

In the early nineteenth century, there were still strong social and ritual sanctions placed on overseas travel by orthodox Hindus. On their return, Hindu merchants, especially Bhatias, compensated for this violation by donating to religious institutions and by undertaking a pilgrimage to Vaishnava religious sites. On the whole though, in Kachchh, migration or *deshatan* was encouraged. The Sanskrit word *deshatan* signifies leaving one's country of origin. In the eyes of Kachchhis, migration in search of a better life was a progressive act. Migrants who returned to

Kachchh periodically were looked upon highly by other Kachchhis, and they enjoyed *vag* or social status and influence in society. Although the 'ban' on travel abroad did not prevent traders from travelling overseas, it did seem to make them reluctant to settle overseas on a permanent basis. The mercantile castes generally practised strict endogamy. Exogamy of varying degrees was seen as 'polluting'. Perhaps for this reason, those who cohabited with local Africans in Zanzibar or east Africa usually did not marry or take up responsibility for any children from those relationships. According to Claude Markovits, some merchants who lived alone had a tendency to enter into local relationships of a 'quasi-matrimonial' nature. Thakkur Jairam, a Bhatia, during his visit to Zanzibar in the early 1890s, closely observed the lifestyle of Bhatia merchants settled there. He contemptuously noted that some of the Bhatias were not living 'pure' lives and had developed illicit relationships with African women. He warned his Bhatia compatriots about the dire consequences of such associations on their families back home. Most Hindu females of these traders' families remained behind in India, in part to ensure that their husbands would come back. Shifting the burden of the ritual prohibition on overseas travel to women may have been a way to legitimize such travel for male merchants. Markovits writes that the women of the household did not travel beyond the seas, seemingly to ensure the continuing purity of the household, and perhaps also to argue that the ban did not apply to men. Simpson and Markovits have argued that the gender element in the ban on travel was in keeping with existing traditions of patriarchy in India.

The Rise and Fall of Mandvi

The rise and fall of great port cities usually has a little to do with geographical changes—the silting of harbours and the decline of hinterlands. It also has something to do with history, when political power shifts from one region to another. The story of the rise of Mandvi in Kachchh can be portrayed at one level as the mirror image of the decline of Surat. The subsequent decline of Mandvi has as its obverse the rise of Bombay. But the truth was more complex. Mandvi's rise had much to do with factors unconnected with Surat, and the port actually did not decline rapidly with the arrival on the scene of Bombay. It even had a spurt of growth before finally giving way to the preeminence of Bombay.

In the eighteenth century, the ruling Raos of Kachchh established a firm, symbiotic alliance with merchants and financiers. Maritime trade flourished. It was perhaps the firm roots of the trading traditions of Mandvi in the earlier century that enabled the merchants of Kachchh to hold firm even during the turbulence of the early nineteenth century. Lt Postans observed that Mandvi was a very opulent and busy port, carrying on considerable trade inland with Pali and other places in Marwar, Sindh, Gujarat, and Jaisalmer and by sea with nearly all the ports of western India, the Red Sea, the Persian Gulf, the eastern coast of Africa, and occasionally as far as Mozambique. The coastal trade of Mandvi tended to cluster largely in Sindh and Kathiawar to the north, and in Bombay and Malabar to the south. Voyages both northwards and southwards were quite frequent. The bulk of trade was within the maritime zone of Bombay and the Gulf of Kachchh.

The building of Mandvi port corresponded with the consolidation of Jadeja rule during the time of Rao Khengar I in the sixteenth century. His successors contributed to the growth of Mandvi port. In the eighteenth century, Mandvi's close association with Bombay actually helped it build a network of trade in the Indian Ocean. Mandvi served as an entrepôt and as a depository for goods from the Indian Ocean rim. The credit for Mandvi's success clearly belongs to its entrepreneurs who were adventurous seafarers and good managers of capital. They played a dynamic role in connecting the triangle of Arabia, Africa and India. During the 1760s and 1770s, trade relations with Arabia and Africa grew stronger. An uncongenial political climate did not hamper the development of inland, inter-coastal and overseas trade of Kachchh, as it happened with the port city of Surat, which gradually lost its importance.

Surat was traditionally the richest trading city in India, as it was the entrepôt for the whole of Hindustan, absorbing everything that was brought here. Ashin Das Gupta notes that access from the port to its primary hinterland—the vast reaches of the Gangetic valley—was gradually blocked by wars and military movements. The stoppage of trade, triggered by military movements, is evident in the remark of the East India Company's Board at Bombay in 1728: '. . . these armies prevent the usual recourse of merchants to Surat'. In the mid-seventeenth century, small boats i.e. *hodis,* could still easily reach Surat. By 1720, a new complex of shifting sandbanks near Surat blocked access even for *hodis.* Surat's trade with Persia also steeply declined at this time because of wars; the caravans were no longer coming to Bandar Abbas. The shifting fortunes of Surat resulted in the formation of newer interest groups and the rise of new ports. The traders from Kachchh and Sindh were trying to secure a firmer position in the Persian Gulf, Bombay, Calicut, Cochin and Calcutta. Ashin Das Gupta described it as the 'northern boom'. He also explains that Banias and Parsis migrated from Surat and sought new alliances. From Surat, Parsis went mostly to Bombay, whereas Banias migrated partly to Bombay and partly to the ports of Kathiawar and Kachchh. Port towns like Mandvi in Kachchh, and Porbandar and Bhavnagar in Kathiawar, gained importance as the Mughal metropolis of Surat was eclipsed. Many of these Banias established commercial connections with Muscat. By 1804, trade from Arabia, the Persian Gulf and Africa was significantly diverted towards the Gulf of Kachchh. The most important development of the eighteenth century was the rise of the colonial port city of Bombay. Bombay's unquestioned prominence was based on the east–west orientation of the bulk of India's foreign trade. But one must not overlook the importance of coastal trade and inland trade. Bombay required a trading centre that supplied goods from the Gulf of Kachchh, Sindh and Marwar. Mandvi quickly occupied this place. This rise of Mandvi has sometimes gone unnoticed because of the rapid rise of Bombay. In many respects, Bombay and Mandvi complemented each other.

The seaborne trade of Mandvi was both inter-coastal as well as that of the high seas. The interdependence among Zanzibar, Muscat and Mandvi actually led to Mandvi becoming more of an Arabian or African port rather than a purely Indian one. Mandvi had the highest relative market share in the Muscat and Zanzibar trade. The value-add brought to the table by the Mandvi merchants, who possessed information on the local markets of all three regions, could not be replicated by the Arab and Swahili merchants. In the 1830s, Mandvi also carried on one-third of the Somali trade—known as *buradur*—in the region. In contrast to trading with east Africa, trading with the Somalis was difficult. There was no regulated tax or duty on the cargo. Instead, a present was given to the rulers of the place. The Somalis did all the transactions of purchase and exchange on the coast. They were considered fair dealers, but 'merciless in case of shipwreck and misfortune'. It seems to have been a curious precursor of our contemporary times when the Indian Ocean is faced with a new incarnation of 'Somali pirates'! Lt Postans drew a good description of the 'Swahili trade' during the 1830s. The merchants of Mandvi eagerly awaited the arrival of the Swahili boats, and to get intelligence of their arrival they were willing to pay liberal fees to the messenger. 'The western bastion of the city wall is generally occupied by some dozen possessors of telescopes of all sizes and denominations, who by long practice, are enabled to distinguish various boats at a great distance. Bets are also offered to considerable amounts, indeed this and other species of gambling at Mandvi, form a part of the revenue of the Rao.' By the 1850s, the rising trade at Mandvi alarmed the British. Fearing the rapid progress of the port, the British, in 1857, suggested the appointment of a Commissariat Agent as a 'native' agent at mandvi for preventing the entry of foreigners.

Way before the British developed interests in the Gulf of Kachchh, the Dutch had established trading relations with Kachchh and Kathiawar. By the 1750s, the Dutch were mainly interested in tapping the textile resources of Kachchh, as was the case in other parts of Gujarat. The period of the prolonged decline of Surat—and before the rise of Bombay—was clearly Mandvi's opportunity. Through the interesting research of Nadri G.A. based on Dutch sources, a picture emerges of increasing traffic between Kachchh and Mocha, Jeddah, Basra, and Muscat irking the European companies who had their own commercial designs. In 1753, the arrival of at least twenty-five ships from Kachchh at Mocha frustrated Dutch efforts to acquire gold ducats because of allegedly indiscriminate buying of this specie by the Kachchh merchants. In 1759, the Dutch carried out an expedition in the Gulf of Kachchh and took possession of a vessel returning from Mocha with its cargo. A petition signed by twenty merchants demanding restitution of the vessel and the goods belonging to them was made to the Raja of Kachchh and conveyed to the Dutch authorities. Annual shipping and freighting from Kachchh to the west-Asian ports continued, attracting merchants and merchandise from other parts of peninsular Gujarat such as Porbandar and Navanagar. The brokers of the Dutch Company often consigned a part of the merchandise they purchased to these regions for distribution in the interior. The Dutch brokers at Kachchh in the 1750s were the two Bania merchants Khushhal Manji and Jawaharchand Roopchand. Concurrently, ports like Bhavnagar, Goga, and others on the Kathiawar peninsula attracted trade and traders, largely on account of Kathiawar being a cotton-producing region. Along with Mandvi, Bhavnagar too emerged as a major entrepôt in northern Gujarat. In the eighteenth century, the Europeans considered Kachchh and Kathiawar as prominent depots for cotton and textile production. Cotton from Kathiawar was in general about 10 per cent cheaper than in Bharuch and Jambusar, and often of better quality too. By the 1750s, the Dutch factory at Surat, in its quest to expand, explored the possibility of establishing new factories elsewhere with the help of Johannes Peacock. In 1751, the Dutch established an outlet at Mandvi as a possible source of cotton and textiles. From there, they expanded to the southern shores of the Gulf of Kachchh and got access to the pearls of Navanagar. According to Nadri, this was also partly a measure to guard the Company's commercial interests against the threat of English presence in Sindh and Bombay. The initial results in Kachchh were promising, as the Dutch Company's officials at Mandvi were able to sell their imports at a reasonably good price. However, a dispute with the Rao of Kachchh regarding customs and gifts resulted in the expulsion of the Dutch from Mandvi in 1758. The failed mercantile equation between the Dutch and Kachchh opened the doors for British influence.

Although the Dutch venture in the Gulf of Kachchh ended abruptly in 1758, Mandvi remained the most important textile production centre, providing textiles for export to Arabia and Africa. Mandvi's manufacturing sector expanded rapidly in the 1750s as a number of artisans and manufacturers redeployed their activities from Surat to Kachchh, Kathiawar and Bombay. The peasants of Kachchh were able to raise excellent cotton, which was much cheaper than in other parts of Gujarat, and which, at 1753 Surat prices, could still result in a

20 per cent profit. The secret of the success of Kachchh cotton was that it was free from arbitrary imposts and levies. From the late eighteenth century, the demand for Kachchh textiles expanded rapidly on account of the growing African appetite for cloth. Kachchhis could penetrate the central and east African interior with their large supply of fine cloth. The growing share of Kachchh in the cotton trade caught the attention of the British. In 1800–01, Bombay merchants had imported Rs 3 lakhs' worth of Kachchh cotton, against Rs 28 lakhs' worth from Gujarat. By 1802–03, the corresponding figures had shot up to Rs 8 lakh and Rs 36 lakh. And from 1804–01, the figures were Rs 12 lakh from Kachchh and Rs 31 lakh from Gujarat. The argument started to be advanced that to protect the East India Company's interest in the China market, it was highly advisable for the government of Bombay to control the frequent dissensions among the chieftains of Kachchh!

Mandvi emerged as a central link in the manufacture of a wide range of piece goods. Mandvi was known for its patterned cotton cloth and sailcloth that catered to the demand from overseas markets. Kachchh produced both fine and coarse cloth, primarily for the African markets. Those of the coarsest kind, *pankora* (unbleached), were manufactured in Marwar, and those under the denomination of *seeah kupra*, or black cloth, of which there were twenty different kinds, all distinguished from each other by their colour and the number of threads in the warp, were woven at Mandvi with English thread. Different shades of indigo were used to create bright borders in the making of this cloth. The measures used were the *guz* (33.5125 inches to one *guz*), and the *tasu* (24 to 1 *guz*). *Pankora* worth 20 *koris* sold at Zanzibar at a price ranging from $7 to $12. Exports in a year ranged up to 1800 *guz*. The *burane* of Mandvi manufacture was a very thick cotton fabric used for sails. The *kaniki* was a narrow, coarse cotton cloth from Marwar that was dyed black in Mandvi. About 60 bales of it were exported annually. Cotton bedcovers, called chintzes, were also part of Mandvi's exports. Raw cotton produced in Kachchh and Kathiawar formed 150 bags annually. In the nineteenth century, the Euro-American trading firms and Kachchhi merchants fiercely competed with each other in east Africa. The growth of the textile industry in Mandvi was not unique to the place. Growth also occurred in other textile centres like Ahmedabad, Broach, Bhavnagar, Cambay, Navsari and Jambusar. In the early 1750s, there were 4000 looms in Kachchh, suggesting that a considerable portion of the population of Kachchh and its vicinity was involved in this craft. Mandvi dyers used colouring substances such as *majith*, *surangi* and alum to dye fabric. The one product for which Kachchh was a significant market was alum. Alum is an essential caustic in the dyeing process of textiles. Alum was chiefly procured from the vicinity of Madh. Since alum was available only near the Ashapura temple, it was associated with the miracles of the goddess Ashapura. The manufacture of alum was a royal monopoly, and the Rao controlled its sale. The workmen manufactured alum at their own expense and received 2 *kori* per *maund* for their labour. For the sale of alum, the Rao usually gave the contract to Khoja and Memon merchants.

Due to the increasing demand for textile and ivory, the towns of Mandvi and Marwar had become hives of industry. The Hindu as well as Muslim weavers (*vankars*) manufactured piece goods for the local and foreign markets. Weavers tended to customize their products to suit customers of distant markets. Textiles were frequently converted into woven products. The manufacture of woven products became a specialized activity for weavers belonging to the Khatri community. There emerged the need for an inter-regional engagement, linking Indian weavers and product manufacturers with African consumers. Indian merchants provided this linkage. Their presence in the Indian Ocean, as we have noted earlier, was of a longstanding duration.

Apart from woven cloth, woven products and indigo-dyed cottons, copperware, ironware, glassware, enamel work, silver jewels and art items of gold were also manufactured in places like Mandvi, Anjar, Bhuj and Mundra. These goods came to be collectively referred to as Kachchhi work. The artisans involved in these manufacturing activities had their own system of guilds and a Mahajan body, which claimed to espouse a code of conduct complementary to Hindu dharma.

Specialized quarters emerged in villages and cities where these artisans were concentrated. Imitating the merchants, the artisans too migrated to neighbouring and overseas destinations. At Kathiawar, Kachchh blacksmiths were most prized. Kachchhi carpenters were of great repute and provided their services to the shipwrights of Muscat.

Overland trade emerged as complementary to maritime trade. Mandvi became the terminus from where trade in commodities was carried on with neighbouring Lakhpat, Jakhau, Mundra and Anjar and with the more distant Sindh, Pali, Marwar and Makran. Sindh especially was a major trading partner in the inland trade of Kachchh. Sindh exported rice, turmeric, lotus seeds and salted fish. In return, Sindh imported from the merchants of Mandvi, via Lakhpat, iron, steel, lead, tin, sugar and rice, betel nut, dates, dried dates, teak wood, cloves, English thread, silk thread and cotton. The excellent business relations of Kachchh with Bombay helped Kachchhi merchants, as both local products and foreign goods were largely sold in the Bombay markets. Their trade covered a wide range of articles, including ghee from Thar Parkar, rice and timber from the Malabar coast, turmeric and thread from Bombay, English and Indian fabrics, and piece goods from Kathiawar and Marwar.

The second half of the nineteenth century witnessed the gradual decline of Mandvi. The port was unable to anchor steamers. The formation of sandbanks hurt the port. The entrance to the creek or *karee* (as it is locally called) was very narrow. Progressive encroachments on the left or eastern bank of the Mandvi river caused a large quantity of detritus and silt to be deposited outside the mouth of the creek. During the southwest monsoons, approaching the port became risky. Local craft required at least nine feet of water, and when this was not available, they were forced to discharge part or all of their cargo into smaller boats outside the creek. With all these precautions, they were still liable to be wrecked because of the shifting nature of the sandbanks and the scant depth of water. The Kachchh government did make attempts to reconstruct the breakwater site, but the attempts were either inadequate or untimely. The government was alerted about the siltation of the port by the 1860s. A breakwater to protect Mandvi harbour was under construction in the early 1880s. But the work of building a jetty was not over till 1883–84. Colonel Parr believed that with completion of the palace, built near Mandvi, heavy expenditure on it would cease, and money would thus be set free for public works of importance. Lack of finance or lack of attention of the ruling class resulted in failure to meet the urgent requirements of the port. Mandvi's shipbuilding activities were confined to sailing ships. Mandvi did not become a centre for building steamships. The development of the Rajputana railway network connecting Rajasthan to Bombay hurt Kachchh and Mandvi. Goga and Ahmedabad benefited at the expense of Mandvi and Anjar. After the British conquest of Sindh (1843), a railway line was laid directly from Sindh to Rajasthan, bypassing any need for Mandvi. The Kachchh government tried to improve the competitive position of Mandvi by substantially reducing duties on the Rajputana frontier. It was with the same end in view that the state paid for the survey of the country through which a railway line might be laid from western Rajputana into Kachchh. But this line did not get built. Mandvi merchants still relied on camels and couriers for the transport of goods. The war in Afghanistan increased the military's demand for camels, and this proved injurious to land trade. The railways also diverted a part of the traffic from the Mandvi river. The ivory trade with Marwar too diminished in the late 1870s. The quantity of ivory annually imported at Mandvi dwindled to 48.5 candies. State income from customs at Mandvi started to fluctuate: in 1873–74, it was Rs 1.74 lakh; in 1874–75, Rs 2.07 lakh and in 1875–76, Rs 1.87 lakh. The income declined steadily during the subsequent years. In 1879–80, the income at Mandvi was Rs 1.72 lakh, against Rs 1.94 lakh in 1878–79 and at other ports, (Mundra, Lakhpat and Jakhau) Rs 1.58 lakh, against Rs 1.85 lakh.

Occasional spurts of revival punctuated a longer-term declining trend. For instance, the customs duties at Mandvi rose from Rs 1.89 lakh in 1875–76 to Rs 2.68 lakh in 1883–84. The quality of merchandise imported and exported remained at par with the previous years', although values decreased. Sources of information of those times expressed regret at the reduced shipbuilding activities in Mandvi resulting from the introduction of steam navigation. Nevertheless, the new technologies were learnt and shipbuilding was restarted at Mandvi with the aid of modified techniques. But Mandvi was no longer able to match the sheer trading volumes of its earlier times.

Among other ports, Lakhpat, situated at the meeting point of the Kori creek and the Rann of Kachchh, was of considerable importance. Its principal focus was trade with Sindh. One of the narrow streets of Lakhpat is still known as Madai Bazaar. Goods from there were transferred to Mandvi or Madai. Fateh Mohammed had taken keen efforts to improve the condition of this port. This small town, which had a population of one thousand Banias, was depopulated partly because of the earthquake of 1844, and partly because of the change of the course of the Indus river in 1851. Only a few families of fishermen were left in the town. One cannot speculate whether a vigorous, princely government as in earlier times, or a less indifferent British resident, might not have maintained towns like Lakhpat as vibrant centres of trade had they intervened appropriately. Today, all that is left here are the sands, which are said to have the texture of currency notes, and a lone fort guarded by the Indian military.

The other minor ports of Kachchh included Mundra, Jakku, Koteshwar and Tuna. Mundra was a base for

Bhatia merchants. Mundra has figured conspicuously in Kachchh history. Tuna port, situated eleven miles away from Anjar, was built by Fateh Mohammed in an attempt to create a rival to Mandvi. However, despite emerging as a shipbuilding centre in the eighteenth century, Tuna never lived up to its promise. The merchants of Anjar themselves downplayed Tuna and opened offices in Muscat, Bombay and Calcutta.

Although Mandvi was preeminent in all trades, Kachchhi traditions do associate a degree of specialization with different ports: Cotton was prominent in Tuna–Anjar; Mandvi is remembered for its textiles and ivory; Lakhpat Bandar had strong associations with ghee and rice; while Mundra was the home of cotton piece goods. Not quite completely ghost towns, these places still hold the ornate houses of the merchants of yore, and their warehouses, dockyards and rest houses.

The Horse Trade

No account of Kachchh and Kathiawar can be complete without a reference to their famous horse trade. According to some Mughal chroniclers and their many contemporaries, Kachchh was known as the place where the best horses in south Asia were bred. The *aspan-i Kachhi* (Kachchhi horses) were famous and in demand. Prior to the eighteenth century, the so-called *baehr* or 'sea' horses were brought to India from Fars, Iraq or Arabia in large numbers. But by the eighteenth century,

Gommans writes that horse trade with the Persian Gulf was limited. The bulk of the horses now originated from ports in the Gulf of Kachchh, namely Porbandar, Goga, Mandvi or Sonmiani. In the early nineteenth century, the character of the horse trade changed as demand for horses from the British army rose. The trade moved from being overland to becoming seaborne. For instance, horse exports from Iran reached India by sea. The government at Madras decided to bypass the overland network and buy horses from Kathiawar. Arabian-like horses, mainly from Kathiawar, Kachchh, Rajasthan, Baluchistan, Afghanistan and Turkistan, fetched a medium price of around Rs 500 an animal. Genuine Arabian horses cost up to three to four times this price. Perceived differences in the breeds accounted for this enormous price difference. Despite the market's preference for Arabian horses, the Kathiawar breed had long had its own supporters. In the opinion of Lt Col. L. Stanhope and officers of the 17th Dragoons, their regiment, which was supplied horses chiefly from Kathiawar, was in 1813 better mounted than any other corps. Local chiefs like the Kathis kept mares in their personal stables. The cost of transporting a horse from Kachchh to Calcutta was Rs 760, while the cost of transporting one from Basra to Calcutta was Rs 838, thus providing an opportunity for arbitrage. The horse trade was a capital-intensive business. Those who were able to invest large amounts could make inordinate profits. The entrepreneur Sunderji Shivji Khatri, who at the end of the eighteenth century had gained a near monopoly of the horse supply from Kachchh and Kathiawar, was known for his fabulous wealth. Sunderji's activities and network extended to Kalat in Baluchistan and to Kabul and Kandahar in Afghanistan.

Sunderji, also known as Sunderji Saudagar, from Gundhiari in Kachchh, was given the contract for horse remounts for the Presidency of Fort St George by Captain Montgomery. Sunderji, acting as a representative of the government of Kachchh, paid an official visit to Bengal in order to pay his respects to the Marquess of Wellesley. The government of Bombay now endeavoured to obtain information about Kachchh, which was becoming increasingly interesting to the British by reason of the connections involved. Sunderji served as an agent of the British and may have been in some respects a predecessor to Hansraj, who later invited the British to Kachchh.

Sunderji's personal story is quite fascinating and is worth recounting. From his younger days, he is supposed to have been passionate about horse riding and gambling, and was even given to occasional theft. Sunderji's father Shivji Hirji, fed up of his son's bad habits, finally disowned him in 1790 after giving him a parting settlement of 2000 *kori*. Within a few days, Sunderji squandered away this money, and then proceeded to embezzle his wife's money in order to keep up with his gambling needs. His angry wife asked him to leave the house. Since he was no longer trusted by anyone in his village, Sunderji headed for the big city of Mandvi. There he lucked out by being able to persuade Nagarsheth Mansang Bhojraj, a friend of his father's, to lend him 7,000 *kori* to enter the horse trade. By this time, Sunderji had turned into a diligent businessman. He scoured all of Kachchh and bought seven horses, which he shipped to Bombay and sold for a handsome profit. His new patron lent him more money, and Sunderji parlayed the funds into investment in fourteen horses, which he exported to Cochin. The prodigal was now a businessman known for his integrity. The steady expansion of his business and his 'honesty' impressed Col Montgomery, who purchased horses from Sunderji at Rs 535 per head, advancing him Rs 1 lakh in cash from the Madras government! Sunderji went into a major expansion mode. He set up his own agents in Sindh and Kathiawar whose job was to procure remount horses. In a short while, Sunderji became a major supplier of horses not only to the British, but also to the Nizam and to Tipu Sultan. . His letter, written in Persian to the Governor of Mumbai in 1801, suggests that he purchased 225 horses for the British army. In another correspondence in 1801, it is evident that Sunderji was actively involved in the purchase of horses for the Company . By the years 1810–12, he supplied the Company agents at Bombay with 1800 horses. The young gambler who had stolen from his wife had come very far indeed. It appears that he had even recognized the need to diversify his wealth and his investments, and invested in the pearl trade and bought several ships too. In the 1830s, it was listed that around seven ships belonged to his family. Owning ships provided him not only a measure of diversification but also ended up being synergistic with his main business of transporting horses. His proficiency in several languages may have led to his appointment as an agent of the British East India Company, who assigned to him the job of surveying the Okhamandal coast to find out details about the so-called 'northern pirates'.

Sunderji had a flair for salesmanship; his candid confessions regarding flaws in the horses he sold established him as a person of integrity. He was trusted so much that David Seton, on his mission to Kachchh, was instructed to rely only on him. Sunderji's understanding of local politics and culture was also put to use by the British in order to negotiate the issue of piracy with the coastal chiefs and temple priests of the Gulf of Kachchh. These chiefs justified their acts by arguing that they had no option but to resort to piracy. To bring some sort of settlement between the British and these chiefs, Sunderji extensively toured northern Kathiawar. He was curious about the interesting details of the surrounding local customs and conventions, especially those of Okhamandal, Dwarka and Bait. He was a sharp diplomat, with enormous powers of persuasion. He was regularly appointed as an arbitrator to settle disputes among princely states and between them and the British. He was also a banker for some princely states like Morbi, who in times of need would mortgage their estates to him. As payment for his services as arbitrator, he was frequently granted landed estates by the princely rulers. He impressed Rao Raidhan, who offered him the influential post of the Diwan, which he declined. However, his pro-British attitude won him the enmity of Jamadar Fateh Mohammed, who suspected British designs in Kachchh.

It is reckoned that Sunderji had established twenty-two branches of his firm in Bombay. Other than in Bombay and Kachchh, his mercantile house had branches in Ahmedabad, Mysore, Mangrole, Pune, Coomta, Calicut, Malabar, Baroda, Rajkot, Dhoraji, Jodia, Navanagar and Sindh.

Sunderji was not only a great diplomat of his period, but was well known in the entire Gulf of Kachchh for his charity. In 1813, when Kachchh and Kathiawar went through a severe famine, he generously kept his coffer open for the famine victims. This magnanimous act of donation did not go unnoticed in the eyes of the British, with whom Sunderji allied big time. About his charity it was noted that:

> Sunderjee Sewjee, a merchant of Mandvie chiefly residing at Porbunder and known to Company's Government, has been unbounded in his well-timed charities, and considering the extent of a single man's agility, these charities require but a simple recital of the donor.

During the last twelve months, Sunderjee has fed at Mandvie in Cutch 8000 people on dates, at the daily expense of 300 rupees. At a village named Gindella near the same place, he has fixed establishment for charity which during the late scarcity disbursed 60 rupees daily by distributing grain.

At Porbunder, Sunderjee gave great encouragement to a subscription made at the place for the relief of the poor by contributing 9000 rupees. At Jooria Noanuggar and Surya particularly at the former place, the half famished people of Kattyawar have been also fed at an average charge of 90 rupees everyday and it will be found that Sunderjee's name is inscribed in the list of subscription handsomely made by the native communities of Bombay. It is not possible to ascertain precisely the amount of charities at the sacred Teerhuts of Bate Dwarka & Co., nor those privately administered but from the information of a gentleman on whose accuracy dependence can be placed, it is estimated that during the last year the charities of Sunderjee altogether have considerably exceeded the sum of two lacs of rupees.

This is not the first instance in which Sunderjee has afforded his assistance. In the dreadful famine of 1792 when his mercantile concerns were more limited, this person also expended a lac of rupees. Notwithstanding that there are powerful claims on public respect and attention it is remarkable that the

> same spirit which pervades his charities, animates his
> personal demeanour exhibiting a model of humility
> and disinterestedness which can only be allied with
> the purest behaviour.

These acts of Sunderji's benevolence won him much applause, not only from the locals of the Gulf of Kachchh but the British too. He was also known for his religious endowments; he built and renovated several temples in Kachchh and Kathiawar. From being a gambler, a banished son and a petty thief of his wife's money, Sunderji rose to become a merchant prince and a diplomat. His authoritative biography, which is yet to be written, would be a fascinating read, and would also shed light on that twilight period before final British dominion over the Gujarat coast.

The Sailing Tradition

Before the advent of steam, in the age of the sail, Indian Ocean voyages were dominated by the 'monsoon factor'. The northeast monsoon, or the retreating monsoon, which begins in September, was called *kaskazi* in Swahili and *saji mausam* in Gujarati. The southwest monsoon, whose winds started from April, was known as *kusi* in Swahili and *aakhar mausam, chheli* ghos or *safar* in Gujarati. The fair season lasted from October to April—from 281 *naroj* to 301 *naroj*. The dry and strong winds prevailing from November to April facilitated speedier ships. From June through September, the southwest monsoon lashes many parts of India. From September onwards, the sailors of Mandvi would harness the gentler winds to sail towards the western Indian Ocean. Coastal trade too was briskly carried out at this time. The formal kick off of the business season in September was referred to in Kachchh as *mausam khulvi*. For Captain S. Napier Raikes, acting Political Agent, Kutch, who had developed an understanding of the maritime calendar of Kachchh, the fifteenth day of *Bhadro* i.e. September, marked the commencement of the trade season, while the closing was reckoned as the fifteenth day of *Jeth* i.e. May/June. *Suwallee* (Swahili) boats from Zanzibar arrived in Mandvi just before the southwest monsoon set in. From May to mid-August, sailing the high seas was hazardous. This was a good time for refitting the Kotias in their home ports.

The seasons governed the marine insurance business. Insurance was usually available only for voyages in the fair season—from 281 *naroj* to 301 *naroj*. For claims to be valid, they had to be made within the open season. Before the introduction of modern techniques, Kachchhi sailors were guided by bearings from the land, the sun, and the colour of the water during the day; the moon was their guide by night. The sailors had developed a comprehensive familiarity of the sea. The brisk season for the staple export items such as cotton and seed was in April and May, and for other goods from October to April. Of the various festivals that were conducted by the sea, the principal one was *nava naroj*—not to be confused with the Parsi *Nawroz*—and literary means 'from the new day'. During *nava naroj,* merchants and their constituents honoured the sea, entering the waves to seek blessings for the forthcoming trading year. The Banias in Zanzibar adopted the system of recording accounts as per *nava naroj* or the 'trade new year'. The Zanzibar Custom House accounts for the previous year were settled. Financial documents were replaced with new ones at the commencement of *nava naroj*, which fell in the month of August. *Chatri Chandar*, the Kachchhi New Year in April, and *Ashadhi Bij* in July, marked the start and close of the trading season.

The turbulent period of the eighteenth century turned into an opportunity for Kachchhi shipbuilding. Barendse says that while navigation of Mughal ships in the Gulf steeply declined, 'the waters of the Gulf still teemed with such humble and inconspicuous small vessels from Kachchh and Kathiawar. The Maratha invasions hurt the tall ships of Surat; merchants began to shift to smaller ships and to the ports of Kathiawar and Kutch, which were in turn connected by small barges to the cities of central Gujarat.' Skilled carpenters and other workers from Surat shifted to Mandvi and Bombay.

Rao Desalji I, Rao Lakhpatji and Rao Godji were all active supporters of Kachchhi shipbuilding. The technical and engineering expertise acquired by

Ramsinghji Malam in the Netherlands came in handy. The shipyard or *jahajwado* of Mandvi operated from both banks of the Rukmavati River. Tuna, Mundra and Jakhau were also significant centres of shipbuilding. The seagoing vessels built in Kachchh were of various types, going by the names of *Kotia, Navadi, Machhava, Dhan, Tar* and *Hodi.* Bombay ships, on the other hand, were known by the names of *Padav, Konkani, Fatehmari* and *Valsadi Batela.*

The Kachchhi nomenclature for vessels derived from the shape of their hulls. Carvel built ships, i.e. ships built with flush rather than overlapping hull planks, were popular in Saurashtra and Kachchh. The *Kotia* was the main Kachchhi vessel; all the others such as *Ghanja, Dhangi, Batela, Navdi* and *Padav* were more or less offshoots of the *Kotia.* The *Kotia* was reputed for its speed and sturdiness in stormy, deep seas. Even an empty *Kotia* was reputed to be strong enough to sail in windy seas or through obverse winds. Its tonnage ranged from 80 to 225, although in some cases it even exceeded 500. The *Kotia* could be as long as 135 feet. The larger ones frequently stepped three masts. The stem or *mora* of the ship resembled a falcon's beak; this became the hallmark of the *Kotia.* Another distinguishing feature of the *Kotia* was its rig. It sometimes carried a small square topsail in fair weather. The *Kotias* were fast ships designed for the high seas, and constructed to withstand strong winds. The Kachchhi Vahan resembled a *Kotia.* This ship was specifically constructed in a manner that made it suited for longer voyages. Kachchhi shipyards, known as *wadhas* specialized in the 80–225 candies tonnage. The Kachchhi *Navadi* was a special type of *Kotia*; it was 27 feet to 40½ feet long and 10½ feet to 16½ feet wide. The distinctive feature of this ship was the absence of a platform, enabling it to load more goods. Navadis required between four to twelve sailors to operate, and easily sailed all the way to Muscat and Zanzibar. While the regular Kotias were largely built in Mandvi, the Navadis usually came from the port of Jakhau. Smaller outriggers called *Machhvas* were used for ferrying and fishing. Usually, 9–18 feet long and 3¾ feet wide, *Machhvas,* weighing between 2 and 6 candies, could easily slip into river deltas and coastal creeks with goods that had been unloaded from larger vessels. The large *Machhvas* of 80 candies, 27 feet in length and 10½ feet in width, were used for ferrying goods between Mandvi and Karachi.

Omanis probably link the Arabian vessel *Baghlah* to the increased contact between Oman and the dockyards of the East India Company at Bombay. But Kachchhi sources emphatically claim that Arabs converted the Kachchhi *Kotia* into a *Baghlah* by modifying the stem-head, adding carved ornamentation at the stern, and by removing the painted decoration, which was often found in stripes at the forefoot of the *Kotia's* bow. The increased maritime contacts between Oman and Kachchh could have produced the *Baghlah* and its sister ship, the *Ghanjah*. The *Baghlah* stem was curved and topped with a distinctive bollard-shaped figurehead. The *Ghanjah* was halfway between a *Kotia* and a *Baghlah*. The substantial point of difference was in the stem-head ornament, which was a small, rounded projection carved with concentric circles surmounted by a trefoil crest, with an iron ring taking the place of the *Kotia*'s falcon's beak. Kachchhi shipwrights worked in the shipyards of Oman, especially at Sur.

Kachchhi sailors were known as *Bhadala Nakhwas* and *Kharwa Malams*. There were both Hindu and Muslim *Kharwas*. The etymology of the term *Kharwa* is traced from the Sanskrit, meaning 'carrier of salt'. Kachchhi shipwrights, who were known as *Wadha suthars,* started with a design in mind without any graphic representation. Nevertheless, they guesstimated the keel and the hull of the ship. They repaired ships using a variety of hardwoods imported from the Malabar coast and Saurashtra. Vessels required many different types of wood for the stem, the outriggers, and the hull. The wood for the mast was specially imported from the Konkan coast. Kachchh also at times imported wood from Burma.

Work started with the placement and stacking of wood. It then involved teams of persons lifting and manoeuvring sections of timber. This was heavy work that required 'organization, technique, and skill; brute strength alone was not enough'. At first, the length of the keel was estimated. Pieces of wood of one square foot each were stitched to a length of around 80 feet to 100 feet. Garboard planks were placed over the structure. Scaffolding was made from waste wood and was fastened with rope. The scaffold itself gave the shipbuilder insight into different types of wood and their tolerances. We are told that a shipbuilding yard was transformed into an active, noisy space for eight long months in order to construct a ship. In the course of the eighteenth century, Kachchhi shipbuilders were influenced by Europeans and started using steel, iron and nails. Despite the rapidly increasing use of iron, most vessels were generally stitched as this made the ships better suited for the monsoons and more resistant to collision than European ships of similar size. The stitched boats easily survived getting stuck on sandbanks, where nailed European vessels would shatter. The flip side of this was, of course, that the capacity of the stitched ships was low.

Kachchhi ships were equipped with ammunition for their protection. Avoiding nautical hazards was an ingrained tradition. For instance, at Mandvi, vessels were anchored at *Bharakanthe* or the eastern waters. Kachchhi mariners were known for their skill in dealing with various exigencies of the high seas. They relied on maps and charts; they were also experts at reading weather signals and at making deductions based on the colour of the sea. Their traditions required them to take their bearings from the stars, a tradition that preceded the magnetic compass. Their *roznamas,* which passed from one *Malam* to another, recorded guidelines for the *Malam*. It listed the details of previous voyages and provided notes on the use of astrolabes and other devices. Such charts and diagrams in their textual form were referred to as *Malami hisab*. Some of the *roznamas* contained shoreline silhouettes. Directional instructions were sometimes presented in the form of riddles, along with a coastal map and calculations.

In the second half of the eighteenth century, the Kachchh fleet comprised more than four hundred ocean-going ships. The demand for seamen for these ships increased. Kachchhi sailors usually also acted as stevedores. According to Simpson, the division of labour was remarkably similar at all shipyards in Kachchh, and was reproduced among the crews when ships were at sea. The shipyards were dominated by Sunni Muslims of the Bhadala caste. However, those who worked for them were from different ethnic and caste groups. The organization and deployment of the crew was much closer to the Arab than the European prototype. Terms of Arabic origin such as *Malam, Nakhwa (Nakhuda)* and *Khalasi* were combined with others such as *Sarang* to describe members of the crew. *Tandel*s were in command of the ship. Crew were ranked according to their work profile; above the *Khalasi* was the *Panjari* (lookout man). Above the *Panjari* was the *Sarang*, who could sometimes be the second in command. Training to be a *Malam* or navigator was part of the job description while serving in this position of the *Sarang*. The word *Khalasi* derived from the tradition of paying sailors for the season's work in grain with a lump sum known as *khalas*. Of highest rank were the *Nakhwas* (captains) and just below them the *Malams* (navigators). Both were recruited weeks before a voyage, and participated in supervising the construction of the ship. The experienced *Sarang* (foreman) mediated conflicts and organized the division of labour among the *Khalasis*. He was also responsible for the instruction of apprentices in ship design and technologies of production. The shipowner occupied a position of unquestioned authority over the entire crew. Despite their position in the circle of seafarers, the shipowners or *Bhadalas* did not occupy a high position in the society, however. According to Simpson, this was mainly because sailing was considered a low and 'dirty' profession, consisting of people who were usually 'hot-headed'.

Members of the crew were promoted up from one rank to another. However, in times of necessity, all pitched in to performed essential tasks. The *Nakhwa* was responsible for the navigation of the ship; he was also expected to ensure adequate provisioning and even oversaw commercial transactions on behalf of both the owners of goods and the owners of the vessels. Sailors also frequently traded on their own accounts. Many of them possessed knowledge of basic accounting. Many shipowners allowed them a limited amount of private trade in addition to their wages. Local digests of the

1880s list the payments and reimbursements made to sailors. *Khalasis* received for each *ghos* (voyage) cash i.e. *khalas* and *bhatu* i.e. daily meal allowances. The *Sarang* received 1¼ times the share of the *Khalasi*. *Nakhwas* and *Malam* received double the *khalas* and allowances from the shipowner or the renter (for the whole season). *Petbalio,* as the name indicates, was an apprentice who was not paid but was given a meal to fill his stomach or *pet*. He went through a rigorous apprenticeship before sailing. The men employed to build a ship were split under the categories of carpenter (*suthar*) and labourer. The carpenters were predominantly Hindu, while the labourers were Sunni Muslims. Lowest in rank among the labourers was the *Petradio or Petbalio* (assistant, galley hand), who had to obey the commands of the *Sarang,* their supervisor and trainer. A system of apprenticeship was in vogue in the shipyards of Mandvi. Simpson describes apprenticeship as a social and collective activity, inevitably riddled with the same contradictions of the underlying societies.

The shipwrights of both Muscat and Mandvi experienced a setback as steam took over from sail. But sailing ships have retained an amazing persistence. The *Bhadala* have always continued to run their small vessels between India and East Africa. Even in contemporary times, a small number of *Bhadala* men have prospered, sailing between Dubai, the free port of the Emirates, and India. In the twentieth century, Kachchhi vessels continued to circle between Basra, Muscat, Zanzibar and as far as Madagascar, even as the volume of trade had declined considerably. In the 1930s, Sampat observed that shipbuilding activities entered a depressive phase. But World War I caused an increase in demand for Kachchhi ships.

While the very rich merchants owned ships, most medium-sized and small merchants preferred to rent ships either for a single season, *saji mausam,* or for a single trip, *ghos,* when the ship was referred to as a *noori* or *ghosi* ship. A single ship rented to multiple merchants was also considered a *noori* ship. The renting rates of the *noori* or *ghosi* ships depended on either weight or bulk, i.e. on per candy or per carton. The seasonal renter remained in possession of the ship during the open season lasting from 271 *naroj* from the ports of Kachchh and 281 to 301 *naroj* from the foreign ports. This system incentivized the renter to arrange for the timely return of ships.

The expenses of the ship, including the state taxes, were borne by the shipowner. The renter paid the rent in three installments—the first at the time of departure, the second at mid-season on the second day of the waxing moon in February—*Maha Sud*—and the third on Kachchhi New Year's day, the second day of the waxing moon in July. In the case of long voyages to ports like Aden, Swahili, Mozambique, Vibu and Kumer, rent was paid once the voyage was completed and the ship returned to the owner. Owners recruited crews, either for a single voyage or for the whole season.

The cost of the first 'servicing' and attendant repairs were assumed by the shipowner, who compensated the renter in case he had happened to pay for these costs. The renter for the season was responsible for crew allowances i.e. *khalas bhata* and taxes i.e. *durbari lagat,* along with subsequent maintenance costs.

There were established norms for payment of brokerage. If a ship was rented for the whole season, the intermediary earned half a per cent in brokerage. The brokerage rates for *noori* ships varied by port. In the c.1870s, for instance, *noori* rates at the ports of Sindh and Kathiawar was 2 *kori*; along the Bombay and Malabar coast 5 *kori*, and at other ports up to 10 *kori*. The register of goods was known as *satmi,* and in it were noted down the name of the owner, the description and value of goods, and the location of the recipient. The owner of the ship or the renter or his agent prepared the *satmi.* The *Nakhwa* would have custody of the freighted goods and would be responsible for handing them over to the recipient. The *Nakhwa* was accountable for compensation, in case of any shortfall in goods. Loss of goods on account of their being stolen by an enemy of the state or when a ship sank, were not set against the *Nakhwa's* responsibility. Similarly, in the case of vessels from *veparkanthe* i.e. from the coasts of Mozambique, Zanzibar and Kumer, shipowners were on the hook only when the ships were near Mandvi, Mundra or Tuna. Thereafter, shipowners were not held responsible.

Marine Insurance

Kachchhi merchants involved in maritime trade sought ways to insure their ventures. The genesis of marine insurance in Kachchh is veiled in antiquity and lost in obscurity. However, it is clear that from the seventeenth century onwards, marine insurance, which was known as *dariyayi vima* was a well-established custom. From Lt Leech's observation, it appears that insurance had become virtually mandatory. Before unloading, stevedores would ask questions as to the identity of the insurer of the cargo. If there was no insurance, no stevedore would come forward to unload the vessel, and no agent would agree to work on sale of the cargo. Usually, ships and cargo were separately insured, with the coverage extending to a range of 60 per cent to 100 per cent of the value. Insurance was provided both by individuals and by consortia of merchants. The insurer or *jokhmi* was entitled to *viradh* or premium. If the ship faced hazards (*kaja*), then the *jokhmi* reimbursed the sum that was contractually due. Sometimes, insurance and credit were combined. Under the terms of the *aavang*, in the event of total loss of the vessel, the insured was excused from the obligation to repay the loan contracted for the vessel or the cargo. If the voyage was successfully completed, he was required to pay the insurer interest in addition to repayment of the principal amount borrowed within a stipulated time. In another type of insurance, the owner of the goods, directly or through an agent (*aadatia*), drew a bill known as a *jokhmi hundi* on a third party, who actually paid the owner in advance before the voyage was completed. Once the vessel anchored at the harbour, then the holder of the *hundi* received money from the owner of the goods or his agent. In all three cases i.e. insurance (*vimo*), *aavang* and *jokhmi hundi*, the premiums were set by the market. There was also a market for the insurance contracts themselves, which could be sold/traded. The deductible losses on *jokhmi* payments were usually 5 per cent. Changes made to the voyage route or transshipment of goods rendered the insurance instructions. Towards the end of the season (*aval aakhar mausam*), at first sign of rain or gale, insurance premiums would run up.

The hull or the cargo of a ship was insured until the time the ship safely anchored at the scheduled port. The contract ensured that the owner's vessel was actually seaworthy and that he did not try to make claims for damages incurred before the voyage. The cargo was insured separately and a separate premium, called *viradh* agreed upon. The owner of the goods provided the list of the details either to the *jokhmi* or *aadatiya* (agent) for their records. To deal with the moral hazard of inflating values, agreements ensured that the *jokhmi* received his premium at a fixed rate. If values were understated, the *jokhmi* did not have to cover the excess. Marine insurance was combined with credit, with insurers having a stake in the vessel and/or the cargo.

There were professional insurance brokers in Kachchh. The broker would make triple entries—in his books, in the books of the insurer and in the books of the insured. These entries were used for settling claims at a later date. In cases of dispute, the values in the broker's account books were treated as authentic evidence.

Insurance income was subject to both government and ecclesiastical taxes. Tax payments were made both to the durbar and and to religious tax collectors. The religious tax, *dharmau lagat*, was paid at the onset of the new year, on *Ashadhi Sud Bij*—the second day of the full moon of July. The state strictly enforced the law that insurance fraud not only rendered contracts void, but would result in judicial intervention and punishment of persons who, for instance, might deliberately damage goods and then make insurance claims.

In any port of Kachchh, if a ship sailed in with an open sail, then all observers would know that its voyage had been a safe one. A closed sail, on the other hand, suggested a perilous voyage and damage to the vessel or loss of cargo. In such an event, the *Nakhwa* was required to promptly report to the owner/the insured. Subsequently, the broker would attempt to settle the claim. If there were disputes and attempts at settlement failed, the Mahajan of that place would intervene and take custody of the goods. The Mahajan would then act as the judicial authority to decide on the validity and the extent of the claim. While this system worked at most ports, the sheer volume of insurance activity in Mandvi called for additional resources. In the 1880s, the durbar had appointed six of its representatives to deal with insurance claims. In typical Kachchhi tradition, the durbar and the Mahajan had cooperative rather than competing jurisdictions in all these cases.

The Banking World of the Goswamis

A *hundi* is a document ordering the payment of money drawn by one person on another. Its main objective was to facilitate transfer of money from one place to another. *Hundi*s were effective instruments that supported long-distance trade. Kachchhis were not the inventors of the *hundi*. This reputation is traditionally assigned to the Multani *hundi* bankers from Shikarpur, which is today in Pakistan. Multanis extended their business to Bombay, Madras, Rangoon and Ceylon. In Gujarati tradition, the hundi was the suitable mode of money transfer from Vastupal Tejpal, the banker of Ahmedabad to the Sheth of Junagarh, Narsinh Mehta. Seven details were considered essential for a *hundi*— the names of the drawer and the drawee, the name of the holder or recipient, the place where the payment would be made, the due date and lastly, the type of *hundi*. Kachchhis used various types of *hundi*s, which went by the names *Namjog hundi*, *Shahjog hundi* and *Endhanjog hundi*. In all these notes, the duration or time limit within which money was required to be paid was indicated. *Tarat hundi*s were honoured after a day. The *Darshani hundi* was paid at sight. The *Muddati hundi* was paid within a stipulated time. The grace period allowed for the *Muddati hundi* varied by region. A five-day grace period was granted at Bhuj, Mandvi and Mundra, and one or two days at Anjar. In Mandvi, Mundra and Anjar, the *hundi* was issued or received through brokers. In Bhuj, there were no brokers. Honouring the *hundi* in all circumstances, including the insolvency of drawer, was key to its success.

A promissory note could be rejected either on its presentation or on the expiry of the term. But if the banker once bound himself on oath to accept a bill, he could not reject it even if the issuer of the bill became insolvent in the interval. If the note was lost, then documents known as *penth*, *per penth* or *kagar* were issued. In all these documents, the information contained in the original *hundi* was repeated. The notes were sold like any other commodity, by making entries in the seller's and buyer's books. In Mandvi, Anjar and Mundra, the bill passed through the hands of brokers whose rates were 1/12 per cent. Apart from regular *hundi*s, there existed the *jokhmi* (insurer) *hundi*, where the holder of the *hundi* undertook the risk of safe transport of goods from one place to another.

Records concerning *hundi*s issued during the 1860s are preserved in the monastery of Dnyangiri Nirmalgiri at Mandvi. These records indicate that *hundi*s were transacted between Muscat, Zanzibar, Bombay and

Mandvi. The monasteries acted as banks. *Hundi*s were issued from Mandvi by monasteries and then counter-issued in Zanzibar by firms such as those of Jairam Shivji's and Thariya Topan's.

Monasteries not only maintained Shiva temples and Sanskrit *pathashalas*, they also operated as business conglomerates. They owned valuable land in Mandvi, Bombay and Karachi. They were funded through donations of the pious, bequests that they got when people died without heirs, business profits, including profits from the opium trade, lease rentals from landholdings, and profits from banking operations. Kachchhi monasteries seem to have resembled Armenian religious shrines that accumulated capital, leveraging their role as clearing banks for overland trade. The Goswami network, spread across Mandvi, Bombay, Karachi, Muscat, Zanzibar and east Africa, resembled that of the Chettiars who were famous for their widespread operations in Burma, Ceylon and Malaya.

A Kachchhi businessman had three options for obtaining credit. A loan from relatives or from firms known to them could be convenient, but the amounts would necessarily be limited. A loan from a substantial merchant was the second option. The third potential source were the monasteries of the Goswamis who had access to a wide network. The Goswamis were true bankers, not just moneylenders. They accepted deposits as well as made loans. There were a total of forty monasteries or *math*s, as they were known in

Kachchh. By tradition, the Dnyanagar Nirmalgar *math* was considered the chief or head *math*. This *math* acted as the central bank and clearing house for other *maths* and indeed for Kachchh itself. The heads or mahants of the different Goswami *maths* were selected by an informal but very effective process of mutual consent. The mahants could not be hereditary as all Goswami monks were required to be bachelors. The *maths* also provided safety deposit services for clients who needed to store their gold, silver, and other valuables. Secret store rooms in the building of the main *math* in Mandvi are a testimony to this aspect of their business. The *maths'* short- and long-term credit were both productive and remunerative; their banking set-up was deeply embedded within broader Indian Ocean networks. The Goswamis had considerable political clout. Their services were frequently sought by the *durbar*. Riddhgar Goswami was known to have been personally welcome at the royal court at all times. The tradition of the Goswami banker monks is so unique to Kachchh that their existence perhaps answers Claude Markovits' question asking after the secret behind the magical success of Kachchhis overseas.

The Language of Business

Kachchhi entrepreneurs had a love affair with accounting. According to one Kachchhi tradition, the account book is compared to a mirror that reflects the financial façade of a merchant. It could also be a talisman that saves merchants from making losses. It was therefore perilous to ignore the account book. Double entry bookkeeping and difficult compound interest formulas were completely internalized by Kachchhi businessmen. The daybook called *rojmel* was the fundamental financial record for a business. This carefully recorded financial transactions at the time that they occurred. The bookkeeper's next device, the journal known as *avro*, was the bridge between the daybook and the ledger. On a monthly basis, the bookkeeper copied the financial information from the daybook into the journal. The journal included a bill register called *hundini nondh*. The goal of the journal was to organize transactions by customer and by date in order to facilitate the creation of the ledger. The ledger or *khatavahi* contained a summary of all entries made in the *avro*. Details of transactions with a client were carefully entered in the ledger. The ledger was many a time treated as evidence for future claims or settlement. Kachchhis believed in planning and forecasting future profits. This task was assigned to experienced accountants. Cash was king for all Kachchhi merchants, and cash was meticulously tracked in a cashbook referred to as *rokadvahi*. For other items, a notebook known as *hathavahi* was maintained. Some bankers kept separate books for principal amounts and for interest, called *vijavahi*. The bill register, known as *jangadvahi*, showed all bills of exchange issued and discharged.

In Gujarati, accounts was known as *namu* and the accountant as *Mehtaji*. The account books and other financial documents of firms such as those of Ratansi Purshottam's make for fascinating reading. An interesting feature of Kachchhi letterheads was their professional 'logo' which was carried prominently: traders printed weighing scales, swords or tridents, potters' wheels and seafarers anchors for logos. Another fascinating aspect of Kachchhi legal documents was that the name of the first witness to the execution was always the sun i.e. *Shree Suraj ni Sankh*. This custom transcended religious differences. The tradition of Kachchh was that documents and agreements were prepared and signed during the day in the presence of the sun. For this reason, during the monsoon, when the sun was rarely visible, matters that required documentation were avoided!

From Apprentice to Merchant

The apprenticeship system was the bedrock of the education and training of Kachchhi merchants. The Kachchhi love for numbers is illustrated by the frequent references to *gantar* or numeracy skills as being more valuable for survival and progress than *bhantar* or formal book-learning. For Kachchhis, the bazaar was the best school. Sampat describes the apprenticeship period set for a Kachchhi boy to turn him from a novice into a seasoned businessperson. When a boy was around fifteen years of age, he was sent to a firm i.e. *pedhi* to start his business lessons. Like apprentices the world over, he was first put to work cleaning the shop, lighting the diya (lamp), buying groceries and so on. At the next stage, he was taught accounting; he learned to keep the books of account and draw up rudimentary balance sheets. He then moved on to learn how to scrutinize the quality of products and commodities, where to warehouse different articles and how to keep track of expenses. In a span of ten years, almost all details pertaining to the *pedhi* were learnt. Travellers like Ruschenberger have attested to the fact that far from Mandvi, in distant places like Muscat and Zanzibar, the Kachchhi system of apprenticeship flourished. Bartle Frere's observation at Zanzibar captures the graduation of the apprentice:

> Arriving at his future scene of business with little beyond credentials of his fellow caste men, after perhaps a brief apprenticeship in some older firms, he starts a shop of his own with goods advanced on credit by some large house and after a few years, when he has made a little money, generally returns home to marry to make fresh business and then comes back to Africa to repeat, on a large scale.

Many firms had residential quarters; the apprentice literally spent day and night at the firm. Living without parental support, many apprentices learnt to make multiple adjustments. Apprenticeship was a great leveller. A few apprentices were orphans or had a single parent; many came from a poor background. In contrast, some of the others were wealthy, and some even future heirs of the firm. There was little distinction in the early stages in the training of this diverse group. Laddha Damji, who controlled the big business concern of Jairam Shivji's at Zanzibar, came from a poor family headed by a single parent. He went through the standard apprenticeship module, starting with cooking, dusting and cleaning. It is said that he rose up the ranks partly by watching closely the conclusion of trade deals, and partly by virtue of his good handwriting and accountancy skills. In just a few years, he rose to the top of the firm. Caste and religion were not barriers for clever, hardworking apprentices. Thariya Topan, an Ismaili, learned the ropes at the Hindu firm of Jairam Shivji and eventually set up his own big business firm. Jivraj Balu, Sheth Narsi Natha worked their way up to be eventually ranked as 'Sheth' in the business world of Bombay. Khatau Makanji was born in Kachchh–Tera, and came at a very early age to Bombay, where he became an apprentice in the flourishing Bhatia firm belonging to his maternal uncle Jivraj Balu, which was then run by Dwarkadas Vasanji. Khatau's natural intelligence and keen business instincts resulted in his speedy admittance as a partner in the firm's establishment at Coomta (Kanara); a few years later, he was entrusted with the management of the headquarters of the concern at Bombay. Khatau possessed a brilliant mind and had uncanny commercial instincts. He was quick and accurate in his judgement of men. Highly respected in business circles and beloved of his own community, he made for himself a name that was honoured in many provinces in India. He died in 1876, leaving behind two sons. His surviving brother Jairaj Makanji managed the firm Khatau Makanji and Company. There were many stories similar to that of Khatau's.

After the tough training period came the *veparni aanti guti*, i.e. twists and turns of the trade or wheels within wheels, which the novices were expected to explore before they earned a reputation in the market as established traders. Local usage and customs guided their trading pursuits from start to finish. The *Digest of Local Customs and Usages*, published in 1881 by the state of Kachchh, explains in depth the processes and norms that a trader was required to follow.

Each trader was placed at a different level in the pecking order. A big businessman was one who had his own warehouse (*vakhar*) and who bought and sold commodities through brokers. Brokers maintained samples of goods or *vanki*, to be shown to customers. Once the sample was chosen, the rates were fixed and goods were handed over. Thereafter, the trader claimed money from the buyer. This type of trader was called *vakharwala vepari*, or wholesale merchant. The *nichatia vepari* or retailer displayed his goods in an open shop from where buyers purchased them at the retail price. The peddler, or *feria vepari,* purchased goods and travelled around selling his merchandise. Each commodity or product had its own sales tradition. Rhinoceros hide and alum were sold for cash. Silk was paid for in fifteen or twenty days. Some commodities were sold either for cash or in a postpaid mode.

Different forms of partnerships or *pantiada* were in vogue in Kachchh. These collaborations could be based on unwritten rules or cemented through a formal agreement. Some partnerships were similar to contemporary venture investments. One partner invested capital—*rash*—while the other contributed his talent and efforts. In most cases, the firm was established in the names of all its partners. Sometimes, the names of inactive or sleeping partners were not mentioned. Some partners preferred that their names not be known; in such cases, a *tryat,* i.e. a third person having nothing to do with the business, may lend his name to it. The person in whose name the business was carried out was known as the *prassidh* or known partner, and the others were called the *gupt bhagidar,* the hidden or anonymous partners. Whatever the form of partnership, rules were laid out pertaining to roles, and responsibilities, and distribution of profit and losses.

The most senior employee of any business was the manager or *munim.* Good *munims* were known for their integrity and acumen and were highly respected. The services of a broker (*dalal*) were essential for smooth transactions. In Kachchh, broking was a registered profession and anyone who wished to join the profession was required to take permission from the state revenue officers. A broker was required to pay a part of his income to the *durbar*. If a broker used faulty weights and measures or worked in a fraudulent manner, he was suspended from business. The broker kept a book (*vahi*) to note down the deals between buyers and sellers; he also registered the same details in the customs collector's record. This note was used as evidence in case of a dispute. A broker in a particular business was not allowed to become a principal in that business, whether solely or in partnership.

Kachchh had an unusual, but important and integral member in its business community—the recommender, or *bhalamaniya*. The trader banked on a recommender to get his transactions done in a methodical manner. In return, the recommender was paid his share called *haksi*. He was also tipped handsomely for odd jobs.

The utilization of a firm's office space and its appearance are quite intriguing in their details. The office could be a single or multi-level building. It was furnished with mattresses and desks. We have a very interesting description provided by the explorer Charles New, who writes, 'Tailor–fashion he sits upon his low couch- a mattress spread upon the ground- and surrounded by a row of cash and other boxes . . .' The *pedhi* of Jairam Shivji's in Zanzibar was multi-level and resembled a palace, conveying the strength of the big business house. Intentionally or otherwise, Charles New draws attention to the practical skills (*avadat*), managerial acumen and passion for business of the mostly Kachchhi Hindu merchants of Muscat and Zanzibar. He observed: 'See him at his books, and you see a man lost to all the world.'

2

PEARLS, DATES AND ARMS: KACHCHHI ENTREPRENEURS IN MUSCAT

Muscat, in the kingdom of Oman in southeast Arabia, is blessed with a fine and deep harbour where all types of seagoing vessels can anchor safely and comfortably. In the nineteenth century, Muscat emerged as the twin city of Mandvi. Whether Oman was an extension of Kachchh or whether it was the other way around is an argument that need not detain us. Suffice it to say that Arab traders of Muscat, in alliance with Kachchhi merchants, dominated not only mercantile activities in the western Indian Ocean, but also pretty much ruled the roost apropos of east African commerce. The story of this trade covers goods as diverse as precious pearls, sweet dates and sinister arms!

The Rise of Muscat

One must give credit to the Portuguese who, five hundred years ago, figured out the strategic value of Muscat. For the next two centuries, they used the military fortresses they had built to fend off the Ottomans, the Dutch and the English from Muscat. But they were not able to tame the Yarriba power which made frequent inland attacks. The Yarribas first attacked in the 1630s, forcing the Portuguese to seek peace and possibly pay tribute. By 1643, the Yarribas took over Sohar and gained independent access to the sea, enabling them to bypass the Portuguese export licensing system. At the time of Portuguese rule, the Indian traders who were active in Muscat were Kachchhi and Thattai Bhatias from Sindh. An early reference to the Indian presence in Muscat appears in a tale of Ibn Ruzaiq. It describes the life of an Indian merchant Narottam who acted as a supply agent for the Portuguese. Narottam disapproved of the Portuguese commander Pereira's wish to marry his daughter. In an attempt to rebuff the proposal, it is said that he helped the Yarriba ruler expel the Portuguese from Muscat. The Yarriba ruler returned Narottam's favour by exempting Hindu merchants from payment of taxes to the Yarriba government. Whether this story is true or not, there is no doubt that there existed friendly relations between the Yarribas and Indian merchants. There is also no doubt that in 1649, Sultan

b. Sayf al-Yarriba stormed Muscat and took it from the Portuguese. The Portuguese remained strong on the seas and continued the war there. Even as they gave up hopes of recapturing Muscat, they continued to blockade the port. The Imams skilfully used the Dutch and the English to counter the Portuguese and build up Muscat's coffee trade with the Persian Gulf, India and south Arabia. With great foresight, they ensured that no foreign power, then or later, was allowed to establish a factory in Oman. Oman under the Yarribas did not remain peaceful. The country plunged into a civil war, which invited Persian interference. The civil war more or less ended when Ahmad bin Sai'd was recognized as Imam c. 1743–44. With the return of peace, Muscat began to develop again and grew in importance. As both the Ottomans and the Persians were relatively weak, there were no foreign rivals, and Muscat's trade flourished, especially in coffee. This changed somewhat in 1783, when the Qwasim and the Utub captured the island of Bahrain, which emerged as a maritime rival.

The dynamics of the growth and decline of ports in India—Mandvi, Bombay and Surat—had a mirror image in the Persian Gulf too. The interplay of European forces represented by the Portuguese (who ceded Bombay to the British) and the Dutch, who were active in Kachchh till superseded by the British, also had parallels in the Gulf. Muscat gained importance over other ports of call, unfolding an interesting chapter in the history of Oman. During the eighteenth century, when Persia came under the rule of Nadir Shah, Dutch influence received a setback. With the British, Nadir Shah's relations were positive, although always clouded by some level of ambivalence. In 1741–42, the British obtained a trade-related *rogom* from Nadir Shah. This *rogom* gave away various concessions to the British, who established their trading station at Gombooron (Banda Abbas). As per British accounts, under the *rogom,* the Company's trade was carried on with considerable success so long as Persia was tranquil. A ship was annually consigned direct from Europe; in addition, many consignments were made from Bombay. Sales consisted chiefly of broad cloth and a small quantity of iron and lead; returns were in wool, copper and specie.

After the death of Nadir Shah, the general disorder that ensued changed equations in the Gulf. Earlier, Bandar Abbas, where both the Dutch and the British had factories, was the most important port. After Nadir Shah's death, Bandar Abbas declined under the oppressive rule of Mulla Ali Shah, with the Dutch and the British shutting down their factories there. Commerce at Bandar Abbas was also adversely affected by developments that took place in 1758 in the interior of Persia. These developments isolated Bandar Abbas from other parts of the country. British trade suffered further from a surprise French attack. After Mulla Ali Shah's reign, Arab unrest increased. All these circumstances affected British trade at Bandar Abbas.

The British retreat from Persian trade is captured in sombre tones by the Company's London documents:

> We have taken the epoch of the abandonment of the Gombroon factory, as the conclusion of the ancient state of commerce between Persia and India . . . after the removal of the agent and council to Bussora, the trade was diverted to different quarter. Though still a considerable part of the goods sent there entered Persia by way of Haiza, yet the troubles that shortly after broke out in that quarter prevented its being carried at best on the part of the company to any great extent.

Bandar Abbas was abandoned in favour of Basra. By 1763, no Dutch or British trading stations were left in the southern end of the Gulf. Basra and Bushire were the gainers. According to one report, 'In 1763, a factory was established at Bushire under articles of agreement with Sheikh Soddoom, and confirmed by a Royal grant from Carium Caun, but we do not find that any considerable trade was established.' The only relatively secure and profitable location for European commercial outposts was the northern head of the Gulf at Basra, which was alternately under Ottoman and Persian control. Even Basra's position became tenuous. After the death of Shah Karim Khan in 1779, Persian control declined rapidly as Persia plunged into civil war. Three major ports of the Persian Gulf—Bushire,

Bander or Bandar Abbas and Basra—all went into decline. In the late eighteenth century, Persian control from the Shah's court over the ports, islands and coastal districts of the Persian Gulf further declined. The Gulf was transformed into a theatre of conflict between different fleets of Arab raiders. Well-armed British and Dutch ships continued to operate here.

As the Persian empire continued to fragment and decline, a new maritime power emerged in eastern Arabia—Oman. In the first half of the nineteenth century, Muscat, the capital of Oman, overtook Bandar Abbas and Bushire that had earlier been ports of consequence. On the other side of the Arabian Sea, Surat was in decline and trade volumes were down. Sultan Hamad bin Seyyid (1785–92) of Oman was a far-sighted ruler who took prompt action to lessen the impact of the overall decline, one of the key reasons for the rise of Muscat. He decreased the import duties collected from Hindus and Jews, from 9 per cent to 6 1/2 per cent ad valorem. Such measures were meant to make Muscat an attractive port. This is evident from the following report:

> Great part of what had been carried on from India, immediately with Persia, seems to have been transferred to Muskat, which is very conveniently situated for a Depot of goods intended for the Gulph, at a time when an unsettled state of government renders it hazardous to risk property

in the country. From a judicious encouragement given by the Imam at that port he has brought it to a degree of consequence, it would without that and above circumstances never been attained. The Imaum himself has now Fleet consisting (it is said) of Twelve sail of 500 tons each & upwards, besides a great number of Dows, dingeys & which, though many of them are armed, he employs occasionally on voyages to different parts of India & up in the Gulph; ships of different nations carry to this Port the merchandise required for the consumption of Persia, which is purchased by the Muscat merchants & by them again transported in small vessels or Boats to the Persian shore.

Timely state intervention was to the benefit of Muscat, even as overall trade declined in the Gulf. Simultaneously, the changes in exchange patterns afforded new scope for developing Oman's trade in distinct ways. The increased import of Mocha coffee into the Gulf and Muscat was aided by the formation of the Omani convoy system carrying the annual coffee fleet to the Gulf. This buttressed the key position of Muscat. On account of all these measures, by 1775, Muscat had clearly emerged as the principal trans-shipment centre between the Persian Gulf, the Red Sea and India. The Omanis provided cover for the Kachchhi Bhatias to move to the eastern littoral of Africa, establishing the India-Arabia-Africa triangle.

Muscat became the key vertex of this triangle. Wellsted aptly said of Muscat:

> This town is entitled to a high rank among Oriental cities, not only as the emporium of a very considerable trade between Arabia, India, and Persia, but also, in reference to its extensive imports, of some note as the seaport of Oman.

Various Indian products like cotton, timber, rice, sugar, spices and ghee were brought not only from Kachchh and Bombay, but also from Calcutta, to Oman for both home consumption and re-export. The rise of Muscat enabled Oman to consolidate its power in the Arabian waters with the occupation of Gwadar on the Makran coast and by taking Qishim, Hormuz and Bandar Abbas and its dependencies on lease. Without becoming a monopolist himself, the Sultan demonstrated his keen interest in trade by building up his own fleet of fifty ships between 1790 and 1802–03. These ships crisscrossed the sea, covering several destinations. The ships went as far as Bengal to pick up Bengal muslin and piece goods; to Bombay and Malabar on India's west coast to collect timber and pepper; to the eastern islands to fetch drugs and spices; and to Mauritius for coffee and cotton. In the seventeenth century itself, Muscat had been a major market for textiles from Punjab sent via Surat. Muscat had extensive trade relations with Mysore in south India. Hyder Ali and Tipu Sultan leveraged

Muscat to develop business relations in all of Arabia. Tipu Sultan, following the European fashion, built factories at Muscat and Kachchh. The fear that Oman might follow Tipu into the camp of the French was one of the reasons for the first agreement with Oman by the British in 1798. By 1800, Muscat emerged as a trading emporium, carrying on lucrative dealings with Kachchh, Baluchistan and Sindh. The rough division of labour involved the Arabs managing the shipping and the freighting while their Kachchhi counterparts handled sales, collections, storage, purchase and finance.

Oman benefited from the Anglo-French rivalry. The French did not hesitate to target English colours even when their ships were sailed by Indian merchants. Indian vessels found it convenient to acquire the neutral flag of Muscat in the absence of British ability to protect them. Another reason for the success of the Omani merchant fleet was that the freight rate of an Omani ship was between half to one-third that of a British ship.

Trade and Settlements in the Persian Gulf

At the turn of the eighteenth century, Muscat's preeminent position was illustrated by the reckoning that more than half of Indian imports at Bushire and Basra, and the bulk of imports into Bahrain, were received through Muscat. Lewis Pelly, a British

Political Resident, described the trading web of Arabia as extending from Europe in the west to territories to the east of India—spanning western India, Muscat, east Africa and the Aden coastline of Arabia. While Muscat was the leader, several other trading posts were important too. One caravan route commenced from Mished Tbrah and other places in southern-central Asia down through Zend to Bandar Abbas. Another caravan route came by way of Teheran, Isfahan and Shiraz down to Bushire. Goods were also funnelled through the Tigris on a river steamer or boat to Basra. Some trade also took place along the western coastline between Kuwait and 'Frains' to the north and Ras al Khayimah to the south. Kachchhi merchants, though small in number, were located throughout the Persian Gulf and were found in places as diverse as Yazd, Bandar Abbas, Kerman, and Lingah, apart from being found in the principal Indian centres of Muscat, Basra and Bahrain. British official records indicate that a handful of Kachchhis, along with their Sindhi counterparts, managed to trade in the less favourable regions in the area traditionally avoided by foreigners. At Bandar Abbas, there were sixty Khojas, thirty to forty Shikarpuri Banias and four or five Kachchhi Bhatias. They were principally *gumastas* or agents of Sindh and Bombay firms. They were prosperous. Their main complaint was about the difficulty that collection of goods and money from the interiors entailed. For instance, they had ordered and paid advances to cotton growers in the province of Kerman. But when the crop was ready, the Persian governor of Kerman refused to allow the goods to pass unless the merchants would consent to his taking half of them at the price at which they had advanced them to the producers. This deprived the merchants of profits accruing from price changes. The governor gave priority of export to goods that he had seized. The merchants had to deal with the asymmetry of tackling inventories when prices fell, but of not benefiting when prices rose. Kachchhi merchants tried to limit their direct operations in the interiors and stay focused on the coast. They mitigated their risks by dealing with correspondent or commission agents at Kerman and Yazd, while altogether avoiding transactions with Persian subjects residing in the capital of Persia. In 1856, at Lingah, a port on the Persian coast, British Indian traders complained of an attempt to increase duties on their goods. The demand was resisted, as the treaty between Persia and England of 1841 did not allow more than 5 per cent to be charged. Sadlier Forster noted that 'There were neither Hindus nor Christians residing at Katif.' The uncertainties in these places made Muscat even more attractive to Kachchhis.

Indian Capitalists and Business Practices in Muscat

Unlike the ports of Persia, Oman was a safe haven for many different types of merchants including

Kachchhis. Abraham Parson, who visited Muscat in 1775, saw immense quantities of goods in the town piled up in the streets without a guard. The bazaars of Muscat were well supplied with grain, dried fruit, chinaware and coarse cloths. In the early nineteenth century, Muscat had the appearance of a cosmopolitan town; its streets were packed with Arabs, Jews, Hindus, Baluchis, Turks and Africans. The Albusaid rulers borrowed money from Indian financiers. This capital was also used to ship Omani troops to east Africa. For Indian traders, this helped them establish a commercial link to Zanzibar. At Muscat, the Sultan himself was a coffee merchant and had great empathy for all merchants, irrespective of their ethnic or religious affiliation, and encouraged them to invest and settle in Muscat. He maintained a competent police who guaranteed security of life and property not only for the locals but also for the foreigners. Kachchhis found Oman particularly attractive because the Sultan gave considerable religious freedom to Hindus, which was unusual for an Islamic country.

Sampat believes that their trading acumen and mastery over finance helped the Kachchhis gain importance over their Arab counterparts in Muscat. The Bhimanis and the firm of Shivji Topan were among the early Indian traders in Muscat. The success of Kachchhi Bhatias in Muscat was followed by their success in Zanzibar. They replaced the Sindhi Bhatias who had been dominant in Muscat from the eighteenth century to the 1820s.

The rulers of Oman, while mindful of their position as Muslims and as Arabs, also seem to have had an instinctive understanding of early globalization trends in the Indian Ocean. Until 1833, import duties were 7 per cent for non-Muslims and 5 per cent for Muslims. The Sultan and his close merchant associates did not pay anything. In 1806–07, Seyyid Said became the Sultan of Muscat. With his far-sighted vision, he signed commercial treaties with America in 1833, with Britain in 1839, with France in 1844 and with Germany in 1856. These treaties reduced the ad valorem duty rates to 5 per cent for all non-Muslims, and to 2.5 per cent for Muslims on all goods brought into the port of Muscat. No export duty was levied; transit goods having once been paid for on import, paid nothing, whether consumed in the country or exported to any other market. The annual income from customs shot up to Rs 20 lakh despite the reduction in duty rates as the volume of trade expanded tremendously. That Oman had clearly become a trading nation was demonstrated by the fact that the Imam earned less than Rs 1 lakh in revenues from agriculture. The Sultan ensured that regulations were fair and their administration competent. The good reputation of Indian merchants is attested to by the fact that the task of monitoring the customs administration was assigned to Indians. In the c.1790s, customs collection came under a wealthy Kachchhi Bhatia merchant named Mowji, of the Bhimani family firm. Despite being surrounded by Islamic extremist groups like the Wahabis and Qasimis, the Sultans of Oman seemed to understand that it was liberalism and not chauvinism that would contribute to their own prosperity. In 1802, Sheikh Mansur, who was in the service of the Sultan, reckoned that there were in Oman 4000 'Beniani' i.e. Banias, whom he found conspicuously industrious. Though Mansur's numbers appear to be a tad too high, there is no doubt that a large number of Indian merchants were settled in Muttrah, a town between Muscat and the Batinah coast, and of course in Muscat itself where the Sultan granted them several rights and where their presence was tolerated and respected because of their disciplined conduct.

Joseph Osgood, a western traveller, was a keen observer of the trading practices of Indian merchants. He described the Bania's way of finalizing a business deal with a customer. The buyer and the seller would negotiate with their hands under a cloth. Pantomimic finger language fixed the prices. Osgood adds: 'When the terms of purchase have been agreed upon the strings of tongue were loosed by the exclamation "Halas!"—"Tis finished!" and the contract is ratified by the ancient method of striking hands.' According to Joseph Osgood, while this mode of dealing had the advantage of secrecy, it also afforded dishonest brokers 'grand opportunities' to cheat their employers. Osgood, who stayed with several Indian merchants, was of the opinion that some of them were 'shrewd, artful and rapacious'. According to William Palgrave, Sultan Said himself knew that whatever might be the energy and enterprise of his own subjects, their commercial transactions would never attain real importance except with the cooperation and under the lead of Indian merchants. Accordingly, he encouraged the Banias of Kachchh and other Indians to settle in Muscat; not only was a policy of religious toleration followed, but specific privileges were given to 'a half-Hindu colony'.

Kachchhi merchants advanced funds to date growers and producers of handicrafts, either through their own employees or through independent brokers working on a commission basis. Despite the unsettling conditions, there were many intrepid Indian Banias in Basra. They traded either through direct channels with Mandvi and Bombay or through Kachchhi Banias in Muscat. The Kachchhis of Muscat acquired dominant positions in coffee and pearls, which they marketed in India.

Kachchhi merchants evolved a bankruptcy code. If a merchant was not in a position to pay his creditors, then his transactions were stopped and he was declared insolvent, or *devaliu* or *nadar*. The insolvent merchant would then close his shop or warehouse and show his books of account to the creditors to find a way out to clear the dues. In another custom, a trader would sit during the day in his shop with a candle burning before him, which publically signalled his failure.

Western travellers noticed that members of his caste, or his creditors, would many a time condemn him publicly and in some extreme cases even beat him up. Despite these rituals, in actual fact he was given a fair amount of time to re-establish his business and pay back his debts. In Kachchh, some cases of insolvency would be formally declared before the durbar. If the insolvent merchant did not take responsibility for repayment of his debt but absconded, then his creditors would approach the court. Creditors would mutually consent to check the accounts of the debtor, and would approach a third party, the Mahajan or the formal court to settle the matter. Before confiscating the insolvent's property, selected personal items, such as cooking vessels, household material and clothes were handed over to the insolvent. The intention was not to deprive the insolvent of items that were vital for his daily needs. An appropriate instalment schedule was put in place to liquidate property and cash so that the insolvent could pay back as much of his debts as possible. Unlike modern codes, the formal bankruptcy of a Kachchhi merchant did not absolve him of his obligation to pay all his debts in full; paying back a debt was considered a moral duty, and the obligation was assumed by his children. According to prevalent Hindu religious belief, it was essential for sons to clear the debts of a dead father, as otherwise the soul of the deceased would not rest in peace.

A Little Kachchh in Muscat

Kachchhi Hindu Bhatias and Muslim Khojas thrived in Oman, most notably in Muscat and Muttrah. J. R. Wellsted noticed that the Banias were in greater numbers in Muscat than in the other ports of the Persian Gulf as Hindus in Muscat were allowed to practise their religion and were not required to adhere to a humiliating dress code which was strictly enforced in the cities of Yemen. According to Buckingham, Oman ensured personal liberty and safety, and was hospitable to strangers, thus encouraging traders to settle there. An American ambassador, Edmund Roberts observed: 'All religions within the Sultan's dominions are not merely tolerated, but they are protected by his highness; and there is no obstacle whatever to prevent the Christians, the Jew or the Gentile, from preaching their peculiar doctrines, or erecting temples.' The Sultan of Muscat permitted them to construct temples for worship. Two temples—Ma'bad Al-Banyan and Bayt Al-Pir—were established in the Hindu quarter. While these two temples do not exist today, there is a temple in existence for over one hundred and fifty years at the Al-Hawash quarter, called Hawash Al-Banyan. There was one crucial difference between the Muslim Khojas and the Hindu Kachchhi traders in Muscat. The Khojas brought along their womenfolk and settled in Muscat, living more or less as complete families. Despite the story of Narottam Bania having brought

along his family with him as early as during the time of
the Portuguese, Hindu traders as a rule did not bring
their families overseas. The Khojas tended to view their
move to Muscat as permanent. Hindus thought of
themselves as transients. It is not clear whether Hindu
women were left behind due to concerns for their
safety in an Islamic environment. Climatic conditions
too played a major role in this decision. Some Kachchhi
merchants did succumb to the effects of the extreme
heat of Muscat. Many died annually from apoplexy and
other heat-induced diseases. An Arab writer, Abdur
Razzak, has left a description of the Muscat heat: 'The
heat of the sun,' he says, 'was so intense that it burned
the ruby in the mine and the marrow in the bones: the
sword in its scabbard melted like wax . . . In the plains
the chase became a matter of perfect ease; as for the
desert, it was filled with roasted gazelles.' The wild and
dense jungles and the unhealthy climate of east Africa
too deterred the Hindus from taking their women to
Zanzibar.

The Hindu settlement in Muscat did not have
any resident women, but was otherwise a full-fledged
one. The settlement was in the eastern part of the
town, where the Hindus had their temples as early as
the seventeenth century. They lived either in the Al-
Waljat or in the Banyan quarters, both of which were
located inside the old walls of the town. In Muttrah,
they had their own quarter of shops. Their houses were
of stone and cement. The 'people from Kutch, who

monopolized considerable share of the trade, occupied
the largest and best.' A row of shops had their own *delas*
(a dwelling with an inner yard) in the narrow streets.
Muscat was truly a space transformed, where one could
imagine oneself as living in Mandvi. Here, Kachchhi
Hindus wore traditional Hindu clothes, ate a vegetarian
diet and even maintained *goshalas*. As part of its policy of
religious toleration, Oman did not force Hindus to bury
their dead. Hindu crematoria were located in Kalbuh,
a place between Muscat and Sidab, which was accessed
by sea. The Kachchhis as well as other foreigners felt
pleasantly welcome in Muscat because its excellent
police force protected their quarters and ensured them
security. Religious beliefs led to a division of labour
between Kachchhi Hindu Banias and Kachchhi Khojas.
Hindu merchants, given their vegetarian traditions, did
not deal in fish. The business of dried fish was a Khoja
monopoly. The Khojas doubled up as shopkeepers,
carpenters, shipbuilders, artisans and small merchants.
They traded in textiles, grains and dates. Sir Bartle Frere
saw the Kachchhis' business enterprise as 'a very thriving
labyrinth, of fish, meat, with grain, and vegetable
sellers, shoemakers, cutlers, and hardware sellers, and
the shops of beads and ornaments such as M and K.'
While Khoja community traditions depicted their
arrival in Oman as having happened centuries earlier,
Ibn Razyak's historical documents date the period of
the 1740s as the time of their connection with Oman.
British records mention their settlement here from the

1780s onwards. Bartle Frere checked an inscription over a door in the Khoja quarter, which suggested that the building had been constructed two hundred and forty years earlier, i.e. in the later medieval period. The Khojas, also known as Lutyanas or Lawatiyas, seem to have originated in Persia and India. They established themselves chiefly at Muttrah, a town three miles away from Muscat. Muttrah connects Muscat and the Batinah coast, and was an important commercial centre. The Khojas at Muttrah lived in a separate quarter or Sur, which was known as Sur Luwatiya. It was a restricted space, and no outsiders were allowed to enter without prior permission. Khoja women moved without veils within the quarter. The Sur at Muttrah was a distinct space, with inner windows and doors, substantial walls and inter-connected houses. While the Hindu Bania generally lived above his shop, the Khoja merchant commuted to his shop in the markets at Muscat and Muttrah. Daily, they took the ferry; some, as Frere describes, in 'smart' boats of their own, while others in 'omnibus' boats and canoes. Their dress resembled that of the affluent Arab merchants. Khoja females adorned themselves with considerable jewellery. The Khojas were a close-knit group and had a detailed system of community rules similar in many ways to those of the Hindu Mahajan. The community worshipped in a *jamatkhana* within the walls of its Sur. It had a stipulated hierarchical structure, and had a reputation for being disciplined and organized.

Indian Investors and the Pearl Trade

Kachchhis were ubiquitous in the trade networks of the Persian Gulf. Besides the Arabian Dhow, the Kachchhi Batela was almost invariably sighted in the waters of the Arabian Sea. David Seton, in 1804, reported that Arabian and African products were chiefly exported to Mandvi, from where they would be transported inland to Marwar, Multan and the interiors of India. The products of Arabia were re-exported to local and other foreign markets. In return, Kachchh chiefly supplied grain, alum, iron and steel to the Muscat market. Kachchhis had a virtual monopoly over trade in articles like Indian cloth and piece goods. Shields exported to Muscat yielded a good profit margin. For example, if the cost of shields at Kachchh was 10 to 20 *koris* a piece, they were sold in Muscat at 30 to 40 *koris*. Pearls had been traded in the Persian Gulf since ancient times. In the 1830s, Kachchhis dominated this trade, which was reported to be worth $1.5 million annually. The lucrative coffee trade was largely in the hands of the Kachchhi 'Banians'. Pearls and coffee were brought into Muscat and then re-exported.

Pearl fisheries flourished in the Persian Gulf in the nineteenth century, as demand for the 'luminous' objects on account of new European fashions augmented the traditional demand from the oriental courts. The management of the pearl trade generated substantial profits for the Indian Banias. Thattai Bhatias from Sindh, who were settled in Bahrain, and Kachchhi Bhatias and Khojas who were settled in Muscat, were the chief players in the market. They not only owned most of the boats, but advanced provisions, cloth, and other essentials to the pearl fishers. The industry operated chiefly on credit extended by Banias to pearl divers, both during the non-diving season and in the spring when boats were provisioned with supplies of dates and rice that could last for many days. Control of the supply chain ensured high profits for the pearl merchants. One British report claims that the Banias were a necessity 'for the reckless Arabs who were in the habit of spending whatever they had and getting back to the Bania to keep themselves supplied with food and raiment for the rest of the year.' It further notes that the Arabs rarely kept accounts or signed any agreements. For this reason, entries made in a Bania's ledger were taken as evidence of the veracity of each transaction. The Bania supplied the *Nakhuda*, or the master of the pearling boat, with every necessity, including the clothes, food, and tobacco required for the trip. At the end of the season, the debts were settled using the proceeds from the sale of pearls. A bad season for the divers would lead to debts being carried forward. There is evidence that some Banias settled in places like Sharjah operated as goldsmiths, apart from financing and dealing in pearls.

The *Nakhuda* would borrow chiefly from a Bania or a *Mussaqam*. On return from the fisheries, the *Nakhuda* would make over to the Bania his whole packet of pearls, the gross value of which would be determined. The Bania would take a commission of 20 per cent. From the remainder 80 per cent, the earlier advances made to the *Nakhuda* would be deducted and the amount that was left given to him. The Bania probably made a margin of between 20 per cent and 35 per cent on the input supply side too. While this was lucrative for the Bania, his risks in the event of a bad season or a drop in pearl prices were also high. Luckily, the value of the pearls of each season was universally known. Disputes were rare and transactions were easily effected.

The few disputes that did arise were submitted to a marine court called *salifeh-ul-ghous*. A decree was usually issued, allowing the *Nakhuda* to pay off his debts in yearly instalments. Having recovered the money, the agent supplied a paper of release that formally freed the *Nakhuda* from further obligations. He was now free to seek a new financier. The new financier was liable for his previous dues if the earlier ones had not been paid and if the formal release had not been obtained. The formal release protected all parties. In case a third party trader bought from a *Nakhuda* without the permission of the *Mussaqam*, then he became responsible for the entire debt of the *Nakhuda's*, even if it exceeded the actual pearl purchase. The contractual bond tied up the *Nakhuda* and his crew to the Bania and vice versa. Some Banias found it more convenient to take a discounted sum rather than wait for the *Nakhuda's* instalments.

With this, the Bania's claims would be over and the Nakhuda became a free man able to enter into new contracts. His house and other onshore property could not be touched. He usually got himself a fresh crew and hired a boat at the recognized rate of 20 per cent on the value of the season's harvest. The trade 'was built on a structure of debt . . . (in which) the merchants owned the ships . . . and owned the *Nakhodas* as well as the ships, for the *Nakhodas* could scarcely ever expect to be free of debt.' However, there was a system in place to render borrowers time to pay back their debts. In unfavourable seasons, merchants usually deferred their claims until the third year, when they either expropriated the boats of the debtors or figured out an arrangement that would allow the debt to be paid off over time. A promising trading season meant that the *Nakhuda* could pay off his debts, and if he was fortunate, clear a tidy profit for himself as a bonus.

The pearl trade benefited the Banias, the *Nakhudas*, the divers and the Sheikdoms who derived tax revenue from it. But, given that it was built on an edifice of debt, default was a risk. British records frequently refer to absconding divers. Migration of debtors engaged in pearl fishery and trade from one jurisdiction to another with a view to evading their liabilities, was a significant matter of concern. In 1868, Colonel Pelly took steps to extradite such individuals from the chiefs who harboured them, but with very little success. On 24 June 1879, an agreement for the mutual surrender of fraudulent, absconding debtors was accepted and sealed by the Trucial Sheikhs. However these Sheikhs, unlike the Sultan of Oman, did not follow a far-sighted policy of supporting trade. Some of them were not above making attempts at extorting money from traders. In 1861, the Sheikh of Bahrain, for instance, compelled British Indian subjects in his territory to pay for premises they held in the bazaar, though these premises were their own bona fide property by right of purchase. He also extorted from them a sum of $200.

Bombay-based British capitalists showed some interest in the pearl trade. However, the British Resident in the Gulf persistently warned them against it, advising them to stay away for two reasons. Firstly, in the opinion of the Resident, the British merchants were no match for the Kachchhi Banias and other Indian traders. Secondly, he was concerned about armed intervention by the Arabs, as the British did not possess the right to fish for pearls in the fishing grounds. The Resident cautioned British capitalists against 'so precarious a speculation'. Based on negative feedback from the Gulf, the British government in Bombay flatly informed the firm of M/s J. and W. Watson that the government did not sanction their operations. Defying their own government, some English entrepreneurs decided to try to enter the pearl trade anyway. In 1872, certain English speculators contemplated the establishment of a pearl fishing company to obtain pearls from the Persian Gulf with the help of steam power and modern appliances. Lt Walter Grant, agent of these speculators, approached the chief of Bahrain to secure concessions, which the chief rejected. He declined even to entertain any relations with parties through the English government. Grant was discouraged by the Resident from proceeding to Oman because of a supposedly disturbed state of affairs. But, given the climate of the times, the British could not be kept completely out of the Gulf. They emerged as the chief arbitrators settling ongoing disputes among the Sheikhs.

In all the principalities of the Gulf—Bahrain, Qatar, Abu Dhabi, Dubai, Kuwait, Sharjah, Ras al-Khaimah, Ajman, Umm al-Quwain—the inhabitants were chiefly pearl fishers, and the main source of income for these Sheikhdoms was the tax collected from the pearl industry. Lorimer noted of Bahrain: '. . . the principal pearl market of the Persian Gulf . . . if the pearl beds were to fail, the Shaikhdom would shortly be reduced to comparative insignificance.' The famed pearl banks of Bahrain attracted trading vessels. Out of the four hundred ships of large or medium tonnage operating there, two hundred were large boats (carrying a crew of one *Nakhuda* or captain, twelve divers, and twelve assistants) while one hundred were of intermediate size transporting one captain, six divers and six assistants each. Bahrain's pearling operations prompted Abraham Parsons, in his account in c.1775, to reckon that Bahrain's fisheries could yield £187,500 in a good year, and seldom less than £112,500. Exactly a century later, it is known from the Residency trade returns for 1873–74, that pearls worth Rs 79 lakh were exported to India alone. In 1875–76 and 1776–77, the Calcutta, Bombay and Karachi imports altogether were clubbed at Rs 11.99 lakh and Rs 13.87 lakh respectively. In 1887, Bahrain exported pearls valued at Rs 24.94 lakh and in 1888, pearls valued at Rs 32.07 lakh. The exports from Muscat to India were computed at $30,000; in addition, there were 1000 bales of nacre worth $30,000. The pearl diving season of 1888 was so successful that total Persian Gulf exports hit a level of about Rs 60 lakh, about Rs 10 lakh higher than exports in 1887. The value of pearls exported in 1904 stood at £1.5 million and by the 1920s at £3 million. In a span of a century, the pearl fishery expanded six-fold in terms of value. The statistical information on the pearl industry suggests near complete dependency of the Arab states on revenues from pearling. From the mid-eighteenth century, and through the nineteenth century, the value of the pearl trade increased continuously.

The pearl bazaar was vulnerable to fluctuations and uncertainties. Consistent demand could exist for a few years, but could easily be followed by a sudden drop in demand. In Bombay, for instance, imports of pearls from the Persian Gulf in the years 1871–72 and 1872–73 amounted to Rs 16.07 lakh Rs 16.38 lakh respectively. But in 1873–74, they steeply declined to Rs 13.13 lakh. The fall or rise in demand was never properly explained, but attributed to a 'myriad', vague factors. The pearl trade in the Gulf in 1883, for instance, was 'unfavourable' because yield was good but demand for pearls not up to the expectations of the dealers! Pearls were usually sold in packets, which could include pearls of different sizes and quality. If a buyer wanted to pick a single pearl from a packet, it was not unusual for him to have to pay a fancy price. In the absence of a standardized currency, the coins given in exchange for the pearls could also vary in value each year. Sometimes the coins were not of standard weight. Merchants could not always gauge the fluctuations in weights, coins and value of pearls in the market. They had to engage skilled bookkeepers to help them. Despite all efforts, the pearl trade could not be reduced to an exact science. The impression of contemporary observers seems to have been that in the nineteenth century, there were serious challenges for supply to keep pace with the demand.

The Bahrain–Muscat–Kachchh–Bombay Axis

In 1790, Manesty and Jones listed a number of markets to which pearls were directed from Bahrain, including Surat, Sindh, Calcutta, Bushire and Mocha via Muscat. From Bushire and the Indian ports, the pearls were exported to 'Kandahar, Multan, India, Tartary and China.' In 1800, pearls worth Rs 2 lakh were exported to Persia from the southern shores of the Gulf. But the Indian/Kachchhi stranglehold over the pearl market was firm. In a period of three decades, three-quarters of the produce was shipped to India, with the rest being shipped to Persia, Arabia and Turkey. In 1819, Evan Napean, a British officer, observed that perfect pearls were reserved for Surat, from whence they were distributed throughout India. His analysis was as follows:

> [A]ll the pearls that are fished, are generally sold in the Indies because the Indians are not so difficult as we, and by differently the rough ones as well as the smooth, taking the whole at a fixed price.

In the 1830s, the Persian Gulf pearl trade was estimated at Rs 40 lakh annually. Muscat had a commanding market share. Nearly two-thirds of the shipments came into Muscat and were conveyed to India, usually on Kachchhi Bagelas. The Parsis of Bombay are supposed to have exported a lot of pearls to China. Uneven pearls went to Constantinople and other ports in Turkey where they were used to decorate arms, headdresses and other embroidered work. Indian and Persian rulers and magnates had a reputation for hoarding fantastic amounts of nacre and pearls.

The Kachchhis developed a vocabulary around the weights and measures in the business. The *rati* was the principal measure, and counting was done by *chavs*. One *chav* equaled 100 *dokdadokda*. Testing involved pressing the pearl with a strong object. False pearls broke but real pearls did not. Kachchhis referred to a false pearl as a *phatakia*—one that breaks instantaneously. The Indian market preferred pearls of a yellowish hue and of perfect symmetry. The Baghdad market valued white pearls. Smaller pearls too went to Baghdad. As the nineteenth century progressed, pearl dealers of Muscat started freighting shipments from Bahrain to Bombay by the British India Steam Navigation (BISN) mail steamer. Kuwait's pearls and shells too were exported to Bombay. In order to make payments, Kachchhi and Sindhi pearl dealers imported large quantities of dollars and rupees from India to the ports during the fishing season. We have access to some statistics related to this. In 1884–85, import of pearls to Bombay from Muscat and elsewhere was valued at over Rs 20 lakh. By the close of the 1880s, this figure showed an increase of Rs 1.4 lakh; re-exports of pearls and other jewels increased correspondingly. The pearl trade received an impetus from the Paris Exhibition of 1899. India's imports were valued at Rs 91.97 lakh, and her export of jewels increased by Rs 55.31 lakh; unset pearls alone accounted for the bulk of the increase, contributing around Rs 54 lakh.

Bombay's strategic location between the pearl fisheries of the Persian Gulf and the Gulf of Mannar made it the pearl capital of the world. Kachchhi Banias, along with a few Sindhi Banias, came to be known as experts in classifying and valuing pearls. Even those Kachchhis whose primary business interests were elsewhere liked to dabble in the pearl trade. Khatau Makanji, a Bhatia from Kachchh, managed several cotton mills and public companies. He and his successor Govardhandas Khatau passionately pursued the pearl business, both in their individual capacities and through a syndicate formed in 1908. They maintained commission agents in places as far off as London and Paris. The syndicate was dissolved in 1910, and Govardhandas Khatau again assumed full control of the business until the time of his death in 1916.

All good things must come to an end. By the end of the nineteenth century, Paris replaced Bombay as the pearl capital of the world. Once Parisian jewellers gained control of pearl classification, they became the arbiters and standard-setters. The US emerged as an important buyer, preferring to deal with Paris. Both Europeans and Americans were paying extraordinary prices for pearls. Time does not stand still. Even as the trade began to witness the substitution of nacre with plastic and the exhaustion of natural beds, cultured pearls replaced natural ones, and by the middle of the twentieth century, control of the pearl market moved to Tokyo.

Turbulent Times

After the death of Sultan Seyyid Said in 1856, Omani politics entered a crisis. With the shift of the capital to Zanzibar in 1840, Muscat experienced many troubles. In Seyyid Said's absence, his regent in Muscat was indifferent to issues regarding trade. A letter of Lewis Pelly's, penned in 1863, remarked that after the division of Muscat and Zanzibar in 1861, the position of Muscat as 'a first rate Asiatic Maritime Power declined because the naval force was divided, dismantled; the trade declined. The British antislavery squadron contributed to the decline of the slave trade between Zanzibar and Arabia.'

The fundamentalist ideology of Said Azzan bin Qais (1868–71) resulted in many restrictions on trade. Ibadi principles required a lack of respect for religions other than Islam. Though he mockingly claimed that he did not wish to interfere in other religious practices, the new ruler objected to various religious rituals and practices of the Hindus, including the use of drums. People were required to grow moustaches in the fashion of the *Mutawas* (the moral police). The tobacco trade was frowned upon. The government abandoned its earlier policy of protecting commercial interests and focused on becoming a religious police state. Azzan and his associate Khalili attempted to remove the Bhatia business house of Bhimani's from the post of customs collector. This attempt failed and they had to give the post back to the Banias.

In 1869, a number of Kachchhi traders reported to Lewis Pelly that they were struggling as trade was in decline. Seyyid Turki's reign was a troubled one. The civil strife between Ibrahim bin Qais and Seyyid Turki caused trouble for Indian traders. The 'tribes' used their power to fleece merchants in order to maintain supplies to their marauding bands. In their correspondence, the British consuls reported many such instances of extortion. Although some references exist, on the whole it does not appear that the harassment was a response to any manner of exploitation by the Banias.

State revenues plummeted as trade declined. The Zanzibar subsidy ceased. The abolition of the slave trade in 1873 was a major setback for Muscat. In 1877–78, around 1000 Arabs left Oman, attracted by the greater security and prosperity of Zanzibar. Many firms across Muscat, Bombay and Zanzibar went into insolvency. Steam navigation hurt many merchants who had relied on the sail.

Despite all these problems, the Kachchhis did not abandon Muscat. They emerged as financiers to the Sultan who was in financial difficulty, and as agents of European and American firms, especially in the newly emerging trade in dates and arms. Firms such as those of Gopalji Walji and Ratansi Purshottam moved in to leverage these opportunities.

Oman to America: The Date Trade

While all of Arabia was known for dates, those from Oman were considered preeminent. In the markets of Muscat, one could find over a hundred varieties of dates known by different names. Date products— date syrups, dried dates, date vinegar, oil and alcoholic beverages (date wine and *araq*) were plentiful. John Johnson, a British army man, noticed the many uses of a date tree: 'The date tree in Arabia supplies the place of the cocoa tree of India; and like it seems to furnish the natives with the most of the necessaries of the life. The fruit is food for men and cattle. The leaves and fibers of the tree are wrought up into mats and ropes with which the huts are covered.'

Date trees were most abundant in Batina, Wadi Samail and Sharqiya. In Batina, date plantations formed an almost continuous belt, sometimes seven miles deep along the coast. In Wadi Samail, the palms were estimated at 600,000; in the Badiyah division of Sharqiya, there were about 158,000 date trees. Large groves existed at places in Dhahirah, especially, at Ibri where the trees numbered about 50,000. The well-known varieties of dates in Oman were the Misbali, Fard and Khalas. The Fard was a small, dark-coloured date grown mainly in Wadi Samail. The palms of Badiyah and Sharqiyah were chiefly Mibsali. Initially, production of the Fard was restricted to Wadi Samail, where conditions were best suited for it. But when the demand for the Fard raised its value, its cultivation spread to other regions. In many places, the Fard was grown to the exclusion of other varieties. This variety could be preserved for a year. It usually began to mature in late August when it became available for shipment. Steamers from Muscat and Muttrah would take them to America, which soon became the most important market for the

Fard. Kachchhi commission agents were active in the packing and shipment process. Shipments peaked in September and October. Retailing in America peaked during Thanksgiving (late November), Christmas and New Year. The dark Fard with its strong flavour appealed to the American consumer as it was easy to serve as a single piece rather than as a congealed mass. It required great care while packing to ensure that its skin was kept intact and dry. The *Digest's* reference to date shipments makes it evident that Kachchhi consumers were acquainted with the Fard. Its popularity among them, though, was limited.

Date production was dependent on the monsoon rains. Untimely rainfall sometimes lowered yields. For a good crop, it was essential that, along with normal rainfall, certain hot dry winds blew to help the dates ripen. Records show that in 1877–78 the date harvest was very good and that exports more than doubled. During harvest time, there was an influx of labour into the interiors. The date trading season lasted for about two months.

The date tree first blossoms in February. In March, one can see bunches of blossoms that are milky white in colour. The fruit begins to form in May. In September, when the fruit is ripe, the tree sheds an edible part known as 'superabundance'. At this point, the fruit is known as *khumal* and is green in colour. In June and July, the fruit is known as *kharek* and is either red or yellow in colour. It is fit to eat and is sometimes sold in this form. In August, the date turns soft and juicy. It is known as *ratab*, and is sold in the bazaars, but it is not yet in a fit state for preservation. The dates plucked in September, known as *khurma*, are ideal for preservation. The dates are gathered in a trough and exposed to air and sunlight. The fruit throws off its extra juice and hardens sufficiently to allow it to be packed in baskets. The juice is gathered and stowed in skins or jars; it was called *dushab* and was used as a sugar substitute. The juice was also preserved using a mixture of sesame seeds, powdered ginger and walnut kernels. This preserve was called *khurma-shirah* and was prized in the Persian Gulf. The *zahidi* date was usually ripened only up to the *ratab* stage. It was exported to distillers of arrack in India. Wet dates and higher quality, more expensive dates from the interior were traditionally exported to Arabia. When Seyyid Said moved to Zanzibar, he wanted Omani dates there. This created an opportunity for Kachchhi merchants to extend their network. *Kharek* or dried dates were preferred in India, where they were required for wedding ceremonies and religious festivals. The word *kharek* had become so common in Gujarati and Kachchhi that it is assumed to be from Indian rather than Arabic roots. A popular adage in Kachchhi is *'Bhokh lage tade kaharku matthi'*—when one is really hungry the kharek tastes the sweetest. The Mibsali dates from the 'Badiyah' region were also liked in India, and were exported in sizeable quantities from Sur to Bombay. The Fard was so popular in America that an attempt was made to grow it in Arizona. This attempt was not successful. In 1868, the British tried to introduce the date palm in India. The Chief Commissioner of Oudh and the Conservator of Forests in Mysore and Coorg were supplied with plants. Some shoots were forwarded to Rajputana where the climate seemed suitable. It is quite surprising that neither the British nor the Kachchhis thought of cultivating dates in Kachchh itself, something that has happened only in recent times.

In 1821, James Fraser reckoned that a date tree was valued at between $7 and $10, its estimated yield being valued at $1 to $1.5. He also estimated that an estate had around 3000 to 5000 date trees. Muscat dates chiefly competed with north African varieties. Prices ranged from $1 to $4 between 1880 and 1900. Basra and Bahrain offered competition to Omani dates. The districts that grew dates stretched from Abu al-Kahsib in the south to al-Haritha in the north. Kotias from Kachchh remained the dominant means of transport. Since dates came from the interior of Oman, disturbances in those interior regions were a risk to the trade. In 1892, political disorder in Wadi Samail interrupted for a time communication between the Sharqiyah district and the port of Muscat.

Along with pearls, dates were also often treated as quasi-currency. Abraham Parson writes:

Dates are more plenty in this city, and it's neighborhood, than perhaps in any other part of the world, and give bread to innumerable quantity of people, who are employed in gathering, packing and transporting them to every port and place in the Persian Gulph and India. The poor people have little other food than dates, which are esteemed very nourishing.

As in the case of pearls, it was the Kachchhi traders who provided capital and credit for the date trade. Two- and three-year loans were advanced against future produce from specified tracts and plantations. The middleman was required to retain the title to the plantation so that at least one *jarib* (area occupied by 100 palm trees) of date palms served as guarantee for the advance money that the trader committed. Some evidence exists of direct negotiations without a middleman between date planter and date merchant. The story goes that in order to access the best crop, Gokuldas of Khimji Ramdas avoided middlemen and personally travelled all over Oman on a donkey. American importers sometimes provided letters of credit through a bank in Bombay. Kachchhi traders required Arab brokers and planters to sign a bond so that the crops were sold only to the person who had extended credit in the first place.

The date trade was a significant source of revenue for the Omani state. At Muttrah, before shipping, the government collected *zakah* on them. The packing of dates was an elaborate process. Each merchant had his own *chardagh* or temporary hut made of woven reeds. Women and children were employed to pack the fruit. Packed dates, which were earlier shipped on Baghlas or Dhows, were later moved on British steamers. The dates that were not exported were sent inland to Kuwait, Zubair, Suq al Shuyukh and the Najd. Americans introduced case-wood in place of palm frond bags for packing dates. Quality control of the packing process also got attention. The exchange of cables between the American importer William Hills Jr. and his Kachchhi agent in Oman, Ratansi Purshottam, makes for interesting reading. Hills insisted that Ratansi use American packing materials sent on his steamers. Hills specified the numbers of cases, the numbers of the boxes in each case and the weight of dates in each box. Apart from case-wood, he sent grease-resistant paper, straps, nails, hoops and wax paper too. This is mentioned in one of his cables dated February 1906. Hills in turn got his shooks from Dodge & Bliss Co., iron bands from Cary Mfg. Co., paper from Coy, Hunt & Co. and double presses from Fogarty & Co. He bought nails from United States Steel Product Export Co. He purchased hammers, bronze bells and handsaws from Alexander Pollock Company, who were described as manufacturers and dealers in railway, steamship and contractors' supplies. Cary Manufacturing Co., who were suppliers of bands and straps, were described as specialists in the manufacture of varieties of wire and metal straps. Hills charged the costs of these supplies to Ratansi and extended credit to him. Once Hills did not supply nails on time. This proved costly as he was then forced to ship the dates through Bombay and London in order to get the packing right. Hills expected Ratansi to arrange mats on his own, as Gopalji did for his principals. Mats were stowed between decks in order to ensure that the goods arrived in a proper state. Hills emphasized that shipping should be done only under these conditions. Ironically, in May 1907, Hills laments about the problems involved in shipping case-wood and paper from his side: '. . . past three weeks shipping was seriously interfered with because of labour difficulties which prevented the steamship companies from obtaining sufficient stevedores to handle consignments. The balance of the shooks and waxed paper therefore awaited the strike call back.'

The specific instructions on packing make for interesting reading. Too much pressure needed to be avoided. While the dates needed to be packed regularly in straight rows and in layers, it was preferred that the press not be used to such an extent as to make it difficult to separate the dates. Small merchants needed to sell dates in less than full boxes. Given the sticky nature of dates, it was important to have wax paper between the layers of dates in the boxes or at least between every other layer. Inserting a sheet of paraffin paper after every four or five layers enabled dates to be broken apart in better shape at the consumer's end and gave much better satisfaction to all buyers. Hills looked to Ratansi to try out various methods to eliminate rival brands. Hills wrote: 'While the quantities shipped by these people (the rivals) is not important, still it is quite sufficient to make a bad market here, and if their packing and shipping can be eliminated, it is highly advisable that this should be done.' Occasionally, Hills did compromise on quality. In order to get large quantities, he permitted the packing of *phurphuria* dates as his competitors were doing, but he tried to keep the quantities down.

The operations of sorting, packing and repacking dates required around one hundred days, from mid-August to early December. From Ratansi's documents, it is evident that the date factory owner employed a range of employees—foremen, carpenters, women supervisors and packers, porters, water carriers and servants. These employees were hired on a daily payroll, with incentives like holiday bonuses. The exporter was also required to hire boats and manage the weighing and steamer loading operations.

In 1866, an American named William Jack Towel opened his own establishment in Muscat. A New England seaman, Towell worked in close collaboration with the Indian date merchants. Initially, the principal Muscat-based exporters to the US were Mohammed Fadl, a Khoja who partnered with Towel in 1894, and Gopal Walji, a Bhatia. With the entry of Ratansi Purshottam, the American date trade became more interesting. Gopal Walji dealt with Hills Brothers of New York, and W.J. Towell was the agent for Arnold

Cheney of New York. William Hills, whose agent was Ratansi, encouraged him to cartelize operations with Walji and Towell to keep prices down and control the market. Hills wrote: 'It has been my understanding that Messrs. Towell & Co. and Gopaljee Waljee have had an arrangement together whereby they have divided the receipts of dates fit for packing which come to market, purchasing more or less together, thereby avoiding any rise on account of competition.' Hills was prepared for Ratansi to enter into an arrangement with these two firms, but only on condition that sufficient dates be reserved for his account through Ratansi, as it would enable him to pack the entire quantity of shooks which Hills had shipped. Ratansi was open to joining the cartel, but was apprehensive of appearing to be in a monopoly position in Muscat. Any arrangement was tricky, as American demand was confined to a short, three-month period. It seemed more convenient to cartelize at the American end. William Hills first reached out to Hills Brothers, based on Ratansi's request. The final arrangement led to all three leading exporters—Towell, Walji and Ratansi—agreeing upon a single price to be paid for dates, and dividing the supply into Muscat for the US market equally among themselves, thus cutting the cost of dates supplied to the Americans.

There was an element of cloak and dagger in the date trade. A.W. Bance, a Basra-based representative of William Hills, informed Ratansi that a certain Mr Chalk of the rival Hills Brothers was going to visit Muscat, suggesting that Ratansi should spy on Chalk. Ratansi was under pressure to supply dates of a quality equal, if not superior, to those shipped by Towell. Ratansi was supplied with specimens of Towell's Diamond A and Diamond R brands of dates, which he had to measure against Hills' Monogram and Camel brands in order to achieve his goal. Ratansi was urged not to use competitors' ships.

The focus on turnaround times at the ports of Muscat and Muttrah had a very modern flavour. Ratansi would receive cables from Basra about the imminent arrival of ships, and he would be ready to load the dates quickly. Leftover dates would go through Bombay and London at the lowest freight rate obtainable. Dates to be sold in the American west coast would go through Bombay and Hong Kong. This route was found to be very economical. Keeping packing and shipping costs down was the overall objective. There was agreement between Hills and Ratansi that both needed to make reasonable profits.

Minimizing customs duties was another objective. Hills writes: 'In as much as the duty into Canada is an ad valorem one, I beg you will reduce the F O B cost of these to just as low a point as you can conscientiously do so that the duty upon entry in that market may be reduced to as small a figure as possible.' However, this procedure seems to have had its limitations and was not actively pursued. The necessity of good documentation was emphasized in order to avoid costs at the destination like demurrage, which could be as high as £1 per hour. In keeping with the conspiratorial atmosphere, shipment details were communicated by code. Settlements of all payments were completed at the end of each season. Even while complaining about inadequate shipments, Hills expressed hope of good supplies for the next 'campaign'. The use of the word 'campaign' captures the spirit of the Kachchhi-US partnership in the date trade.

Dealings in Explosives

The last quarter of the nineteenth century and the first decade of the twentieth literally witnessed a boom in gun trade in the Gulf. The Kachchhis of Muscat were quite central to this trade. There had always been an old tradition of gun trade between Muscat and Zanzibar. Guns had been essential to support the east African trade in slaves and ivory. With the British drive against slave trade, gun manufacturers, who were primarily European, looked for new markets. Afghanistan, Baluchistan and the Gulf itself emerged as lucrative destinations, and Muscat became the key trans-shipment centre. Again, Kachchhis were the key intermediaries. Given that the guns and bullets were largely used against British Indian armies during the various campaigns against them in Afghanistan, the British had an interest in curbing this trade. The passing of the General Act of the Brussels Conference in 1890 (ratified in 1892) should theoretically have helped this British endeavour. But the ban was limited to territories below the twentieth North Parallel, which excluded Arabia and the region of the Persian Gulf. Most importantly, there was no treaty that forbade entry of arms into Muscat. There was ongoing pressure on the African arms trade, noted by the fact that in 1888, the British authorities in Bombay refused permission for trans-shipment of bullets to Zanzibar from Bahrain. At the same time, Oman was under some stress. The Sultans had lost revenues from the slave trade. The British were supposed to pay them a subsidy, but this payment was irregular. The Sultans were running into debt and risked losing control over the interiors of their country. Kachchhi merchants in Muscat were also facing stress. The move from sailing ships to steamships had hurt them. They needed activities that helped them diversify from the date trade on which they did not want to get too dependent. The opportunity to import European guns and ammunition and re-export them to destinations in the neighborhood of Oman was irresistible. Soon, Muscat emerged as an arms emporium. The British political officers in the so-called 'tribal territories' were not pleased. They conducted a series of inquiries during 1899, 1900 and 1902 to monitor the availability of arms in the Gulf. In 1903, the Government of India warned the British government that of the weapons sold in the Persian

Gulf 'a proportion reaches the "tribes" on the North-West Frontier of India, with results that constitute a grave menace to the peace of the border.' The real problem, of course, was that many of the suppliers of guns were British manufacturers!

Muscat was well positioned to serve the Afghan markets through Karachi and Gwadur on the Makran coast, and by way of reaching out to Afghan buyers who made the Hajj pilgrimage to the Hejaz. Kachchhis in Muscat leveraged their connections with Bombay merchants to import raw materials to sustain local arms manufacture in Oman. Ironically, the Bombay government of the British received several applications from merchants to obtain licenses for the trade. Seyyid Turki demanded two hundred blocks of lead from Bombay merchants. To fulfil this demand, Sachubhai Khakuani of Bombay applied for a license. European firms continued to ship arms directly to Muscat. Ratansi Purshottam imported rifles and cartridges from his London-based exporting agent Schwarte and Hammer, who in turn sourced products from an arms maker at Liege, Belgium. Germany prohibited its traders from selling arms in Muscat in order to adhere to the Brussels convention. This did not seem to constrain the British, French and Belgian arms exporters. Birmingham and Liege emerged as key origination centres for the trade. Their arms were usually made of cast iron. Bucharest in Romania, which used high quality steel to make arms, was a minor source. On the demand side in

Afghanistan, the Adam Khel Afridi 'tribe' emerged as key buyers.

The negotiations between Kachchhi importers in Muscat and European exporters ran pretty much along the lines of trade in any other goods. The Kachchhi would suggest colour changes and reduction of gold carvings. Exporters pushed back with a delicious sense of irony that the gold trimmings were necessary, as they were very anxious 'to cultivate this business in good faith'. Here is an example of a complaint letter from a European exporter to his Kachchhi agent in Muscat: 'We cannot understand how your client can say that the Muscat market is dull as Liege is filled up with orders for Martinys (sic) and the prices are raising a little nearly every week. Our competitors however, appear to be making a cheaper grade of guns and we think this is the reason why your client asks for cheaper prices. If required we can also make a lower quality, but do not very much like to do so.' The agent turned around and said that he was forced to cut profit down to a minimum in order to secure the order.

In order to reduce his risk, the exporter insisted on a deposit from the Muscat importer. The exporter justified the deposit fearing that shipping of arms and ammunition to Muscat may at any time be interrupted by unforeseen circumstances. Therefore, he wished to be sufficiently protected against any eventualities. This stance was not unjustified, as the threat of British naval embargo in the Gulf loomed large. The importer earned interest on his deposit. The correspondence shows an instance of 5 per cent interest on a deposit of £200. The commission agent insisted on receiving deposits well in advance as factories would refuse to proceed with orders until this was done.

Customization of rifles to include Arabic inscriptions or floral designs was quite common. The system ran smoothly, with sample rifles being sent in order to confirm the requirements. Too many deviations from the standard, of course, increased risk of delay. As to be expected, manufacturers resisted alterations so as to not face negative feedback later. Weapons were packed in solid wood cases that were lined with tin; the cases were bound with solid iron hoops. To avoid rusting, rifles were greased with Vaseline both inside and outside, and then wrapped in a special white wax paper. They were packed in hay to form five lines of five pieces each so as to make for twenty-five pieces in each case. The tin case was hermetically closed and the cover of the case was screwed down. During the supply process, code words were used to represent rifles and cartridges.

There was a symbiotic relationship between Muscat and Bombay. Dwarkadas Khimjee of Bombay dealt with bills of lading, insurance policies, letters of credit and drafts, and played the role of financier to Ratansi Purshottam in Muscat. While the arms may have been headed to Muscat, the shipping documents were sent to Dwarkadas Khimjee in Bombay. Exporters frequently complained about excessive cable charges and their small profit margins! Importers complained about unforeseen delays, as when the railways in Belgium were blocked on account of heavy snowfall. In other words, the arms business was pretty much business as usual!

The profits, however, were quite unusual. Weapons purchased for as little as Rs 25–40 in Muscat could be sold to Afghans for ten times that amount. A Lee-Enfield costing £6 would be eagerly purchased by Afghans at approximately £60–£80. To make sure they did not lose out on the pickings, the Muscat government raised tax on the arms trade from 5 per cent to 6 per cent. The principal weapon sold was the Martini Henry carbine. About 60 per cent of those imports found their market in the Persian territory where 'Martini Khan' was the recognized arbiter in 'tribal' disputes. Almost every European company made its own Martini model. There also existed strong and continued demand for the Austrian Werdnl rifles. Both Arab and Afghan buyers who visited the warehouses were able to differentiate among the various makes and preferred certain models over others. Ratansi was aware of the fact that his customers preferred La Francotte Martini rifles. He tried to persuade other manufacturers to imitate the La Francotte. This was expensive, as the lever or handle, as well as the shoe of the rifle, would need to be changed. Most manufacturers therefore refused. And everyone refused to inscribe the patented name. Schwarte and Hammer wrote: 'Our works, as well as we ourselves, are on friendly relations with the firm of Francotte, and you will therefore understand that we should not like to infringe on their name and number too closely.' Other Belgian works were making the same kind of rifles for the market with the inscription 'Martini Muscat' instead of 'Martini Francotte'. Ratansi directly approached the makers Auguste Francotte to import their sporting rifle Martini Francotte 303 bore, which carried their name and special inscription. The makers replied that Messrs Times Dharwar & Co. of London enjoyed monopoly on sale of the Martini Francotte and therefore they were not ready to supply such rifles to other firms, however high the prices offered may be. Besides, they had a backlog of very big orders and had to refuse a new one. The wily Kachchhi in Ratansi would not give up. To somehow or other become an agent of Francottes', he asked them if they made or could make Mauser rifles. Eventually, Ratansi had to give up as he received a negative response.

Given their Afghan headaches, the British authorities in Bombay were finally forced in 1880 to stop granting licenses for the export of heavy consignments of arms and ammunition of war consigned to the Persian Gulf from other countries. Subsequently, the British persuaded the Persian government to prohibit export of percussion caps from Persia in 1881. Despite this and despite prohibitions placed at repeated British insistence by Persia (in 1881), Bahrain (in 1898), Kuwait (in 1900) and the Trucial States (in 1902), rampant gun-running continued. Oman gained when, by 1903, the arms trade had been nominally prohibited at all ports in the Persian Gulf region with the partial exception of Muscat and Oman, where ostensibly, internal traffic was carried on. In 1891, the Sultan of Oman had agreed to restrict import of arms into his Makran enclave of Gwadar. But he refused to do so in Oman itself. He did not intend to lose his important source of revenue—the customs duty on arms. From 1891 to 1897, the Sultan's own steamers brought in arms from Zanzibar to Muscat. At Muttrah, three prominent Khoja merchants were engaged in the arms trade. From 1890 to 1892, 11,500 firearms were landed at Muscat. Europeans too directly shipped Enfields from Austria–Hungary to Khoja merchants at Gwadar. In 1895–96, imports were estimated at 4350 rifles and 604,000 cartridges, and in 1896–97 at 20,000 rifles with a proportionate number of cartridges. In 1898, the British Consul at Muscat issued a notification requiring British subjects to inform it about arms or ammunition obtained or disposed of by them. In January 1900, the Sultan was induced to adopt a similar policy. Kachchhi traders found a way out by registering all arms transactions through Arab agents. Over time, European manufacturers supplanted British ones. They sometimes sold copies of British weapons specially manufactured for the North-West Frontier. European shipments increased after Hamburg steamers started operating in the Gulf in 1906. Ratansi's London agent Schwarte and Hammer & Co. decided in 1908 to start transactions with Moritz Magnus Jr. of Hamburg. The British authorities looked on in frustration. In Muscat, Grey estimated that 200 rifles a week were crossing to Makran; in 1907 alone, intelligence department estimates indicated that 30,000 rifles and 3,000,000 rounds of ammunition were being imported annually into Afghanistan and the 'tribal territory'. The arms made in Muscat itself were now all breech-loaders or muzzle-loaders. They had ceased to be saleable in either Arabia or Persia. Some were sold locally to 'tribesmen' from the interior of Oman, some to visitors from other parts of the Gulf, and some to the *Nakhudas* of coasting vessels; the greater quantity were shipped to Bahrain, Qatar and Kuwait, concealed in bales of other goods and in cases of halwa or dried limes. A few were dispatched to minor ports in the Red Sea where there were no customs houses.

In March 1899, M Goguyer, a French merchant, established himself in Muscat and began to deal in arms. He approached leading Kachchhi traders and informed them that his operations would be exempt from British interference. He planned to export arms in local vessels flying the French flag. He extended his business to Bahrain. In 1901, his business began to increase rapidly; in 1903, the Odessa firm of M/S Keverkoff & Co., and in 1905, the Djibouti house of Baijecot & Co. were added to the list of foreign arms-dealers at Muscat. In the early days, arms from Belgium and Birmingham had dominated the Muscat market. But in 1899–1900, about one-seventh of the imports were from France, and by 1905 the proportion of French arms had risen to four-tenth. Hardinge pointed out privately to Count d'Ormeson, the French representative, that French interests controlled 49 per cent of the arms trade (compared with 27 per cent Omani and 24 per cent British), and of that 49 per cent, Goguyer himself handled 60 per cent. D'Ormesson admitted that French interests were large, and added that Goguyer was able to make his voice heard in the Chamber and the press. In March of 1907, Agent Grey reported that more than one hundred Afghanis were in Muscat buying arms, and more than half of them were actually found lodging with Goguyer. Once the arms had been purchased in Muscat, they were moved across the Gulf on *Dhows* using increasingly ingenious methods to avoid capture in Omani or Persian waters. Few guns were seized, even though the British had instituted an anti-smuggling patrol. British interests received a further setback when Sultan Faisal started borrowing from non-British arms dealers, particularly from Goguyer. To make matters worse, just in order to not completely hurt the interests of British manufacturers, the British authorities were forced to be not too stringent in monitoring the regulations.

Failure of the Conference and Expansion of the Arms Trade

A pall of gloom prevailed in the Muscat market when the news broke in 1908 that a new international conference was to take place in Belgium with the specific purpose of discussing ways to check the arms trade in the Gulf. This gloom is evident in the letters Ratansi exchanged with his European trading partners. His partners kept him informed about the conference while reassuring him that changes, if any, would not impact trade. Moritz Magnus wrote to Ratansi: '. . . your apprehensions are going too far. There are so many interests connected to the Arms Trade, & English are too good businessmen, as to spoil this important commerce of which even their subjects are taking profit of, in a considerable manner.' Schwarte and Hammer wrote: 'We only hope however that the importation of arms and ammunition at Mascat (sic) will not be seriously interfered with, and that you will soon be able to send us your further orders.' The Europeans offered to accept smaller orders till the question was finally settled. The conference ran into an impasse. With respect to the sale of arms to Africans, the German and British proposals were diametrically opposed. When the conference failed to arrive at any conclusion, the arms dealers were greatly relieved. Moritz Magnus blissfully wrote to Ratansi that '. . . the Gun-Trade Conference was adjourned, as officially advertised until autumn next, but as we think to an undefinite (sic) period. Let us hope, they will never meet again!'

The failure of the Brussels Conference enraged the British government in India, as captured in this 1909 note: 'The gravity of the position is such as, in our judgment, to call for immediate and effective action, and we can no longer safely afford to await the uncertain issues of diplomacy. We are strongly of the opinion that any reasonable means and expenditure having for their aim the suppression of the traffic will not only prove economical in the end, but are imperatively demanded to avert a danger which, if permitted to increase, may seriously embarrass our position in India.' Following this, a naval blockade was imposed along the Makran Coast in 1909. It achieved some success with the seizure of consignments aboard *dhows* crossing the Persian Gulf, but failed to interdict the flow of arms northwards through Persia and Afghanistan. British intelligence worked overtime watching steamers from Karachi to the Gulf, looking for known arms traders; the identity of pilgrims to Mecca and Karbala were carefully checked to prevent dealers from reaching Muscat. Spies were also sent into Afghanistan to report on the arms trade; information regarding arms, caravans and gun-runners was passed on to the navy and to troops in the Persian Gulf, who met with increasing success. But Muscat proved to be a stumbling block as its arms trade was increasingly dominated by the Europeans, especially the French.

British search and blockade costs amounted to about £125,000 annually. To make matters worse, British arms manufacturing companies and their workers felt they were being victimized as the naval blockade ended up confiscating only British arms. At the annual meeting of the Gun Workers Union held in Birmingham, a resolution was unanimously adopted by a crowded gathering of workers. The meeting testified to the suffering caused among workmen by loss of wages through the stoppage of trade resulting from the Persian Gulf seizures; in its plea, it said it 'humbly requests Your Lordship to receive a deputation of employers and workmen with the view of including Your Lordship to use your influence with the Persian authorities to permit this trade to be continued'. Leading arms manufacturers and suppliers like Times Francis lobbied for the removal of checks and threats to their trade in the Gulf. London exporters were quite willing to supply Belgian rifles rather than British-made rifles that could get held up by customs or by the embargo authorities. Schwarte and Hammers did exactly that. While supplying rifles to Ratansi, Shwarte and Hammers did away with the practice of engraving their names on the butt of the rifle; instead, they used a non-British naming N. P. Dhotia and used a 'Made in Belgium' label. The British customs authorities would not identify these arms as British, and shipping them from London or any other English port was therefore possible. The British government was increasingly concerned about guns and rifles being exported in greater numbers to the North-West Frontier of India. They resorted to enforcing the Merchandise Marks Act. A rifle required a 'Made in Belgium' label without which the customs authorities would consider it an English-made rifle that would risk confiscation. In Lord Salisbury's view, the content of the cases containing rifles and cartridges had habitually been concealed in the Bills of Lading under the misleading description of 'merchandize' or 'hardware'; and the names of the consignees were withheld by consigning the articles 'to order'. The flip side was that a large proportion of the arms and ammunition exported from Manchester, though shipped as being of British manufacture, was not really of British origin but was made abroad. A representation was made by a leading manufacturer of ammunition in England protesting this evasion of the Merchandise Marks Act. This too received the attention of the government. In any case, by 1907, owing to the tighter British naval embargo, all British suppliers were playing it safe. They avoided the supply of British manufactures and were particular about shipping through Antwerp rather than through Manchester or other British ports. This also caused problems and delays for suppliers. The supplier lost out as the importer would charge a penalty. Schawarte and Hammers were once fined a sum of £22.40 by Ratansi. They sheepishly requested that the fine be reduced to £10.

The blockade succeeded in increasing the price of rifles and ammunition on the North-West Frontier. Slowly, after 1910, arms supply from the Gulf dried up. After 1912, caches of rifles and ammunition were seized in the Persian Gulf and on the Makran coast. The traffic in arms through Afghanistan to the North-West Frontier 'tribes' sharply declined. The profits enjoyed by European traders at Muscat also slumped. By the end of 1911, all but one French company had closed down. An agreement with the Sultan of Oman on Arms Warehouse Regulations forced the closure of the French firm of Goguyer's in December 1912, at long last effectively bringing an end to the arms trade between Muscat and the North-West Frontier. Tim Moreman argues that the trans-border Afghan and Arab 'tribes' had already amassed large quantities of arms and ammunition, sufficient to satisfy local requirements for several years to come.

In retrospect, the role of the Hindu Kachchhi Bhatia in the arms trade remains a source of puzzlement and controversy. The community had traditionally not involved themselves in businesses that involved violence and killing. This principle had been quietly abandoned. The business principles that prevailed were those of seizing opportunities and diversifying their portfolios.

Lewis Pelly's observation, though racist and politically incorrect by today's standards, captures some key elements of the 'low profile'- and 'high success'-nature of Kachchhi participation in the Arab dominion of Muscat:

> The trade is in the hands of British Indian subjects. It is so from the force of circumstances. The Arabs being too indolent to embark in the trade themselves, it falls into the hands of people who are willing to do so, possess the means of doing so and who are contended with small ventures and politically innocuous; and who are patient of dwelling for years in a manner and position which scarcely any other people of equal wealth and intelligence would endure.

3

KACHCHHI ENTERPRISE IN ZANZIBAR

Once again, we have to begin with a tribute to the intrepid Portuguese. It was from Portuguese Diu that Gujarati merchants began their long and continuous contact with Mozambique and the Swahili coast of Africa. This Indian Ocean trade led to the growth of textile production, ivory and tortoise shell-carving, and gold work in Diu. The real opportunity for Kachchhis came when their friends, the Omanis, made inroads into the Swahili coast during the second half of the eighteenth century. By this time, Kachchhi merchants were well and truly embedded in both Muscat and Bombay. Zanzibar was to become the fourth leg of the Kachchhi quadrilateral, as direct visits by ships from the west coast of India to Zanzibar became more common. The early trade in African ivory was entirely with India.

India re-exported the ivory to the European markets. According to Abdul Sheriff, the ivory trade was a key factor responsible for Indian migration to Africa. Kachchhis gradually began to dominate Zanzibar's Indian trade. The British got worried that the French might enter Mandvi. This worry was partly justified, given the strong French presence in east Africa in the eighteenth century, mainly to access supply of slave labour. Consequently, in the first treaty that the British signed with Kachchh in 1809, one of the clauses clearly stated that entry of French and American vessels to the littoral of Kachchh was to be prohibited. Anglo-French rivalry was a sideshow as far as Kachchhi merchants were concerned. The real losers were the merchants of Diu, with their Portuguese connections, as against the Kachchhis, with their Omani-Zanzibari connections. Writing in the 1840s, A.C.P. Gamitto, a Portuguese officer, laments the fate of the Banias of Diu: '[T]he old opulent Banias possess almost nothing today; the commerce they had with India has nearly all fallen into the hands of the Batias, from Kutch . . .' The Kachchhi engagement with Africa was now in full swing.

The Zanzibari Attractions

The island of Zanzibar occupied an important position because of its intermediate location between the east African ports and its large, navigable harbour, which made it safer to dock there than at other coastal sites.

Sultan Said Seyyid (1806/07–56) probably had an intuitive sense of Zanzibar's potential when he relocated his seat of government from Oman to Zanzibar, from where it operated between 1832 and 1840. The Sultan encouraged Omani Arabs and Kachchhis to settle in Zanzibar, its adjacent islands, and even on the African mainland. Within two decades, the impact of these changes began to show. From almost nothing in 1834, Zanzibar's trade grew to an estimated £1.66 million by 1859. Kachchhis were given a protected status and were permitted to use the Sultan's flag. After some initial difficulties, the Kachchhis obtained, by 1828, the privilege of paying a low, 5 per cent duty on imports. They were also allowed to trade in the prime economic zone, the Mrima Coast, which was reserved for the Sultan himself. Although Europeans attempted their best to gain an entry there, they failed. According to Abdul Sheriff, this was a 'guarded privilege for local merchants and formed one of the cornerstones of the commercial empire.'

With the signing of various commercial treaties, Euro-American firms made their entry here. But the Kachchhis remained dominant, retaining substantial control over the import-export trade. In some interior areas, Europeans were unrepresented. The exchange at Tanga was wholly in the hands of Kachchhi merchants.

As the century progressed, the number of Indian residents on Zanzibar island shot up from 200 in 1819 to 1000 by the 1840s. In 1860, the Khojas and Bohras moved into a new quarter of Zanzibar town, and their numbers rapidly increased. Each *Bagela* from Kachchh usually brought a number of settlers. Their departure from Mandvi and arrival at Zanzibar are part of written and unwritten Kachchhi memoirs. The Royal Register had a list of the names of Kachchhi families who were long-time residents of Zanzibar. They were the 'Sultan's Hindees'. Until 1845, they were the Sultan's subjects. After the appointment of a British consul, some of them sought British protection. It appears that in 1869, there were 350 Indians who claimed the Sultan's protection. Some opted for what we would today call dual citizenship, seeking safety and advantage from both sides.

At Zanzibar, just as in Muscat, the Hindus established their separate residential quarters and attempted to create a Little Mandvi in Zanzibar. They spent lavishly to celebrate occasions like the birth of a child, weddings, or the occasion of their sons joining the business. Diwali was an important festival. Kachchhis in Zanzibar were known for their feasting, fireworks, music and dance. But in their daily living they preferred to maintain a regimen of simplicity and frugality. In the late 1840s, Captain Loarer, a French naval officer, estimated that Hari Bhimji, one of the principal Indian merchants at Zanzibar, whose commercial transactions with just one American firm averaged about MT$10,000 a year, spent only about MT$25 a year on house rent, food and living expenses. He also described Bhimji as 'very rich and very powerful'. He added that most other Indian merchants subsisted on MT$5 at Zanzibar and MT$2–3 on the mainland. Unlike their Hindu-Bhatia counterparts, the Muslim Khojas were in the custom of displaying their wealth. They adorned their wives with expensive jewellery. This, apparently, fetched the attention of thieves. Frequent cases of burglary were reported in the Khoja residential quarter. Khoja women made several complaints about being stopped and plundered in the streets. They finally requested the Sultan to ensure strong surveillance of their quarter.

Foreign Trade of Zanzibar

In the late 1830s, Zanzibar became an important trading emporium for European, American, Arab and Indian entrepreneurs. The items of trade included ivory, clove, gum copal, coconut, sesame, orchella weed, tortoise shell, rhinoceros hide and skin. The Kachchhis followed their usual practice of financing suppliers of these products, and made their profits distributing the products as well as providing inputs to the suppliers in the form of cotton goods, beads, ironware and muskets. The slave trade was also a source of significant profits. In the 1870s, British Consul Elton noted that Zanzibar's export trade had increased manifold, shipping large quantities of clove, copal, hide, coconut oil, sugar, ivory, cowries and orchella weed, principally to Hamburg and Kachchh.

Ivory

Ivory became a very valuable trading commodity in the nineteenth century. Ironically, before 1800, ivory was considered an ordinary item and was used to make common seats and bed props. While travelling in east Africa, Charles New had this to say: 'Ivory trading expeditions were thrusting across Lake Tanganyika and far into the north, and the slave and ivory trades alike were causing an influx of firearms into the interior.' The ever-increasing demand steeply reduced the elephant population in the nineteenth century, creating ecological imbalances. Elephant ecologist Cynthia Moss reckons that 825 tonnes of ivory represents 70,000 elephants. Natural mortality could not feed this immense demand for ivory. She poignantly argues, '. . . people forget that ivory is the tusk of an elephant. The word ivory disassociates it in our minds from the idea of an elephant. One tends to lump it with jade, teak, ebony, amber, even gold and silver, but there is a major difference: the other materials did not come from an animal: an ivory tusk is a modified incisor tooth.' The ivory trade resulted in considerable environmental losses in central and east Africa while it enriched Mandvi, Bombay, Hamburg, Connecticut and Holland. The overall demand for ivory, to make knife handles, billiard balls, keys of musical instruments, mathematical scales, chess men and various other articles, was so enormous that Cecil Burns, acting principal of the J.J. School of Art, Bombay, in the 1900s, was surprised to note that 'the noble race of animals, which yield it has not long since become extinct . . .' Way before Cecil Burns, an American traveller in the 1850s, Joseph Osgood, expressed similar concerns when he wrote, '. . . the increasing demand for ivory, and the fact that both male and female elephants are killed, go far to favour the opinion that before long this valuable and noble animal will be exterminated in this part of Africa.'

The journey of ivory is fascinating: extracted by hunters, brought by caravan to the African coast and thence to Zanzibar, shipped from Zanzibar to Mandvi on a six-week voyage by a *Kotia*, shipped again on a coastal boat to Bombay, and taken overland to Marwar, Hala, Kanara and Pune where craftsmen chopped it and carved it into bangles and combs. In Europe and America, ivory was turned into combs, cutlery handles, billiard balls and piano keys. This glamorous trade, we now know, was all the time promoting the killing of helpless elephants and disturbing the balance of the east and central African ecosystem. The exorbitant economic value placed on ivory during the whole of the nineteenth century allowed historian Edward Alpers to identify it as something 'imposed on Africa from without'.

Sadly for the African elephant, the ivory of Zanzibar was preferred to the Ceylonese and Indian for being denser in texture and not so liable to turn yellow. It was soft and more open in grain, and was on account of its elasticity eminently suited for billiard balls and similar articles. New England merchants preferred Zanzibar's soft ivory over the hard ivory from west Africa. Like all trades, even this grisly one developed its own product vocabulary. Prime Zanzibari, Abyssinian or Congo were regional categories of ivory. Chopped ivory was known as Opel. *Kadia* ivory was best suited for bangles. Europeans demanded *babu* or *bab wilayati*. The Kachchhi demand was for *babu ankasha* and *babu kashshi*. According to Burton, the tusk meant for Indian bazaar '. . . must be of middling sized, little bent, very bluff at the point', as it was meant for rings and armlets. The '*bab wilayati*' or 'foreign sort' was dispatched to the European and American markets.

To obtain ivory, well-manned caravans were dispatched from the coastal ports to the interiors. Caravans of 3000 to 4000 people made the return journey from the interior to the coast. The complex caravan convoys included a host of direct participants, right from the head to the porters or *Pagazi*. Kachchhi financiers played a decisive role in raising capital and assembling goods that would be eventually exchanged for ivory. Traders would carry outward from Zanzibar arms, thousands of yards of cloth, beads or wire and even opera glasses, depending on the fashion of the day in the interior, and trade them for tusks. In the interior, territorial chiefs who controlled the ivory trade organized specialist hunting networks. By the 1850s, there were three east African caravan routes into the interior. The most popular and central one originated in Zanzibar and ended in Ujiji on Lake Tanganyika, from where a series of secondary routes radiated outward to Arab-run outposts and assembly camps. This long journey of around six months might win an Arab trader 18,000 pounds of ivory, carried back to Zanzibar in caravans of up to 2000 professional porters. River caravans or canoe caravans were also organized. River caravans often commenced from Kau and Kipini. In the mid-nineteenth century, at Kipini, two Bohra and three Bania merchants, all connected with Lamu Kachchhi merchant houses, made arrangements, including monetary ones, for Swahili or Arab ivory-gathering expeditions up the Tana River. Initially, cotton cloth from Kachchh was the chief export to the Zanzibar market. Later on, the American cloth popularly called *merikani* monopolized the supply. Kachchhi investors looked upon caravan financing as an extension of long-term credit.

Since ivory came from the 'moving frontier', as elephants near the coast were hunted out or migrated inland, stability in the interior from where ivory was procured was important for the merchants. Local disturbances along caravan routes often obstructed ivory supply and made the large investments risky. Ivory traffic was interrupted during the 1870s because of a war with the Mirambo 'tribe' in Unyanyembe. When Sultan Barghash imposed prohibitive duties, there was diversion of business to Mozambique and the Somali country. Due to the disaster of Unyamwezi in 1870, Laddha Damji's expectation of large profits went for a toss, and he had to bear big losses. The business rule of thumb was that for every thousand dollars of capital invested in outfitting, one hundred *frasila* of large tusks were needed in order to defray the expenses and even out the risks.

Kachchhi merchants frequently played off two formidable African trading 'tribes'—the Yao and the Bisa—against each other, trying to see if they could wait it out or were in need of vital goods in exchange. In 1849, the American Consul in Zanzibar wrote to a leading ivory merchant of Salem, Massachusetts: 'There are reports of the Beshu tribe near Kilwa with 3000 *frasila* (upwards of 100,000 pounds) of ivory. The Banians have dispatched upwards of (MT) $100,000 worth of goods and (MT) $10,000 in specie . . .' The sheer size of the financial needs meant that they could not be met in Zanzibar. The financial markets of Mandvi and Bombay had to be relied upon.

In his narrative, Joseph Osgood sheds light on some aspects of the ivory trade. People, whom Osgood identified as 'Manumazees' (perhaps Nyamwezi?) from the interiors would bring the ivory to the coast in caravans after making a three-month journey. At the coast, these people would approach the Kachchhi Bania traders from Zanzibar town. Between them then commenced 'the tug of trade.' The appointed agent of the Bania trader would produce a cotton cloth; upon this the agent of the tribe would then place one tooth as a sample of the ivory they intended to offer for sale. The quantity meant for sale was not revealed until the trade was completed and the prices fixed. Over the tooth, the Banias and the agent of the tribe would negotiate for several days until terms were agreeable to both parties. In between, 'junkets' for the assembled tribe at the expense of the Banias were considered appropriate. At the end of the dealing, the Banias would obtain ivory in barter for brass wire, beads and trinkets. In Buganda, Bunyoro and Ankole, the ivory trade was largely controlled by the ruler, with whom negotiations were carried on. One tusk of every pair belonged *de jure* to the king, who also possessed the right to purchase the remaining one. Ivory also fell into the ruler's hands in the form of tribute. Tribute to chiefs took away a considerable share of the profits of the ivory trade. In the absence of a centralized state in east Africa, tributes to each village chief could considerably ratchet up the costs.

The governor on the coast exacted a high duty, and another duty was paid to the collector at Zanzibar who collected on behalf of the Sultan. The overtaxed ivory was finally exported to Europe, America and India. Kachchhi Banias observed elaborate rituals and ceremonies when the first cargo was shipped out. This was supposedly to ensure good fortune. The slave trade, it must be noted, was inextricably tied up with the ivory trade. Almost every caravan that came back from the interiors had thousands of porters, who were then disposed of as slaves. In financing the ivory trade, the Kachchhis were perforce financing the slave trade too. Even after the British ban on slave trading, this grisly business continued, albeit on a smaller scale.

Mandvi was the centre of ivory trade in India. In the 1830s, Mandvi imported ivory amounting to about 450 candies annually. By the 1870s, Bombay too had become important. Good quantities of ivory were exported to the Bombay market by 1873–74. The import figures for Bombay speak for themselves: in 1871–72, Rs 14.72 lakh, in 1872–73 Rs 15.53 lakh, and in 1873–74 Rs 19.06 lakh. In 1878–79, there was a large falling off in ivory shipments from Zanzibar, which was attributed to overtrading in the previous year.

From Mandvi, ivory went principally to Marwar, transported on bullocks by the nomadic Charan community in return for grain and coarse cloths. Candy and *frasila* were the measuring units for ivory. The import duty was fixed at 250 *kori* per candy. The market price at Mandvi varied from 4000 to 5000 *kori* per candy. Some small quantity was worked on at Mandvi itself and converted into women's ornaments. On the sale of the whole tusk, half a *kori* per *maund,* and on the sale of smaller pieces, 10 *kori* per *maund* was paid in brokerage; sometimes 5 *kori* in *sukhdi* (brokerage) was charged from both the buyer and seller. The table below shows how ivory tusks were classified, measured and sold in Mandvi:

Opel or Chopped Ivory		*Babu Aanksa Variety*		*Kadia Variety*	
Rate	Weight	Rate	Weight	Rate	Weight
35 old *dokda*	1 *sher*	32 old *dokda*	1 *sher*	35 old *dokda*	1 *sher*
44 *sher*	1 *maund*	48*sher*	1*maund*	44 *sher*	1 *maund*

32 old *dokda* equalled 1 *sher* and 50 such *sher* formed 1 *man* or *maund*. One *maund* equalled 487 rial. *Opel* and *kadia* were measured at fixed weights ranging from 10 *sher*, 5 *sheri* and 2½ *sheri*. The whole tusk was weighed in *mani* and *adhmani*. The *babu aanksa* was weighed by *adhmani*.

The ivory shipped from Mandvi to Bombay was chiefly for re-export to various manufacturing pockets. The chief centres for ivory work in western India were Hala in Hyderabad (Sindh), Kanara, Karachi, Pune, Surat and Marwar. Apart from the ubiquitous bangles and combs, toothpicks, buttons, boxes, handles for swords, daggers and knives, small figures, *kayels* (humming tops), *chakardis* (top), *ghughras* (jingling bells), chess boards, balls and chessmen were made in India. Oddly enough, the Hindu religious traditions regarding non-violence did not affect the demand for ivory objects, which involved the killing of elephants. A kind of ritual permission had been given by some state authorities. The Peshwa Savai Madhavrao (1780–95) claimed to have found in Hindu sacred books a law prohibiting Brahmin women from using metal hair combs. This was even followed by a decree supporting the use of ivory combs. One Audutrao Dhandarpalkar came from Nashik to Pune and set up the first ivory comb factory in that city. His example was followed by the carpenter Abaji Ava. Subsequently, Kunbi craftsmen took to the making of combs. The introduction of bone combs challenged the market for ivory combs. However, high-caste Hindu women considered bone combs impure. Three ivory combs formed part of the *vayan* or outfit of an upper caste Hindu bride. Ivory, which has mythological connections with Lord Ganesha, was considered pure. Many Hindus sought comfort by staying under the impression that the ivory they used came from elephants that had died naturally. Osgood's observation backs this unlikely story. He writes, '. . . the traders say that they collect much of the ivory in the large swamps of their district, into which the elephants have entered during the dry season in search of food, and there being overtaken by the heavy rains of the ensuing wet season have perished by drowning.'

The manufacture of ivory goods was a relatively simple process. The ivory was at first soaked in water for two or three days. It was then cut into pieces of the required size and sawn through. While sawing, it was kept vertical by means of a vice. It was then filed, rubbed, and polished to convert it into the final fine product. Combs for use by women were rectangular and had a double set of teeth, while men's combs were crescent-shaped and had only one set of teeth. Small pieces of ivory were used to make dice. The price of a comb ranged from 6 annas to Rs 1.5, varying according to their size, thickness and workmanship. The combs and dice were sold at the workshops by the workers on their own account. Their main customers were high class Hindus. Coloured and dyed ivory was produced in Hyderabad, Sindh. Red dye was extracted from babul trees, and green dye was imported. Considerable trade was done in armlets. Many women covered their arms 'till they look as though they were encased in ivory'.

At Kanara, a few Gudgars, whose chief calling was carving sandalwood and painting, at times carved ivory. They imported ivory from Bombay or Mysore. Ivory-carving in Karachi consisted almost entirely of the manufacture of arm rings, called *bahin* when they were full-sized and *gaabha* when they were for children. Ivory carvers also kept ready-made *gaabhas,* which they sold singly or by set, or *churo* (*chudo*). Chessmen and pieces for the game of *chopat* were usually made on order. During the marriage season, demand for ivory objects was brisk. While in most places, retailers of uncut ivory were Marwaris, in Hala they were Sindhi Banias. The retail commission was between 1 and 1.5 per cent. The craftsmen usually bought the uncut ivory on credit, paying an interest of around 1 per cent per month.

Workmen had to sell the articles they made on their own account and pay the standing balance, including commission and interest, to the Marwari moneylender. Most craftsmen remained indebted to the Marwari.

In Surat, ivory bangles were worn by almost all lower-class Hindu women. Sheriff writes, 'Brides in faraway India wore ivory bangles, while the Chinese even farther east made their unique, intricate carvings using ivory from Africa'. There were a few *hinghratia* or ornamental boxes used for preserving turmeric or vermillion that women applied to their foreheads, much as they do today. As a luxury item, ivory was subject to economic cycles. In 1895–96, famine conditions in India resulted in a drop in ivory imports by about a third. The plague in Bombay added to the market's woes. That year was declared as being the worst of the decade.

Kachchhi purchasers of ivory were often criticized by their contemporaries. According to an American trader at Zanzibar, in 1844, the Indians:

[T]rade with the natives who are very ignorant and know not the value of these articles. The Banyans obtain the ivory of these people for almost nothing, giving a string of beads or small coil of brass wire for a tooth weighing 140 pounds or even more. But the natives within a few years have found out something the value of this article and charge a much higher price for it.

Osgood, too, noted this:

> The Manumazees are met at the coast by Banian
> traders from Zanzibar town, by whom they formerly
> were much imposed upon and duped to trade away
> a valuable tusk of ivory weighing several frazils for
> a handful of paltry beads or small roll of brass wire.

Clearly, over time, African sellers did realize that their ivory was quite valuable. All parties in the trade did try to game the system for their benefit. Caravan leaders had a reputation for not fulfilling their commitments. Porters had a reputation for running off with guns and selling them to African chiefs at a profit for themselves. Entrepreneurs from Salem, Massachusetts, played an increasing role in the direct trade with east Africa; nevertheless, most of the ivory went to Bombay and from there a portion of it was re-exported.

The rise and subsequent decline of the ivory industry is an interesting story in and of itself. It involves an early form of globalization. The crucial raw material was accessed from mainland east Africa through Zanzibar. Hard ivory from east Africa was not so easy to carve as the soft ivory of Zanzibar. It was more suitable for making a different range of products. In the last decade of the nineteenth century, Zanzibar was the source of two-thirds of the world's ivory, while the emerging US economy absorbed 80 per cent of the ivory. In between was the elaborate supply chain, where our very own Kachchhis were so critical. The demand for ivory was driven by the exponential growth of the piano industry, as piano keys were made from ivory. The factories at Ivoryton and Connecticut manufactured keys, keyboards and sounding boards for many well-known piano makers, whose combined production reached half-a-million pianos a year by the early decades of the twentieth century. Roell observed: 'Almost every home, even among the humble, possesses this instrument and some amount of piano music.' By 1890, one American out of every 874 owned a piano; in 1910, this ratio reached one in every 252. Louis Elson wrote: 'There is probably no country in the world where the piano is so (sic) widespread as in the United States.' It also represented the cult of domesticity, an ideal that was exceedingly popular in the Victorian Era. Roell connects the piano's place within the Victorian Era, the era from which the piano was born. Known as the 'altar to St. Cecilia', the piano became a quintessential object in the Victorian home. It also became the epitome of Victorian ideals. The emergence of piano culture symbolized the emergence of middle-class values in the Victorian age. The piano player required sacrifice and tenaciousness, which were markers of bourgeois attributes and culture. Ralph Emerson boasted this purity of the piano in his essay, 'Tis wonderful how soon a piano gets into a log hut on the frontier. You would think they found it under a fine stump.' Piano manufacturers synthesized Victorian sentiments with the consumer trends developing during the 1890s. The companies released unlimited funds to remodel the entire factory system. This also required a responsibility to personally employ every man, an action that was indicative of piano makers' deep conviction for design integrity. The growing piano industries conveyed the shift from nineteenth-century Victorian ideals to twentieth-century consumer culture.' Pianos required spacious homes such as those provided by rising American affluence. Between 1851 and 1864, the sale of ivory, primarily for piano keys, was valued at half-a-million dollars. In 1891 Zanzibar, the principal export entrepôt on the east African coastline, provided more than two-thirds of the world total; in 1894, 80 per cent of their export went to America. By the end of the century, the ivory cutters of Deep River and Ivoryton manufactured more than 50,000 combs and hundreds of thousands of piano key sets each year. The factories processed more than 100,000 pounds of ivory each year, with peak years of more than 200,000 pounds of elephant's tusks. At its peak in the 1890s, the industry employed more than 1000 workers at two principal factories at Deep River and Ivoryton. The villages of Deep River and Ivoryton can be said to have grown into towns leveraging the ivory industry.

Many commercial centres in Germany, the Netherlands and Britain were also established specially to deal in ivory. Before the 1850s, ivory amounting to MT$213,145 per annum and after the 1850s, to MT$213,145 per annum and after the 1850s, MT$547,089 per annum, was exported from Zanzibar to Bombay, and from there to England. All important western merchants obtained their ivory requirements through the Kachchhis. The Kachchhis exploited the fact that ivory had grown to triple the size of the traditional clove market. They continued to view the Indian Ocean almost as a Kachchhi lake as they kept control of various commodities traded there. Omani Arabs were not completely absent from the trade. But it was the Kachchhis—Thariya Topan and Ratansinh Bhimji—who were known as the Ivory Kings of Zanzibar.

As artificial substitutes replaced ivory for combs and piano keys, the trade went into a steep decline. The beneficial side-effect was that the east African elephant was not completely hunted out of existence!

Copal

Between 1830 and 1880, an unusual, rare natural product gained prominence in the trade of Zanzibar. This was copal—a brittle, aromatic resin found in the lowland forests and coastal hinterlands of east Africa. Copal was used in the manufacture of high-value varnishes, and was in demand from varnish factories in New England and Hamburg. Zanzibar copal was different from the copal of western Mexico and New Zealand with which it competed. East African copal had distinct regional specificity. Copal is a product of the *Hymenaea verrucosa* tree, known in Swahili as *Msandarusi* and among Bantu-speaking farmers of the coastal hinterland as *Mnangu*; Arabs called it *Shajar El Sandarus*, and Indians referred to it as *Chandraus*. Copal trees were usually seen on the coastal plains and disappeared west of the coastal hinterland. In east Africa, considerable quantities of copal were obtained from the semi-fossil anime, which was dug from the ground. As with all commodities, sharp trading practices in copal were not unknown. The best copal from fossils was regularly adulterated with inferior copal resin and sometimes even with wet sand and gravel in order to increase the weight of shipments.

According to the British Assistant Consul Fredric Elton, bargaining over copal was a veritable 'war to the knife over the barter of "Animi"', between the Indian and the Washezi, a contest in which Elton found both sides 'unscrupulous'. In some villages, parties with their gum would spend the whole night bargaining with the Kachchhis. Finally, a handshake would cement the deal. Individual trades were not possible, as local people and their chief acted as a collective in selling their copal. Fredric Elton was once confronted by 800 armed men near the Rufiji River who believed he was there to disrupt their trade. Each team of copal diggers was led by a 'big man' (*mtu mkuu*) who determined how the product would be traded and its profits distributed. Copal digging was restricted and controlled using a variety of taboos to determine access to forests in which ancestors were buried or where potentially malevolent spirits resided. Sunseri argues that control of copal provided hinterland polities with the ability to accumulate wealth and that this in turn enabled Africans to negotiate relations of protection with others like the traders.

Kachchhi traders faced considerable harassment and taxes. The African chief extracted a ground rent. Then arrived the *jamadar* who levied an arbitrary percentage on imputed profits, supposedly to prevent dissension. Then came the *ushru* or government tax of 20 per cent. The government also charged rent for storage. The Kachchhis, nevertheless, tried to work within the written legal agreements they had with the coastal agents. After this long drawn-out process, copal was sold to the Indian market or to the foreign merchant. The price in Zanzibar was about $9 per *frasila,* against $1 to $3 per *frasila* in mainland Africa. While Zanzibar had facilities for cleaning and washing copal, Americans preferred to take the unclean gum to Salem, where the cleaning facilities were better.

During their stay in the interiors, the Kachchhis appeared 'quite at home' in their settlements. They would ramp upon an enclosure and plant a garden around a covered and raised terrace on which they met for meals. While varnish manufacture in the nineteenth century gave a boost to copal, it should not be forgotten that the copal trade had its roots in antiquity. Copal was burned as incense in religious ceremonies at Jerusalem and Mecca during the middle ages. It was mixed with oils to coat paintings in medieval Europe, a process which led to its recognition as a superlative varnish (a coating that provides a hard, lustrous, transparent finish to a surface). Increasing European incursions into the Indian Ocean after 1500 led to demand for 'Bombay copal' or 'Calcutta copal'. In 1591, the first English ship to visit Zanzibar left with half a tonne of copal. Copal allowed European varnish manufacturers to make a product that could rival Chinese and Japanese lacquers in beauty and hardness. By the seventeenth century, 'Zanzibar copal' was in high demand in Europe for coach varnish, which was based on intricate formulations and processes that were closely guarded from rival coachmakers. In 1653, a merchant with the English East India Company at Zanzibar was informed by a mainland ruler that he would be able to find good trading there of ivory, beeswax and 'Sanderoos', 'A Gumm like Amber'.

The nineteenth century witnessed a 'copal boom'. Small quantities of copal—a little less than $500 worth, or perhaps 4375 pounds—found a market in Bombay in 1802. The following year, ten times that amount was fetched at Bombay, doubling again by 1815. In the 1840s, some 420,000 pounds of copal was shipped to Bombay annually. This was perhaps its peak level. As is to be expected, the Kachchhis of Zanzibar were the principal intermediaries in this trade.

While commercial varnish makers emerged in Surrey in England as early as in 1791, it was the American interest that fuelled the boom. C. Schrack and Company, established in Philadelphia in 1815, John W. Masury and Son, established in New York in 1835, and Simson, Valentine & Company, established in Boston in 1832, produced varnish for carriage makers, railroad and stretcher builders, cabinet makers, and anyone else requiring a clear, glossy finish to their products. Bridgerport's Parrott Varnish, Newark's Murphy Varnish, Philadelphia's Felton, Rau, and Sibley and Chicago's Heath and Milligan emerged as competitors. In the 1880s, Newark had more varnish makers than any other city. New York and Philadelphia, followed by St. Louis and Chicago, led in the number of paint firms. Francis H. Glidden of Cleveland entered the business in the early 1870s, and though his company would one day be famous for paint, its primary product in the early days was varnish. Varnish sales to industries such as manufacturers of carriages and agricultural implements grew rapidly. In 1849, 1822 firms manufactured wagons and carriages. At the end of the century there were about 6000 firms.

The entry into the east African market of Americans, especially merchants from Salem, changed the dimension of the copal trade. The first Salem ship arrived in Zanzibar in 1826, and the second arrived home in 1827, 'carrying a valuable amount of gum copal'. In 1832, the ship *Black Warrior* returned to Salem 'bringing the largest cargo of gum copal yet received. Makers of fine varnish and lacquers gobbled it up so greedily'. By 1845, American traders dominated the Zanzibar market, shipping 42 per cent of the total copal compared with Bombay's 28 per cent and Britain's 24 per cent. In that single year, a total of 42,500 *frasila* (1,487,500 lb) of copal was traded from Zanzibar, all coming from the mainland's coastal forests.

With the entry of the Hamburg merchants, there ensued a fierce competition for copal between the Germans and the Americans. In 1859, the price of $0.26 per pound of copal paid by the Germans far exceeded that of $0.16 paid by the Indians and the Americans. In such conditions, Indian merchants preferred to sell to the Germans on the spot at the given market price instead of exporting their supplies for future marketing to their agents in India or elsewhere. The Americans were under pressure even from the French merchants. As a result, the price of unclean copal increased to $7.5, and clean copal to $10. In 1859, despite the new entrants, New England merchants took 68 per cent of east African copal. Germany took 24 per cent, with British India taking most of the rest. Burton remarked that Americans, Germans and Indians were the largest consumers of this product from Zanzibar.

In March 1857, a 10 per cent duty imposed on gum copal contributed to a decline in American trade with east Africa. The duties in the US prompted two American firms to bring soda ash into Zanzibar for the purpose of washing copal. It was now more profitable to have copal cleaned in Zanzibar. The Salem factory, cleaning imported gum from Zanzibar, was closed in 1861. The American Civil War added to disruptions in trade between Zanzibar and America. Copal imports steeply declined, by 66.6 per cent. By the end of the war, the American share of copal dropped to less than 20 per cent, against Germany's 45 per cent and France's 35 per cent. In 1870, the last Salem ship with its load of copal returned home from Zanzibar. By the 1880s, Germany, India and Hong Kong were the most important destinations for east African copal, although Copal trans-shipped through British ports still accounted for 10 per cent of American imports from east Africa. Irrespective of whether the final buyers were British, German, French or American, the Kachchhis of Zanzibar remained irreplaceably integral to the long and complex supply chain of the copal trade.

Cloves

Cloves are what it all started with. The twin islands of Zanzibar and Pemba stood for cloves in the worldwide network of Spice Islands. Sultan Seyyid Said made it obligatory for landowners on the islands to introduce at least three clove trees in place of one coconut palm. Disobedience resulted in confiscation of land. Numerous clove plantations sprang up. The Sultan's own plantation was the largest. Waters noticed 200,000 trees in his plantation. In 1840, the returns from the Sultan's clove plantation constituted one-third of his income, which was estimated that year at £120,000. In his report to the State Department, Ward, the American Consul, remarked that Sultan Said produced about 1 million pounds of cloves annually. Soon, clove production took the place of other crops, and Zanzibarians had to start importing the rice and sweet potatoes they once farmed for domestic consumption.

Like the booms in ivory and copal, the boom in cloves benefited Zanzibar greatly. Captain Loarer refers to a clove 'mania'. By 1840, Captain Loarer found Kachchhis owning small *Shambas* or clove plantations. Ibji Shivji, brother of Jairam Shivji, acquired a new *Shamba* in 1844, and another merchant had three plantations when he went bankrupt in 1846. Yet another Kachchhi, Kanu Munji, owned a plantation situated six miles from the town of Zanzibar. By the 1870s, Kachchhis were busy purchasing cloves for which they had made crop advances to Arab growers. Arabs were the principal cultivators. According to Abdul Sheriff, the Arabs felt that as clove cultivation was distinct from clove trading, they did not face much competition from Kachchhis. Wide variations in crop output made clove cultivation a very speculative business. Dried cloves were bought by Kachchhi dealers, who retailed them to English and German clients. Crops on the Arabs' estates were generally mortgaged to the Kachchhi financiers who had advanced money for cultivation.

The clove market was buffeted on both the demand and supply sides. In 1856, the price of cloves in the world market had fallen to a tenth of what it was in 1830. The devastating hurricane of 1872 affected Zanzibar's clove production. Pemba, though, was spared by the hurricane. However, the abolition of the slave trade in 1873 held back the development of large plantations in Pemba. Unstable clove prices and lavish spending by many landowners, who were caught in the grip of *Kadri* (social status) and *Takashima* (generosity) often led them into debt traps. By 1888, about two-thirds of the clove plantations in Zanzibar were mortgaged to Kachchhi merchants. Norman Bennett argues that since Indians were restricted and then forbidden 'from slave holding, the plantation owners normally were left in control of their property, the moneylenders profiting from the settlements regarding crop marketing imposed upon their debtors.' The upward trend in the clove trade was sustained as the market value of cloves in Bombay grew five-fold. But price fluctuations remained an issue. In 1871–72, the value of cloves traded in Bombay stood at Rs 18.98 lakh. In 1872–73, it went up to Rs 19.22 lakh, falling dramatically to Rs 14.59 lakh 1873–74.

Bombay largely imported cloves from east Africa via Muscat and Kachchh. The principal use of cloves worldwide was as a spice for culinary purposes. In India and the Far East, it was also used to fasten the paan leaf containing betel nut. In Europe and

America, cloves were distilled to produce eugenol, which was used in perfumery, toothpastes and in the manufacture of vanillin. Fluctuations were recorded in clove imports to Bombay. There was a surge of imports in 1890s that was attributed to lower stocks in India in the previous years. Between 1914 and 1917, almost half of Zanzibar's cloves were exported to India.

In the late 1920s, the trade directions changed when direct shipping links were opened from Zanzibar to Singapore and Java. This was probably a direct result of the expanding Kretek cigarette industry in Indonesia. Kretek cigarettes had been originally brought to Java by the Arabs. The cigarettes consisted of a dried maize leaf wrapper around a filling of local tobacco mixed with cloves. Commercial production of Kertek cigarettes began around 1916, and the industry expanded rapidly. Indonesian consumers preferred the smoother taste of Zanzibar cloves.

The supply side of the clove business was hurt with the abolition of slavery in 1897, as plantation owners lost their accustomed supply of labour. To overcome this problem, free passages on government steamers were granted in 1907 to clove-pickers travelling to Pemba. In 1911, these concessions were extended to clove cultivators too. The backbreaking labour involved in clove transportation became easier and cheaper in the early 1920s when a system of tarmac roads was constructed in both Unguja and Pemba.

There was a division of labour between Kachchhi Hindu merchants and their Muslim counterparts when it came to articles of trade. The Hindus stayed away from the cowrie trade as cowrie collection resulted in the death of molluscs, which was considered unacceptable according to the non-violent traditions of Kachchhi Hindus. Ironically, Hindu women freely used cowries for decorative and ornamental purposes! Cowries, like ivory and copal, were collected on the African mainland, brought to Zanzibar and then exported to Hamburg and to India by Indian Muslim dealers. Kachchhi Hindus also opted to give a miss to trade in livestock and meat. Cattle were brought from the interior to the east African coast. American shippers transported them to Havana for the Cuban slaves. Hindu Kachchhis did not allow this traffic to be conducted on their craft. This trade was entirely confined to Kachchhi-Muslim traders. At Mandvi, rhino horns were used to make snuff boxes, knife and sword handles and other ornaments. Kachchhi-Hindu Bania traders did not patronize these articles.

African Consumers

What did the Kachchhi merchants give mainland Africans as items in exchange for ivory, copal, cowries and livestock? The single most important item was cloth or, to put it more accurately, manufactured textiles that were imported into Zanzibar from Boston and other parts of New England. The industrial revolution had resulted first in Britain and then in New England, coming up with a 'plain, coarsely woven, but durable fabric' that could compete with hand-woven Indian coarse cotton cloths. One administrative report noted that American cloth was of a better texture and withstood the rough mode of washing, also lasting almost twice as long as the Bombay article. *Merikani*, as the cloth was called in Swahili, perhaps a variant of '*Amerikani*', dominated the east African markets. In 1859, Americans supplied 51 per cent of the textile imports into Zanzibar, compared with 29 per cent from British India and 21 per cent from Britain. American cloth imports into Zanzibar rose steadily from 4250 bales (one bale equalling 750 yards) worth $239,655 in 1848 to 6950 bales worth $421,850 in 1856.

Cloth, beads, brass wire and other imports 'opened' the economies of the east African interior. Textiles were more than just a basic good for mainland Africans. Jane Schneider has argued that cloth is catalytic in consolidating social relations and in communicating identities and values. African kingdoms and chiefdoms differentiated between the ostentatious cloth used by the elite and the drab cloth used by commoners. Burton noted that almost all Zaramo men and women wore cotton cloth, making them stand out from peoples further west beyond the copal belt. Import of cloth thus allowed Zaramo, Rufiji and other coastal hinterland peoples to establish trading links with people further inland. Elaborate textiles served the political purpose of 'celebrating chieftainship and communicating goodwill. Especially dramatic were the kingdoms and empires that amassed great storehouses of tributary textiles.' Chieftains who controlled ivory and copal trading also presided over cloth distribution, according to established hierarchies of patronage. The ability of a *pazi,* the chief, to accumulate cotton cloth and other commodities, including beads, copper wire and grain, to attract a following and thereby strengthen his position in society, was a key factor in coastal hinterland politics. Around the mid-nineteenth century, traders at the coast could obtain a six-foot long Salem *merikani* cotton sheet for 25 cents and sell it in the interior for $1.

Cloth became part of the African barter system. The following report concerning the Madagascan port of Majunga captures this: '. . . it is the beginning of the rice season & they want cottons to buy rice with'. This establishes the connectivity between cloth and food. Cloth, along with beads, as Charles New observed in his memoir, was the only money recognized in parts of Africa. On one of his expeditions he took along with him eight pieces of Manchester fabric, four pieces of *Kaniki,* and sixteen pieces of coloured cloth. The explorer Beardall noted in 1880 that Kichi and Zaramo people brought copal down the Rufiji river to trade for rice and cloth. Charles New also noted that Zanzibaris imported raw, unbleached cotton from western India for use in their own small weaving industry. They exported local bombax (silk cotton) to Nyamwezi, where it was used as a substitute for cotton.

At Zanzibar, the shifts in competitive advantage started taking place from the 1830s when *merikani* started dominating. Initially, Indian cotton cloth had been in demand. But soon, American cloth or *merikani*, was preferred over Kachchh and Bombay textiles. *Merekani* came in the holds of Salem ships bound for Zanzibar. The popularity of American cotton goods extended beyond Zanzibar, through the bazaars of Arabia, Persia and east Africa. One contemporary source noted the dominant position of American textiles even in Portuguese Indian possessions like Daman and Diu in the 1840s and 1850s:

> They (Americans) introduce better and *cheaper* cotton goods than those from Diu, Daman . . . which until now were used for this commerce, and which they (American textiles) are forcing out of the market.

The American manufactures were indeed successful in

> [E]stablishing among the Africans a taste for finer and better patterned cloths, with grave damage to the manufactures of Diu and Daman, which were sustained by this commerce, the principal resource of those establishments.

Before the coming of American enterprise to Mozambique, textiles from Diu dominated the market. Gamitto, in 1832, saw how the standard bale of cloths in the Zambesi valley consisted of seven different varieties of Indian manufactured cloths; but by the time of his departure from Mozambique in 1853, he noted how cotton textiles of English and American manufacture 'are preferred to the Indian weaves'. Machado notes that this change in preference was also noted by Livingstone, who commented on how English and American unbleached calicoes were the only currency in use in Tete. Ruschenberger went further in his observations and noted the specific distinctions between British and American textiles:

> [T]he American cotton manufactures have taken
> precedence of the English manufactures . . . It is in
> vain that the English endeavour to imitate our fabric
> by stamping their own with American marks, and
> by other means assimilating it; for the people to say,
> the strength and wear of the American goods are
> so superior that lest they be deceived they will no
> longer even purchase from Englishmen.

America's trade with Zanzibar in *merikani* in fact did a lot of harm to the trade of other European merchants. The Americans could successfully compete with Indian textiles, but Europeans could not do the same with American textiles. British firms like Newman,

Hunt and Christopher operated in Zanzibar in the 1820s and 1830s. But the entry of American cloth pushed them out of the market. Hamerton, the British Consul, confirmed that *merikani* was in greatest demand in Arabia and east Africa. He feared that the superior quality of American cottons over British and Indian piece goods would soon drive the latter out of the market altogether. American cottons imported to Zanzibar were in demand even in the Persian markets, where they were considered superior to English fabric. Burton made the following statement of regret: 'I made the mistake of ignorance by not laying in an ample supply of American domestic (*merikani*), the silver of the country . . .'

Kachchhi merchants had no hesitation in importing and selling American textiles in Zanzibar. Curiously, while American textiles displaced textiles from places like Daman and Diu, who saw a decline in their market share in Mozambique from the 90 per cent levels to 25 per cent levels by the 1850s, Kachchhi *kaniki* fabrics seem to have retained reasonable popularity and market share—as Pedro Machado puts it, 'for reasons which are unclear'. Though Pedro Machado is not clear with the reason, in all likelihood, the popularity, the finely inscribed designs, vibrant range of colours and substantial circulation of a variety of Kachchhi textiles withstood the western inroads. The sizeable knowledge of the east African local market and control over the exchanges of other commodities also helped Kachchhis to keep up the importance of their piece goods. However, the prime position of the American textile and the parallel existence of Kachchhi textiles did not continue for long, and as discussed below, because the ever-growing textile production in Bombay mills also challenged northwest-Indian goods during the civil war years. Above all, the British textile manufacturing units through India managed to undermine the Indian textile exports by the last quarter of the nineteenth century. British textile exporters were not that lucky. By 1859, exports of American cotton goods to Zanzibar were two-and-a half times the value of British exports.

Kaniki was coarse white cloth of country thread, partly made in Kachchh and partly in Marwar, and finally dyed in Kachchh. Other varieties of coarse cloth from Kachchh in demand in Zanzibar were the *purin*, *fallin* and *dabola*. The cheapest kind of cloth was *barsati*. Africans called it *kitambibarsati*. It was a favourite article of wear among the poorer freemen, slaves and women. The Nyamwezi favoured the *barsati* or *kitambi banyani*. The *dabwani* was cloth with small blue-and-white checks made in Muscat and dyed with Kachchhi colours. It was in demand in the African interior. The *bandira*, a red cotton bunting imported from India, was also prized in the interior, especially by women. The *shazar*, called *mukungura* throughout the interior, was another cotton fabric from Kachchh. The *khesi*, an infrequent import, was a scarlet silk made in Thane in India. Its customers were Kachchhi-Hindu Banias and Kachchhi

Muslims of Zanzibar. *Seeah kupra,* manufactured in Mandvi from English thread, was actually a term that referred to about twenty different kinds of fabric that were, according to Lt Postans, 'the grand articles' of export, highly prized and with a ready market in east Africa. By 1840, annual exports of different varieties of cloth from Mandvi to east Africa amounted to about 950 bales, on which export duty of 10 *kori* per bale was paid. Clearly, Kachchhi-Indian cloth supply may have slipped to second place in the face of increasing demand for *merikani,* but it was never completely out of the market. In 1859, the value of cotton goods at Zanzibar, by country of origin, amounted to: American, £94,500 pounds; Indian, £54,500 pounds; and British, £38,000 pounds. In 1860, Rigby reported that 46 per cent of the cotton in this African region came from India and 47 per cent from the US. Things reversed substantially in the 1860s. During this period, the American firms faced difficulties because of the Civil War. American-manufactured goods exported to Zanzibar dropped from 12,000 bales before the Civil War to only 10,000 bales during the war, and to less than 7000 bales in 1865. Americans imported cotton goods from England to fulfil their contracts at Zanzibar, transporting their purchases to the US in British vessels. Kachchhi financiers like Jairam Shivji bankrolled American firms that needed credit.

After the Civil War, the Americans never quite recovered their position in Zanzibar. Textiles from the new mills established in India, along with British textiles and Kachchhi *kaniki* cloth, flooded the Zanzibar and east African markets. Sultan Barghash enlarged the Zanzibar customs house to accommodate the new volumes. The British had a keen interest in direct trade between Zanzibar and England instead of trade through India. However, the low cost of shipping between Zanzibar and India ensured that even British cloth went to Zanzibar through Bombay. In the meantime, the underlying economics of production also began to increasingly favour Indian cloth. In 1881, the annual volume of Indian cloth exported to Zanzibar reached 5.5 million yards, overtaking British cloth exported from Bombay. Grey piece goods from Bombay were taken by Zanzibar, Mozambique and Aden. The cloth was coarse, but cheap and strong and much in favour with the people. Over the course of the 1880s, this trend intensified. In 1887–88, Zanzibar imported almost all the unbleached drills, more than half of the unbleached sheeting, as well as nearly one-quarter of all *dhoti* exported from Bombay. By 1888, Bombay exports of unbleached and English cloth to Zanzibar had reached the astonishing level of more than 15 million yards a year. Reflecting the increasing purchasing power of east Africans and the decreasing cost of the industrial units of India, the volume of imported Indian unbleached cloth alone was now 30 per cent higher than the American export trade had been at its apex. East African consumers were also buying

Indian carriages and carts, cabinet ware, furniture, boots, shoes, stationery and rice. British officials were alarmed by these developments. Frederic Holmwood, the British Consul in Zanzibar, in a communication to the Manchester Chamber of Commerce in 1885, sought to encourage English manufacturers to take an interest in the east African market. Thomas Metcalf goes on to add that nearly half of Zanzibar's imports came from India. Much of this earlier consisted of British goods re-exported from India. As Indian textile mills took off from the 1870s onwards, 'cotton of Indian manufacture have seriously interfered with our goods'. Metcalf asserted that 'the comparatively flimsy material which the rising manufacturing industry of India is now producing can be sold at little more than half the cost of the heavier and more durable fabrics of Manchester and Massachusetts.' The British were clearly visibly annoyed that Indian textiles, which were considered to be of low quality, were challenging fabrics from Manchester. British envy did not insulate the emerging Indian textile mills from problems though. Further, though Jeremy Prestholdt projects figures which suggest the rise of textile exports in the 1880s, it was not completely true for the entire decade. The administrative reports clearly indicate that after 1881 textile markets experienced fluctuation owing to a variety of factors. The Bombay exports to Zanzibar witnessed the falling off in country-made grey piece-goods, and the same was the case with Persia. Grey goods, which declined in 1882–83 and 1883–84, fell a little further. Volatility remained a feature of this market. In the famine year of 1887, the textile market was so affected that the year was accounted as unpropitious, and no marriages were performed in the Hindu community. Volatility in terms of sharp declines also happened when there were partial failures of rain. There were other factors which contributed to the gradual decline of the Bombay article which momentously rose from the mid-1880s. The grey and whites' quantity was larger but the value less; while in prints the heaviest fall occurred in shipments to Muscat and Zanzibar. There had been uninterrupted decline since 1895–96, the chief cause of which appears to be the loss of trade with China and to less extent with Aden, Zanzibar and Abyssinia. After recovering from the civil-war effects, the competition of American goods in Aden at any rate had had a share in the result. The enormous exports of Bombay yarn to China point to the development of the handloom industry in that country, which was believed to be the main factor in the decline of the piece-goods trade. In the case of other countries, partial failure of the rain was accountable for the falling off. The local factors combined with colonial rule punctured the promising growth of the Indian textile industry.

In sum, textile was the chief commodity which facilitated deeper inroads of the foreign mercantile groups. It was this article which clothed the Africans but at the cost of their freedom and natural resources. The uncalled changes became Africa's burden which the Africans bore for a longer time to come. Incongruously, on the other side, this same commodity made many millionaires. The history of commodity exchange interestingly unveils dissimilarities of human societies settled in different parts of the globe.

After textiles, beads were another item that Africans demanded in exchange for their ivory and copal. *Sofi* Italian beads of various colours were in great demand. Kachchhis made sure that the demand for beads was always met. They also brought to Africa, in small quantities, many other items: skullcaps, knives, razors, firecrackers, soaps, needles, scissors, looking-glasses, picture books, jumping dolls, rings, daggers, naval and cavalry sabres, cooking pots and Birmingham trinkets.

Given that the underlying exchange with African sellers was through barter, mismatches in goods demanded and supplied happened all the time. William Jelly, an American agent, complained to his firm that a wrong musket had been consigned to Zanzibar. The Salem consigner had difficulty figuring out the kind desired by the Zanzibar market. To meet African preferences, four hundred different varieties of beads, each variety bearing its peculiar name, were exported to Zanzibar. It was necessary for Kachchhi Banias to check, measure and prepare lengthy bead necklaces before barter. Beads of the wrong size or colour would be rejected. The 'caprices and vagaries' in taste of African women in the interior could—and many times did—jeopardize a trader's profit. Cases are recorded where a trader assumed that a blue bead which sold well one year would do so the next. Beads were like any other consumer good. Their value on the coast or in the interior was determined by their size, shape, colour and packaging. In 1886–87, Count Teleki found no buyers for Masai beads because the Dorobo no longer preferred them. He had not figured that fashions might change!

The preparation of a caravan heading into the interiors has been well recorded. The caravan head began the process with 'prayers and incense burning'. Numerous coloured items were usually padded between two bales of white material, and the whole was then wrapped in cheap, white *merikani* or calico, and finally covered with coconut matting. Beads were packed in common sacks, and coils of wire were tied together and tucked up in matting. Finally, each stack was stamped with a legible number, which was then entered in a ledger. Kachchhi merchants relished their central and profitable role in the supply chain. Their intelligence about changing demand and supply positions was pretty good, despite the conditions of the time and place; and at least by reputation, they were supposed to be the early birds in getting vital information, which they kept to themselves. They lived up to Fernand Braudel's dictum: '. . . to be well informed was even more important than to be well-trained . . .' They were also early Braudel disciples in reportedly staying focused on secrecy, and on being first in line with new information.

The other problems in dealing with the complex Zanzibar dominion was of overstocked goods and their disposal. Having lost in the first round of sale, the suppliers were left to dispose of their goods at a compromised rate or to change the venue of sale from a specific to a general commercial centre. For instance, the piled stocks of beads, perhaps rejected, had their saviour market at Ujiji, where bead changers converted hundreds of varieties. If beads were the currency of Africa, then Ujiji was its most important foreign exchange market. The conversion rates reflected the prevalent fashions in demand and challenges in supply. Kacchchhi merchants were not unduly bothered by the moral issues involved in the eighteenth and nineteenth-century trade practices, where African receipt of cloth and beads were exchanged not only for ivory and gum copal, but also for human chattel in the form of slaves. They were more aligned to views that free exchange was by definition fair. But it is difficult to accept this position; getting ivory, gum copal and human beings (slaves) in return for cloth, beads and copper wires suggests immoral and grotesque terms of exchange. Given that they operated in the enigmatic Indian Ocean region, Kachchhis were more focused on bread-and-butter business issues like management of shipment schedules. An American merchant, Edmund Roberts, arrived in 1828 at Zanzibar loaded with cargo consisting of a great variety of textiles, gunpowder and arms. He hoped to exchange his goods for ivory and copal. But he learned about the closing of the monsoons the hard way. The time of year Roberts chose was bad. All merchandise had been shipped out of Zanzibar.

Kachchhis learned quickly about consumer preferences in the African trade. They discovered that the people of Buganda had a love for parasols of a certain kind. Lugard found there a demand for 'opera glasses . . . for which they would pay any price'. Cheaper English chintz found no market as consumers preferred French and German varieties. But the French were not always lucky. Writing in 1857 about French merchandise in general, Colchet says: 'The simplicity, and I will say, the originality, of this Zanzibari taste, will be for a long time an obstacle to the introduction into this country of French products.' It was this kind of Zanzibari preference that permitted Indians first, and Americans later, to negotiate comfortably. Success in trading largely depended on the agents' abilities to read African fashion trends and relay this information to manufacturers.

The Kachchhis navigated a difficult but rewarding world between African customers who, according to Jeremy Prestholdt, were 'capable of rejecting, on the grounds of (the goods) not matching their taste'. However, they were still dependent on the availability of these products from foreign destinations. If the foreign merchants were troubled with rejection phobia, their

African and Arab counterparts were equally stressed to be watchful in supplying the right type of ivory i.e. Bab Vilayati, Ulaya or Gendai and also the superior quality of gum copal. The ivory trader had to know his ivory, which varied from hard to soft. In getting the best and maximum in return, African consumers demonstrated their wit when they called for the biggest man in the village—someone with a 'peculiarly long and simian forearm'—who was summoned when cloth was being measured. In these terms, both the parties involved in exchange of commodities were self-assertive. Here, the most difficult was the role of the Indian middle manager who had to manage constantly to meet the expectations of both the sides and finalize the deal. Indeed, the profit, no doubt huge, came only after several tough rides of transacting and shipping to facilitate the trade of it. Kachchhis were the beneficiaries of the uniformly high reputation that Indian traders in general enjoyed in the Arabian and African littorals. Faced with disturbances in the Somali ports, the Germans whittled down their direct presence and readily appointed Indian agents there. Trust and reliability were important factors, and this resulted in Indians being given a preference. Indian Bania traders were also fixated on first-mover advantages. The importance of being the first to arrive in order to get rich pickings is summed up in the Gujarati saying: *Jenu vahan pehla poche tene vadhare male'*. In matters of business, Kachchhis seemed uninhibited by racial or linguistic prejudice. In the interior, they often employed Swahili as their language of business. In the 1870s, in the Bajunga country, Swahili agents represented two Indian houses.

Early Globalization: Euro-American and Indian Enterprise in Africa

Nineteenth-century Zanzibar was similar to contemporary Singapore or Dubai. A consistent, low, 5 per cent import duty on all goods from Europe and America, no duties on exports, which was quite common in those times, no taxes on shipping, no charges for pilotage, no charges for use of the port, no requirement for manifests or approvals from port authorities before sailing—does all this not make for a trading haven? Add to this the sheer commercial advantage of picking up full cargoes instead of having to sail along the African coast picking up small shipments, and one can see how and why Zanzibar became so important.

Either because of their business practices, their lower overheads or their preference for lower margins, Kachchhi traders almost always offered better pricing than their European and American competitors. While merchants from many littorals participated in the Zanzibar trade, the relative share of the merchants from Mandvi was the largest. Most of the American and European merchants bought and sold goods with the help and advice of a Kachchhi Bania, who sometimes was more a partner than just a broker or agent. Lt Postans noted that the Swahili coast was well supplied with Banias and Bhatias from Mandvi and that they, on behalf of their correspondents, carried on all the trade. Bartle Frere also observed Indian dominance of the trade. He noted that some Arab merchants, especially Suris, traded with the more remote fringes of the Comoros. But the main trade was in the hands of the Banias and Europeans. Key to Kachchhi commercial success in Zanzibar seems to have been the fact that they got in there early. They set up the infrastructure for trading, broking and money transfers. So when the Euro-American merchants arrived, this Kachchhi network was cost-effective in servicing them. Kachchhis followed the Omanis into the African interiors, frequently acting as financiers.

American commercial involvement with east Africa started in the 1820s with trading in Majunga, west of Madagascar, and eventually moved to Zanzibar. The first recorded American visitor to east Africa was Captain Johnson who, in 1823, traded at Zanzibar and Mombasa for copal and ivory. Meanwhile, American traders also began to penetrate the east African market from India. Small quantities of ivory and copal were exported in the 1820s from India to the United States. In 1826, Captain Millet voyaged from Mocha to Zanzibar, buying ivory worth around MT$12,000 in east Africa. Edmund Roberts arrived in 1828 in Zanzibar with a great variety of textiles, gunpowder and arms. Captain Bertram, of the well-known firm Bertram-Shepard, visited Zanzibar in 1831 with gunpowder and $30,000 specie. He managed to pick up part of a large copal cargo worth MT$13,000 from the Sultan, which the latter had earlier planned to dispatch to India. Bertram pioneered direct trade in gum copal between Zanzibar and America. He disliked trading through India as he felt the British Indian Customs officials imposed needless restrictions. Americans brought to Zanzibar a variety of goods for exchange: cotton sheets from textile mills in Lowell, brass wire from Waterbury and Worchester, muskets and rifles from Springfield and Hartford, gunpowder and beads. The arms trade was originally tied to the slave trade as arms used to be exchanged for slaves. Curiously, ivory too was exchanged for arms. American muskets and gunpowder attained a premium position. During his expedition, New observed: 'Often with the help of these weapons, ambitious local leaders were carving out political fortunes for themselves.' The Sultan established Omani domination over parts of east Africa. In 1837, he used superior arms to subdue resistance by the Mazuris of Mombasa. The Sultan was regarded as the principal customer of American arms merchants. In 1840, he sent his ship 'Sultana' on a trade mission to New York. In March 1845 alone he bought American goods worth 35,000 dollars.

British traders did not concede space to the Americans all that easily. In 1836, the firm Newman, Hunt, and Christopher from London established its business at Zanzibar. In a report to George West, John

Waters mentions that six British vessels called at Zanzibar in 1837, as compared with only three American vessels that were called. In 1845, another British firm Dickson, Cogan, Henderson and Co., established a business in Zanzibar. Direct trade between Britain and Zanzibar increased during the 1830s. In 1846–47, British trade with Zanzibar was worth $214,000. Luckily for the Americans, Newman, Hunt, and Christopher incurred losses and had to downsize. In the 1860s, the British firm of Fraser decided to set up a sugar plantation and factory in Zanzibar, in partnership with Sultan Majid. British firms like Smith Fleming of London and Nicol & Co. of Bombay remained active in trade. English cotton manufactures from Bombay and Britain retained their foothold in the Zanzibar market.

The French too kept trying to nibble at the Zanzibar market. In 1844, they signed a commercial treaty with the Sultan. American success in Zanzibar impressed the French Consul Broquant, who prepared a report which cogently analysed the American dominance of Zanzibar's non-Indian foreign trade. The other French Consul, Guillain, felt the market preference for superior American cloth left little scope for the French to enter. Guillain, however, believed that the unfavourable situation could be changed by taking the help of American merchants to develop Mayotte as an alternative to Zanzibar. In May 1849, Sultan Seyyid Said dispatched a vessel—'The Caroline'—to Marseilles, bearing a Zanzibari envoy, Hajji bin Darwish bin

Muhammad, whose job was primarily to increase penetration of Zanzibari cloves in the French market. The Zanzibar trade mission was welcomed and well looked after. The Marseilles Chamber of Commerce managed to sell the produce from Zanzibar and helped the mission purchase products for 'The Caroline's return voyage, in the process ostensibly protecting the inexperienced Zanzibaris from being cheated. The sale of the goods reportedly brought in the exact figure of 398,745.52 francs! The expectation was that there would be much business between Marseilles and Zanzibar. In November 1849, the merchants of Marseilles dispatched the merchant vessel 'Albert-et-Clemence', owned by the firm of Rabaud, to Zanzibar. Vidal Bros. and Rabaud Bros., prominent Marseilles merchants, established their businesses in Zanzibar. In 1854, another powerful Marseilles firm, Regis Brothers, joined the Zanzibar trade. In June 1850, a group of over thirty Frenchmen arrived from Reunion, to begin local manufacture of sugar. French exports to Zanzibar consisted of bullion and Venetian. Apart from cloves, Zanzibar's exports to France included dried coconut and sesame. Despite these efforts, French firms were relatively unsuccessful in Zanzibar, with the firm of Vidal having to shrink its business considerably. French merchandise did not have the draw of American cloth, and was not popular in Zanzibar. Rigby mentions that by 1859, Franco-Zanzibarian trade in tonnage terms was 70 per cent lower than the 1856 levels, 64 per cent less than the 1857 levels and 51 per cent less than the 1858 levels. Nevertheless, the limited French trade with Zanzibar continued.

Not to be left behind, German firms also entered the Zanzibar market. In 1849, the influential Hamburg firm of William O'Swald opened an agency in Zanzibar. Captain Rodatz of the Bremen schooner 'Alf', with experience of two ventures, reported to his firm that Zanzibar was the most favourable place on the east coast of Africa for trading. In November 1848, he voyaged a third time to Zanzibar. In the beginning of June 1849, Rodatz established an agency in Zanzibar. From 1844 onwards, Adolf Jacob Hertz, another Hamburg merchant, began to send his ships to Zanzibar in order to buy cowries and to sell them at a profit on the west coast of Africa. In the beginning, the cowries were bought in the Maldives. But blue cowries from Zanzibar yielded a better profit. From 1846 to 1851, A.J. Hertz plied a couple of ships between east and west Africa. By 1858, Hertz had as many as fourteen ships making voyages from Zanzibar to Palma on the west-African coast. Hertz retained Brothers Horn as his permanent Zanzibar-based representatives. From 1855 to 1859, William O'Swald had four to five ships crisscrossing between Zanzibar, west Africa and Hamburg. In the 1860s, Oswald had ten ships on this route. In 1853, Hamburg-based Hansing built a factory in Zanzibar that focused on cowrie and palm-oil trade from Zanzibar to west Africa. Having entered Zanzibar, Hansing then extended its business into Mozambique and Somalia. The American Civil War became an opportunity for German firms such as Hamburg to overtake others in the Zanzibar trade. The leading enterprise remained William O'swald, ahead of three American and two French firms, as well as one British firm, which were all established on the island in the 1860s. In 1864–65, the decline of the American share in the Zanzibar trade was so steep that Hamburg gained the top place. As Germany expanded its colonial interests in east Africa, the German East Africa Line was set up in 1890 with investment participation by various Hamburg firms—Hansing, Hansing, Woermann, Laeisz and Bolten.

Colonel Rigby's report shows that Zanzibar's trading position was stronger than that of places like Aden and Karachi. In 1856–57, Zanzibar's imports, in pounds, stood at 908,911, Aden's at 594,635 and Karachi's at 685,664. Export values were 1,664,577, 906,904 and 1,430,187 respectively. The British, the French, the Germans and the Americans . . . all preferred to deal through Kachchhis, who remained well-entrenched. The Kachchhis were led by the prominent and affluent firms of Jairam Shivji and Thariya Topan. The largely Kachchhi-Indian community, the British Consul observed, '. . . may be said almost entirely to monopolize the trade of Zanzibar, as although there are European and other merchants settled here, they are supplied with produce for export, and their imports are nearly all purchased by Indians.' In 1864, exports from Zanzibar amounted to £427,016; of this, exports worth £119,631 went to Bombay, and goods worth £100,586 to Kachchh. More than half went to India, primarily through Kachchhis. The other half went to European merchants who also obtained goods from the Kachchhis. The Consul observed that only about one-twentieth of the trade of Zanzibar did not pass through the hands of Indian merchants. Bartle Frere notes that Indians were quietly occupied in trade, either in small retail stores or in large trading houses from Socotra to the Cape colony. New considered a Bania as 'one of the great powers in Eastern Africa'.

In Portuguese Mozambique, the French and the Indians were both present. Indians collected and distributed merchandise for a Marseilles firm. They imported ivory and sesame seed into France. Kachchhis retained a large share of the profits of the African trade, irrespective of which third parties they served. In August 1844, Benjamin Fabens, the commercial agent of Bertram Shepard from Salem, reports rather tangentially that the Zanzibar market was very dull because 'Banians' charged high prices for their goods, which precluded the chances of cash payment. The ultimate evidence that the Kachchhis of Zanzibar were globalizers ahead of their time comes from the fact that their shops stocked cotton textiles from England, America and Germany, hardware from India and France, crockery from Germany, brass and copper items from America, beads from England and Venice, old guns from England and new guns from Germany and France.

The Magnitude of Indian/Kachchhi Enterprise

Kachchhi dominance over the nineteenth-century foreign exchange markets in the Indian Ocean makes for an interesting story. Kachchhis preferred Indian rupees and American gold. All other currencies were seen as having insufficient demand and limited liquidity, and were traded at a discount to their official rates. Indian dominance of the money market irked the French Consul Broquant who asked the Sultan for 'regularization' of the French franc in the market. The moneylenders of the island consistently discounted French currency, while the French wished it to pass at a fixed and favourable rate. The Consul found himself helpless when Ibji Shivji, the acting customs master and brother of Jairam Shivji, declined to consent to a decision that overvalued the 5 franc piece. An influential American merchant confirmed that all endeavours of the Sultan to change the local value of the 5 franc piece had failed before unswerving Indian opposition.

The British too had a grievance that the English gold sovereign was not as popular as the consistently overvalued American gold and the Indian rupee. In 1873–74, it was reported that the English sovereign was scarce and that its value in relation to the gold dollar resulted in remittances to and from England being effected at a heavy loss. The firm of Frasers extended their complaint beyond the English sovereign and felt that even the American Double Eagle was undervalued. No wonder the British Consul, Frasers and virtually all the American firms preferred to get their specie consignments in rupees from Bombay. The Consul ended up on the side of a stronger rupee and a weaker English sovereign!

Throughout the Zanzibar-African littoral, Kachchhis maintained a sophisticated financial infrastructure featuring drafts, loans and mortgages. Arabs, Europeans and Americans relied on this financial system. In addition, Arab landlords employed Kachchhis as bookkeepers and financial controllers, and used their business services. Burton felt that the inability of the Muslim (Arab) *saraf* to manage accounts and banking put great power into the hands of the Banias. Plantations were largely owned by Arabs and Swahilis. About three-quarters of the plantations were mortgaged to Kachchhis. James Christi worried that over half the estates in Zanzibar would be affected if the Indian merchants were 'to insist on the immediate realization of their outlying capital'. John Kirk calculated that Indian capital invested in Zanzibar in 1873 was not less than £1.6 million. Contemporary literature refers to Arabs as reckless borrowers who were not concerned about repayment of loans. Moneylending was risky, leading to high rates of interest. The Kachchhis were willing to take risks, as can be seen from the fact that one firm alone, that of Trikamdas of Pangani, had claims of $26,000 dollars on Arabs or Swahilis. Kachchhi Banias were indispensable to maintaining what was, by the standards of the day, very large volumes of trade—$700,000, not including the value of the slave trade.

Some contemporaries like Henry Stanley, Isaacs Nathaniel, Emily Ruete or Bibi Salme, daughter of Sultan Seyyid Said, have labelled Kachchhis as 'rapacious' and 'unscrupulous'. Even this criticism of the Kachchhis, which echoes the words used by contemporary ideologues against multinational companies, remains a testimony to their role as precursors of what we now routinely refer to as globalization.

4

KACHCHHI MERCANTILE FIRMS

Most of the Kachchhi firms of yore have left little trace
behind, but some have documented histories that are
rich narratives from which one may learn much. Here
are some vignettes from them.

Section I: Oman

The House of Bhimanis: The Resilient Pioneers

The Bhimanis were Bhatias who started operations
in Mandvi and went on to Muscat and Zanzibar. The
origin of the house of Bhimanis can be traced to the
second half of the eighteenth century. It is believed
that Rowji was the first from the Mandvi Bhimani
family to establish trading relations with Muscat. The
Bhimani firm began its Zanzibari connection in the

late eighteenth century, when the Sultan of Muscat took Vasanji Haridas Bhimani and Shivji Topan with him to Zanzibar. During the period of Sultan bin Ahmed, the customs collection contract was given to Mowji Rowji, whom Nadri G.A. mistakenly considers a Parsi, stating that 'the Parsi merchants of Gujarat Bhimji Hirji and Mowji Rowji . . . were settled at Masqat and conducted trade through agents living at Bombay, Surat and many other places.' The firm of the Bhimanis grew in wealth and position under Mowji, who can be called a veritable merchant-prince. David Seton, a British officer, described him as 'a fat cunning man and the richest subject in the place.' During this period—c.1802—the customs rent of Muscat stood at $180,000 annually.

Seyyid Said, the next Sultan, continued the system of farming out customs collection to Kachchhis, both at Muscat and at Zanzibar. The customs franchise at Muscat was renewed annually throughout the nineteenth century. In Zanzibar, it was given on a five-year contract from 1835 onwards. Until then, the firm of Bhimanis managed its business simultaneously at Muscat and Zanzibar. From 1804 onwards, the Bhimanis and their competitor firm Jairam Shivji had been alternately holding the franchise. British records indicate that in 1833, the Bhimanis held the customs contract at Zanzibar. They were known as 'Wad' or 'Wat' Bhima, which in colloquial Omani signified 'son of Bhima or Bhimani'. In 1835, they lost their contract to

Shivji Topan, who subsequently lost it to Jairam Shivji. At Muscat, though, it appears that the Bhimanis tried to stay in control throughout, except for some occasional, minor disruptions.

After Mowji, the firm passed into the capable hands of his son Gopaldas Mowji. His business manager provided financial assistance to the Sultan during the latter's fight against 'pirates'. Gopaldas's contemporary Lieutenant Colonel John Johnson noted his influential undertakings in the following words: 'And accordingly none is appointed; but a Hindoo merchant, a native of Katiawar (Kutch), who is settled here, officiates as Agent for his Majesty and the Honourable East India Company. He appears to be a very respectable and obliging man, ready to assist all persons connected with the English, and acting as money banker, and general agent. He has a large house in the middle of the town, and seems to possess considerable influence on all the other merchants of the place. He supplies the ships touching at this port with such articles as they may require.' 1835 was a year of financial setbacks for the Bhimanis. They lost the customs contracts simultaneously at Zanzibar and Muscat. In Muscat, Lala, brother of the prominent merchant Hirji Kachara Pradhan, took over customs collection. The firm of Hirji Pradhan was formidable. In Bombay, it had two warehouses—one at the Fort and the other on the outskirts of the Fort at Chinch Bandar. The firm also had considerable properties at Mandvi. But the Hirji Pradhan dominance was short-lived. In

February 1840, Gopaldas Mowji succeeded in bringing back the customs contract to his firm, retaining it for three years.

The decision of Sultan Seyyid Said to shift his seat of government to Zanzibar threw the political affairs of Muscat into chaos. In absence of the Sultan, the expenses of the governors went unchecked. To satisfy their constant need for money, governors tinkered with revenue collection. As the system of bidding for the customs post at Muscat was annual, political authorities found it easy to make frequent changes. This is evident from the fact that though in September 1843, the contract was won by Hirji from the Bhimanis, two years later, in 1845, the governor of Muscat abruptly handed the contract back to the Bhimanis. The Bhimanis retained the post of customs masters up to 1882, barring the years 1869, 1873 and 1875.

The Bhimani firm acted as agents for several European and American houses, and maintained extensive business relations with the wealthy Arabs of Muscat. The firm had branches at Mandvi, Muscat and Bombay. In Bombay, the office of the firm was located in 86, Bazargate Street, which was a commercial hub where many prominent trading firms, including Jairam Shivji, were located. The firm traded in a range of commodities—rice, wheat, sugar, ghee, oil and lead. The firm straddled the Persian Gulf and Zanzibar to the west, and Calcutta and Singapore to the east. It advanced money to various Arab traders.

The firm also acted as banker and financial advisor to the Government of Muscat. Managing the seasonality of Oman's money supply had its challenges. Specie would flood in from Zanzibar in April, for instance! The Bhimani firm clearly had some level of core competence in customs collection. They even got the collection contract for the port of Bandar Abbas on a sublet basis.

Gopaldas Mowji Bhimani, in his time, was the clear leader of the Hindu merchants of Muscat. He was made the *Nagarsheth*, or head, in Muscat, of the merchant communities from Kachchh, Sindh and Halar. The institution of *Nagarsheth* among Indian merchants resident outside India seems to have existed from remote times, and is known to have existed not only in Muscat, but in locations as far apart as Bandar Abbas, Baku, Hamadan and Tabriz, as well as in Iraq, Yemen, Bahrain, the Dahlak Islands (off the Sudani coast), Massawa, and Bukhara.

In the 1840s, guarding against interference in their trading, the Banias of Muscat rejected British endeavours to claim jurisdiction over their mercantile affairs. But they conveniently became pro-British after the death of Seyyid Said. They believed in floating with the rising tide. For instance, in 1858, ninety-one Indian merchants led by Gopaldas Mowji wrote a congratulatory letter to Queen Victoria and celebrated in Muscat the establishment of her direct rule over India.

During the rule of Azzan bin Qais (1868-71), the Bhatia monopoly over customs collection was challenged. In 1869, acting on the advice of Khalili, the *wali* (governor) of Muscat, Azzan, appointed an Arab as customs collector. In a very short period, the entire arrangement proved to be unsuccessful, and Azzan approached the Bhimanis to take over the customs collection. However, Disbrowe, the British Agent, saw advantage in acting against Indians. He intervened and prevented the reversion. John Wilkinson was also not sympathetic to Indian administration of customs. He has this to say: '. . . the Azzan bin Qais government abolished this system to go back to correct financial administration.' It appears that Azzan first came under the influence of anti-Hindu fundamentalists like Khalili. Subsequently, better sense prevailed and he approached the Bhimanis again, only to be thwarted by the British.

In 1871, the moderate Sultan Seyyid Turki got rid of Azzan entirely. He gave the customs administration back to the Kachchhis, but this time not to the Bhimanis. The disheartened Bhimji Gopaldas tried his fortune in Zanzibar, as the Sultan of Zanzibar invited him to bid for the contract there. Unfortunately, he was three months too late, and the customs lease of Jairam Shivji's was renewed. John Kirk, Consul at Zanzibar, told Bhimji Bhimani that he could not get the post without clearing the earlier debts of Sultan Barghash. According to John Kirk, whose testimony cannot be taken as final, the Bhimani capital was not adequate for the firm to take up Zanzibar customs collection!

Meanwhile, things in Muscat went from bad to worse. For some time the customs contract was with Purshottamdas Jivandas. But Sultan Turki, who was desperately hard up for funds, abruptly ended this contract and broke tradition by giving the contract to a non-Kachchhi, the British merchant C.H. Mcgill. The naïve Mcgill paid a considerable sum of money and furnished provisions for Sultan Turki's ship, only to be told by the governor that with no notice, the Sultan had ordered the termination of the contract and the reinstatement of the former customs master. Clearly, advances were being extracted from multiple parties. Matters can be said to have come full circle when, in January 1873, just one month before the expiry of the earlier contract, Bhimani Gopaldas was called back to the post! It is to Gopaldas Bhimani and his firm's credit that they stayed resilient and maintained the robustness of the financial system in Muscat, despite Sultan Turki's erratic behaviour. In 1882, trouble erupted again. Bhimani was removed, ostensibly because another firm paid $10,000 more, but really because Bhimani had firmly refused further advances to the Sultan. This caused a great deal of disaffection in the Kachchhi community. Merchants reacted strongly because the Bhimanis, as *Nagarsheth*, enjoyed a high status among Kachchhis. The available sources have little to say about the firm's fortunes after 1882.

Kachchhi Resilience

The Kachchhi love affair with Muscat and Oman has a level of resilience that is quite noteworthy. The political turmoil that usually resulted when one Sultan replaced another was something Kachchhis took in their stride. Through thick and thin, some Kachchhi merchant families and firms always stayed on. While Kachchhis positioned themselves primarily as subjects of the Rao of Kachchh or of the Sultan of Oman, they were quite flexible about asking for British protection or help when they felt the need to, on the grounds that they were British Indian subjects! The nineteenth-century revival of Muscat was dependent on their capital. Kachchhis anticipated the setbacks to Muscat as sail gave way to steam. The opening of the Suez Canal was another setback for Muscat. According to Lewis Pelly, by 1869, frequent political disorder and little competition from Arab merchants, who were only two or three in number, left the commerce of Muscat open for those Indians who did not leave Muscat. But the reduced commercial traffic at Muscat was a transitory phase. The drop-in trade was more during the time of Azzan bin Qais. Once a moderate regime was re-established, the situation changed. In 1871, A.C. Way, Consul of Muscat, reported that business was increasing and confidence had been restored. The financial markets were comfortably extending three-month credit to businesses. It is no surprise that Kachchhi financiers were the major lenders supporting the commerce of Muscat. The American demand for dates came as a boon. The trade in arms and ammunition shot up in the 1890s. Kachchhi traders were the chief suppliers.

Apart from the Bhatias, three Khoja merchants at Muttrah emerged as dominant players. Muscat may have been risky and volatile, but the profits were good; trading margins, according to Landen, were 10 per cent in Muscat, as against 2 per cent in Bombay. According to Landen, ten Hindu-owned firms in Muscat city were reckoned among the thirty-five wealthiest merchants.

Ratansi Purshottam: Serial Entrepreneur, Conglomerate Builder

One affluent Muscat entrepreneur of the nineteenth century was Ratansi Purshottam Purecha. Born in 1845, Ratansi was a Bhatia from Mandvi. He came to Muscat in 1857. His uncle mentored him in Muscat, where he joined his ancestral firm of Natha Makkan. Ratansi learnt his business lessons—especially lessons on the arms trade—at Natha Makkan, which exported iron and steel of British and Swedish manufacture from Bombay to Muscat. In Muscat, the metal was converted into pistols and other arms to cater to the Persian Gulf market. Natha Makkan, as also other Kachchhi and Marwari merchants, used the freight services of Kachchhi and Arab shipowners for exporting their goods. When the firm got into financial trouble, Ratansi seized the opportunity and merged his fledgling firm in 1872 with the moribund Natha Makkan. The official papers documenting each step of the merger are pretty impressive for the times, and there is complete clarity that the assets of Natha Makkan are transferred to Ratansi Purshottam. Ratansi quickly turned around the merged entity to profitability. As business expanded, he established a branch in Karachi. His firm traded in grain, textiles and dates.

Meanwhile, in distant New York, William Hills Jr. was separating from his family firm of Hills Brothers and was starting off on his own. Having done his background checks, Will Hills Jr. decided to formally approach Ratansi to operate as his date supply agent for the new business on a commission basis. William Hills Jr.'s letter states that the offer was the result of recommendations and the belief that Ratansi was in a position to pack boxes of premium quality Fard dates. Hills Jr.'s correspondence indicates that he thought of Ratansi's firm as a diversified conglomerate that dealt not only in dates but also in grain, sugar, coffee, American textiles, and curiously, in arms and ammunition! William Hills Jr. was even ready to open a letter of credit on London bankers in Ratansi's favour. This offer of a trading partnership positioned Ratansi well vis-à-vis the prevailing leading date exporters Gopalji Walji and W. J. Towell. Gopalji Walji had for long dealt with the undivided Hills

Brothers. A 6 per cent commission was offered on dates and freight, excluding materials furnished for packing. Gopalji Walji was probably charging the Hills Brothers more. There was considerable back-and-forth negotiation before the deal was struck. The partnership between William Hills Jr. and Ratansi was finalized with a legal document that included specific clauses pertaining to packing. The banker's letter of credit was then opened in favour of Ratansi to draw credit from William Hills Jr.'s account. Ratansi lodged this letter of credit with his bankers in Bombay and drew drafts as needed, sending the drafts to his bankers in Bombay who cashed them and credited the funds to Ratansi's account. Hills Jr. acted as the importer, wholesaler and credit-provider, buying the dates from Muscat and selling them in the American market. Hills Jr. also had a business representative in Basra to procure Persian dates.

As far as servicing the needs of William Hills Jr. was concerned, Ratansi started by advancing money to Arab planters in the date-growing region for the crop. He then managed a large labour force in a sorting and packaging factory, keeping the packed date cargo ready for quick shipment in *Mashhufs* or lighters (flat-bottomed boats) for two back-to-back shipments. Hills Jr. was tasked with sending to Ratansi case-wood and other accessories for packing. Ratansi had office staff who prepared invoices, bills of lading and drafts under the letters of credit. Hills Jr. was a stickler for quality—both in the matter of dates and their packing. It is to the credit of Ratansi's firm that they imbibed Hills's best practices and achieved high levels of quality control. Unusually for the times, Hills Jr. was in the habit of regularly writing to his business partner about new and more efficient business practices. He found a willing audience in Ratansi, who was keen to keep up with continuous improvement of processes. Both sides aimed for clarity in their correspondence, thus minimizing misunderstandings or complications. Hills Jr. found working with Ratansi a smooth process as Ratansi was both timely and precise in meeting his commitments. The exchange of letters and cables, which went on up to 1925, makes for fascinating reading. It has a contemporary tone to it.

The restless and energetic Ratansi turned to the arms trade and soon emerged as one of the leading arms dealers of Muscat. In this business, his partners were Schwarte and Hammer from England and Moritz Magnus from Germany. Schwarte and Hammer found Ratansi a hard bargainer. The correspondence shows that he secured most deals at around the prices he first quoted. The same appears to be the case with his Hamburg trading partner Moritz Magnus, who complains of the low profits earned in the business. Ratansi had no qualms about annoying his London agent and asserting himself in order to get the Belgian factory to customize some of the arms as per the wishes of his Arab customer. Ratansi was desperate to get rifles identical to La Francotte rifles, which were highly valued in the Gulf. Ratansi bypassed his agents and wrote directly to Auguste Francotte to buy the original rifles. Though the manufacturers refused, the indefatigable Ratansi kept periodically writing to Auguste Francotte in order to register his continuing interest. Ratansi believed in leveraging from one business line to another. He persuaded Moritz Magnus in Hamburg to introduce him to German tobacco firms, although Moritz Magnus were arms dealers and had nothing to do with tobacco. They, of course, obliged Ratansi, who was an important customer. Ratansi had a fairly good intelligence system to keep track of the features, quality and prices of European arms. The financial settlements of Ratansi's date and arms businesses always took place through the mercantile banks of London or Bombay.

Having accumulated multiple fortunes, Ratansi decided to invest in real estate in a big way. In the 1880s, he purchased land along the waterfront of Muscat and eventually became the owner of the entire waterfront, with the exception of the palace, the customs house and the British Political Agency. For reasons that still remain obscure, the British did arm-twist Ratansi into parting with some property that they wanted. By the end of nineteenth century, Ratansi and other Kachchhi Banias owned much of the best property in Muscat and Muttrah. Ratansi's assets included a date factory and a farmhouse at Sidab. In keeping with Omani/Kachchhi traditions, his preeminence was recognized when he got the prestigious post of customs master, as the 1887 British report suggests. Ratansi's firm held this franchise as long as this system lasted. Curiously, in the beginning of the twentieth century, the chief of Bahrain approached Ratansi to take up Bahrain's customs franchise.

Sheth Ratansi bin Purshottam Al Baniyani, as he came to be known in Arabic, had clearly arrived when his office and home occupied prime space within the walled city of Muscat at Bait Ratansi, close to the Sultan's palace. He had another palatial office and home in Muttrah Bay. Ratansi was rightly regarded as King, (*Badshah*) of the trading world of Muscat. Today, his great grandson manages the firm and counts himself as the proud inheritor of Ratansi Purshottam's legacy. The recent entry into the firm of the great grandson's son Dhruv Vimal Purecha brings in one more dynamic link into the chain.

A Banker Monk, His Successor, a Deck of Cards and a Knave of Hearts

From his base at Mandvi, Revagar Kuvargar Goswami carried on extensive business in Bombay and Muscat through his agents. He traded both in Indian and foreign products. He built up considerable property in Muscat. Revagar's financial network was linked to the monasteries at Mandvi. Daulatgiri Manroopgiri was another Goswami, a professional descendant of Revagar. He too worked through agents, and his activities extended from Mandvi to Karachi, Bombay, Muscat and Zanzibar. Daulatgiri was connected with Muscat from the 1860s. In 1868, there were disturbances in Muscat. Daulatgiri joined twenty-six other Kachchhi merchants in petitioning the British saying the merchants deserved to be provided with advance notice if the British apprehended any danger in Muscat. This was critical in order that they save their lives and salvage as much of their wealth as was possible in the event of danger. Four affluent traders became known as the pillars of the Kachchhi Mahajan of Muscat. Daulatgiri Manroopgiri was called the Ace (*Eka*). Virji Ratansi, a banker, also known as '*Bait Bijah*', was the Queen (*Rani*) as he played his business cards cautiously. Damodar Dharamsi was Jack (*Ghulam*) because of his trading business operations.

The British authorities frowned upon the arms trade in Muscat, as most of the arms finally went to Afghanistan and the North-West Frontier where they were used against British and British Indian troops. But, as often happens in market capitalism, the private interests of the British firm Francis Times were at variance with the interests of the British government. The firm found in Dharamsi their 'knave' of hearts. In 1887, they established an agency at Bushire, and in 1891 started operations of their own there. Francis Times made shipments of rifles, pistols and ammunition, as well as of various other articles from London to the Persian Gulf, where they sold them actually on a retail basis. In 1896, they decided to enter the Muscat market. They realized that their best option was to appoint a Kachchhi agent rather than start anything on their own. They appointed Damodar Dharamsi as their agent; among other reasons because, it appears, he was not a Kachchhi or an Omani but a British Indian subject. Dharamsi's trade had been principally in arms and ammunition and had been carried on under a special permit from the Sultan of Muscat. Dharamsi arranged trans-shipment of arms from London to Bahrain. Needless to say, the partnership between Francis Times and the Jack/*Ghulam*/Knave Dharamsi was highly inclined towards mutual benefit and profitability.

Khimji Ramdas

The firm Khimji Ramdas, established in Muscat in 1870, deserves special mention. The father of the founder Ramdas was one Dharamsi who was also known as Bachubhai Dalal. Ramdas traded between Mandvi and Muscat. Despite his initial setbacks in Mandvi, where he incurred losses and became indebted to several merchants, Ramdas persevered. He actually expanded the business, setting up branches at Suvek, Mesna and Sur. His main business was the export of dry and wet dates to India. Khimji found an able successor for his trading firm in Gokuldas, who repaid all the ancestral debts owed to the Mandvi creditors twice over. Gokuldas believed in focused charity. He was particular about female education, and played an imperative role in spreading education among females. He donated a palatial building, which became the Khimji Ramdas Kanya Vidhyalay. He understood the importance of an English education and established two English-medium schools—Ramkrishna High School and Sakarbai Memorial School. In memory of his father, he established Khimji Ramdas Arya Kelvani Mandal in Oman. This is now known as the Indian School, Muttrah. He established the Gokul Hospital in Mandvi, which stands out to this day on account of the high quality of medical services it provides to the people of Mandvi. He was also very liberal in helping Kachchhis in times of drought and famine. All this time, his passion for quality and value with respect to his business was unrelenting. He travelled all over Oman on donkey back seeking the best dates for his customers!

In recent times, the Khimjis have extensively diversified. They have interests in construction, building materials, foodstuff, department stores, supermarkets, garments, electronics and paints. The firm is today a leading business house based in the Sultanate of Oman. The KR logo is a familiar one on billboards all over Oman. Khimji Ramdas secured the honour of presiding over the Hindu Mahajan of Muscat.

Purshottam Kanji Pawani

The firm of Purshottam Kanji is yet another conspicuous and well-established one in Muscat. The founder of the firm, Kanji Pawani, and his son Purshottam started small. By the turn of the nineteenth century, they had established a substantial business. At present, the firm has six branches in Oman, focused on banking and foreign exchange. For money transfers, they have partnered with Western Union. The Pawanis were rewarded for their continued loyalty to Oman when the late Gulabbhai Pawani was honoured with the title of 'Sheikh' by Sultan Qaboos in 2009. The Pawanis are known as equal-opportunity employers who rise above caste and community differences. In Kachchh, they are known for their annual visits to Anjar where their religious philanthropy draws wide attention. They have made substantial donations to fund a girls' hostel in Mandvi.

The Jorjanis

The trading family of the Jorjanis was commercially associated with Muscat, Muttrah and Burka some one hundred and twenty-five years ago in the late 1880s. The Jorjanis were owners of a date factory known for the fine quality of its products. Like most Kachchhi merchants, the Jorjanis ran a diversified business, which extended to pearls, textiles and foodstuffs.

Section II: Zanzibar

Shivji Topan and Jairam Shivji

Looking at the superordinate business success of the firm of Jairam Shivji, the name is enlisted first in the line of business firms in east Africa. Jairam Shivji, the premier Bhatia business personage of Zanzibar, assumed the reins of the firm owned by his father Shivji Topan at the time when Zanzibar's foreign trade with the west was picking up at a greater pace.

Jairam Shivji was born in 1792 in Mundra, Kachchh, and not in Lakhpat as Nicolini has mentioned in her book. His father Shivji Topan started his career operating from Muscat. In 1785, the Sultan of Oman undertook an expedition to east Africa in order to reassert Omani influence there. Two Kachchhi merchants—Vansanji Haridas Bhimani and Shivji Topan—accompanied the Sultan. In 1804, the customs collection in Zanzibar town had been farmed out to a Kachchhi merchant, probably Bhimani, who also had the Muscat franchise. Customs collection during this time was decentralized under various hands. Customs management at Kilwa and Mafia was under the governor of Kilwa, who later sublet it to an Arab merchant and the governor of Mafia. Zanzibar was farmed out to Bhimani, who was referred to as 'a Banyan or an Arab whose rich estates in Muscat guarantee his fidelity to the Prince.' The mainland was under some other authority. In 1819,

Shivji Topan managed to get the contract for Zanzibar customs, as is evidenced by the correspondence of Atkins Hamerton, British Consul. The Sultan was probably diversifying risk in his own way by having different customs contractors for Muscat and Zanzibar. However, a see-saw continued between the Bhimanis and the Shivjis, both Kachchhi Bhatias. Edmund Roberts, an American, had commercial transactions with 'Sewar, Banyan' collectors of customs in the 1820s. In 1833, the contract was given to Wat Bhima (the Bhimanis of Muscat) for two years at the rate of MT$70,000. In 1835, Shivji Topan secured control, with an annual payment of MT$84,000. Subsequently, Jairam Shivji, whom Oonk incorrectly identified as an Indian Muslim, succeeded his father and obtained the customs franchise on payment of MT$110,000. Jairam Shivji's firm thus retained the contract. Jairam Shivji came from a privileged background as his father had left him a readymade business. But he was put through a grinding apprenticeship not only under his father but also under his uncle Madhavji Topan. Only after a year's satisfactory performance was he allowed to enter the Zanzibar branch of the firm.

According to Loarer, a French naval officer, the Sultan consolidated the customs of Zanzibar and the mainland in 1822 under 'Sewji Topan's son Jairam who bought out the previous incumbent Said bin Denine'. By 1837, the customs contract at Mombasa, and for Mrima on the mainland was also acquired by Jairam

Shivji. By the late 1840s, the contracts for Mafia and Lindi passed under his control, although they continued to be sublet to their governors Abubakar bin Abdullah and Muhammed bin Issa. Thus, by mid-century, the firm had the power to collect all the duties on behalf of the Imam on all commerce from Cape Delgado to Mogadishu.' Jairam Shivji was the centralizer of the Sultan's customs administration. From its head office in Zanzibar, his firm fully controlled one thousand miles of coastline. The collectors of customs at ports were mainly Kachchhi Banias. The people of Zanzibar called them 'Port Indians' or *'Banian Forodha'*. Each port maintained its registers. At the end of the year, the numbers were consolidated at the customs house of Kilwa Kiwanji and forwarded to officials at Zanzibar. Bartle Frere regarded Kachchhi customs collectors as skilful accountants. They were entrusted with the books of the government. Internally, the firm prepared accounts on a half-yearly basis. The accounts were written in Gujarati. The annual closing took place at the time of *nava naroj* in August, when, technically, the contract too expired.

Jairam Shivji maintained an armed retinue of one hundred and fifty guards to defend the wealth of the island. The customs house was located in the 'Furzani' quarter, close to the salt bazaar. Jairam Shivji had outstanding persons running each branch office—Laddha Damji at Zanzibar, his nephew Pisu at Pemba Island, Laxmidas at Mombasa, Trikamdas at Pagini,

Ramji Pragji at Bagamoyo and Kishandas at Kilwa. As his family gradually took control of the customs at the ports north and south of the Albusaid dominion, people no longer referred to them as 'Port Indians', but as *Jiram Sewji*. The British authority marvelled at the quality of Kachchhi private intelligence and noted that this was the key to their business success.

Whenever the Albusaid rulers and members of the ruling family required money, they wrote a *Barwas* (chit) addressed to the customs master and drew the funds. It was the duty of the customs master to keep a record of the *Barwas* in their books. In modern parlance, the firm of Jairam Shivji acted as private or state bankers to the royal family. For Jairam Shivji, the large debts of the Sultan and his family were not a source of apprehension; the debts increased the dependency of the Sultan on him. In 1841, the Sultan turned down higher bids in favour of Jairam Shivji. In return, Jairam repaid the Sultan's trust by ensuring steadily increasing revenues. By 1856, the revenues reached the sum of MT$220,000. Jairam Shivji told a French officer, Guillian, that the customs contract was not a major source of profits for his firm, but that the contract gave him the opportunity to dominate the commerce of Zanzibar. Jairam Shivji developed close relations with Sultan Seyyid Said, who even forbade the killing of cows in the vicinity of Jairam Shivji's house during the festival Eid al-Fitr and as a gesture of respecting the religious belief of his customs official.

Jairam Shivji's firm also smoothly managed the Sultan's personal affairs, dealing with the Bombay customs authorities to ensure that the Sultan's personal shipments were smoothly handled. The economic and managerial efficiency of the system stands out. Contemporary sources noted that the Government of Zanzibar derived significant revenues from customs duties, only a fraction of which was spent on the salaries of customs house officials. By the 1850s, the firm of Jairam Shivji had branches or agencies at Zanzibar, Muscat, the Persian Gulf, Bombay, Mundra and Mandvi. The firm had two branches in Bombay, one at Bazargate and the other at Fort. These offices also looked after the Sultan's requirements in Bombay, which included minor consignments and handling of freight. For money transfers, the firm tied up with a strong monastery at Mandvi, that of Goswami Dnyangiri Nirmalgiri. In Zanzibar, the firm issued drafts that Kachchhis could cash in Kachchh. The British Consul Atkins Hamerton vouched for the firm's banking services: '. . . from the Custom Master Jairam Sewjee I can get in a few hours' notice any reasonable sum even to the extent of five thousand dollars.'

Kachchhi-American Partnership: Jairam Shivji and Richard Waters

American merchants, chiefly from Salem, Massachusetts, increased the frequency of their voyages to the ports of east Africa in the 1820s. Jairam Shivji's father Shivji Topan closely observed their voyages to Zanzibar. Jairam recollected an incident from the visit of a Salem vessel and his father's conversation with the captain of the ship. He said:

> [H]is father, learning that a vessel manned by whites was at Majunga, went over in a bugala to induce the captain to visit Zanzibar and open a trade with its people. The captain complied with the Banian merchant's request, and an intercourse with Americans, of a most friendly character, was commenced and has been continued uninterrupted till this day, almost exclusively with the port of Salem. No wonder then that when the ignorant inhabitant of Zanzibar hears the United S. spoken of he thinks a small port of Salem is meant.

Shivji Topan, in his own way, was uncannily right, because initially only a few Salem merchants knew of the potential at Zanzibar, and they wanted to keep this trade secret from their compatriots. Once the commercial treaty with America was signed, the trade could not remain a secret. With the establishment of an American Consulate in Zanzibar, events moved quickly. As it turned out, the first American Consul, Richard P. Waters, came from Salem. He was an associate of the firm of Bertram and Shepard. He assumed his duties in Zanzibar in March 1837. Waters and other Americans at first found it difficult to trade in Zanzibar. Jairam required all foreign merchants, including the Americans, to have their merchandise brought to the customs house by his coolies before being carried to their vessels. In addition to controlling the customs house in Zanzibar, Jairam controlled the labour required to carry cargo from the ships to the customs house. Using that advantage, Jairam added a personal surcharge of $100 to $200 on each shipment of cargo. Americans found this procedure inappropriate and expensive. Waters sought a way to evade Jairam's surcharge by bringing the cargo to his own storehouse. A dispute arose between Jairam and Captain Conant of the American brig over the payment of coolie-hiring charges. Conant and Waters considered it a violation of the commercial treaty of 1833, which stated that nothing over a 5 per cent import tax should be placed on American ships. Waters addressed the Sultan directly and tried to win the Sultan's favour with diplomacy. Waters asked that American merchants be permitted to send their cargoes at the consular house. Waters also accused Jairam of prevailing upon Sultan Said to violate the American treaty. Jairam Shivji was not in a mood to compromise as he had acted in accordance with his agreement with the Sultan. Jairam was a very powerful player in the Zanzibar trade and for the Americans, a tough adversary. The incident proved embarrassing for the Consul and gave a negative start to his business in Zanzibar. Waters backtracked a little bit. Although he agreed with Conant about violation of the treaty, he 'regretted exceedingly that an angry altercation had taken place.' In order to seek an amiable resolution, Waters visited the Sultan and apologized. The Sultan took Jairam's side. In Waters's time, it was to Jairam that all foreign businessmen and agents 'must first apply (and who would then) call native merchants together, make known their offer, then take it upon himself to say through what House the business must be transacted and there was no alternative. Refuse to comply with his terms and (one) would be driven from the market done little or nothing.'

The Sultan wanted to appease the Americans as well as Jairam. Both the Sultan and the Americans were interested in resolving the issue, but Jairam was not. He was determined that if he could not charge for hired labour, then he would find another way to make up the cost. Waters mentions that soon afterwards Jairam began charging a 5 per cent levy to his fellow Banias who sold goods to American merchants. After taking this to the Sultan, Waters was assured that this practice would be discontinued. Waters was annoyed by now as he was trying to grapple with a business environment that was rooted in personal relationships and local practices. His early days in Zanzibar were troublesome as he was unable to undertake business transactions without losing out profits to Jairam Shivji. These experiences made Waters aware that Jairam was a consequential business figure in the commercial world of Zanzibar and that confrontation with him should be avoided. Jairam Shivji exercised a near-monopolistic method over the purchase of import cargoes. The British and American merchants alleged that he prevented other merchants from purchasing goods and diverted the imported merchandises first to the customs house. Next, he insisted that shipments needed to be broken only through his firm. Although the terms of the commercial treaties stipulated 'no monopoly', the Sultan could not in practical terms follow it. Waters realized that his financial and commercial security would be enhanced through partnership with the customs master. Both parties understood each other's position and preferred to collaborate rather than compete. Consequently, in 1837, an informal business partnership materialized between Jairam and Waters.

By 1838, foreign merchants arriving in Zanzibar from Europe and other American ports were irked to see Waters and Jairam as the major players in a local monopoly. This monopoly was an arrangement Waters formed with his once formidable commercial adversary Jairam Shivji. The monopoly worked in two ways: First, Jairam as the customs franchisee of the mainland, in order to stimulate trade from there, abolished any taxes on items shipped from the coastal ports of east Africa to Zanzibar. This meant that nearly all goods originating in east Africa would pass through his hands at Zanzibar. Second, Waters, using his consul-ship, influenced merchants to divert most of their trade towards Jairam. It was an arrangement that made both men very rich.

The Indo-American joint venture was advantageous for both parties. Jairam decided that it would be good to extend American trade to Kachchh. In 1837, he proposed to Rao Desal of Kachchh that American and European vessels be allowed to come from Zanzibar to Mandvi with merchandise. He felt that in exchange, cotton from Kachchh and Kathiawar and alum and iron from Kachchh could be traded. The Rao of Kachchh considered the proposal with interest. He consulted with many merchants, who agreed that entry of American and European trading vessels to his port would stimulate the economy, encourage enterprise among his people, and bring considerable financial advantages to him and his country. But, the treaty with the British precluded him from admitting American vessels. He wrote to the British seeking advice, adding that he would abide by the wishes of the British government.

In reply, the Bombay government wrote to the Government of India that it was not desirable that American vessels should be encouraged to trade with the ports of Kachchh, and that if trade possibilities existed, British vessels ought to be given preference. Revealing some evidence of dissent within the British Indian ruling circles, the Government of India remarked that the proposal made by the Rao could not be discouraged. Finally, the interests of the British merchants prevailed. The British government nixed the proposal. They feared not just American shipping; they feared American textiles even more. They feared that through Kachchh, the superior *merikani* might filter down to other ports of western India, including Bombay. In the treaties of 1809 and 1819 with Kachchh, the British government had forced through clauses that no French and American interests be encouraged in Kachchh. The Rao of Kachchh meekly submitted to the British decision without any marked insistence. The British mercantilist decision to throttle Kachchhi entrepreneurship resembles free India's shackling of visionary entrepreneurs like G.D. Birla and Kasturbhai Lalbhai! The princely state of Kachchh missed an opportunity to develop Mandvi as a truly international port of maritime commerce. A limited quantity of American cloth was imported into Kachchh. The larger opportunity of trading with India through Kachchh was lost to Americans.

On the other hand, American trade with Zanzibar kept increasing. Between September 1832 and May 1834, thirty-two out of forty-one foreign vessels visiting Zanzibar were of American registry. The partnership of Waters and Jairam also prospered. After 1840, Waters became the agent of the firm Pingree and West. Jairam helped Waters by allowing his merchandise to reach the market earlier than those of other merchants. Jairam, as customs collector, could hinder any transactions that Waters did not approve, which did put Waters at an advantageous edge over other foreign merchants. Jairam became the unofficial broker for all Salem merchants trading with Zanzibar. Jairam himself earned enormous profits. In a letter to Jairam's brother Ibji Shivji, Waters writes: '(Jairam) is making a great deal of money this year. I think about one lac [100,000] of dollars!' Waters congratulated Ibji on his new wife and writes: 'When I (Waters) return from America I hope to visit (Cutch) and have the pleasure of seeing your family.' In a letter to his brother William C. Waters, Richard Waters reports, 'Jeram and I [Waters] are on the best of terms . . . I do nine tenths of my business with Jeram.' The Waters-Jairam feud was far behind. It was now substituted by a wary relationship filled with mutual respect. Waters writes: '[Jairam] respects and fears me at the same time. I have his confidence . . . He wants watching but it must be done in a kind skilful manner, so that he will not observe *when* you have your eye on him. And at the same time he must have the impression that you are always watching him.' Again, he writes, 'I wish to give Jeram the preference in offering him whatever I may have to sell and in purchasing whatever I may wish to buy. I can generally make better sales to him, and purchases from him, than anyone else. Not but what I should wish to make trade with others when it can be done to advantage, but taking all things into consideration, a more safe & expeditious business can be done with Jeram, than all the other merchants put together, in Zanzibar.' With the Salem trade behind him, Jairam was soon regarded as the wealthiest entrepreneur in Zanzibar. The partnership is best described in Waters's instruction to his Vice Consul P.S. Parkar at the time of his temporary absence from Zanzibar in 1840:

> After you have engaged to do business of any vessel, you do well to hold a conversation with Jairam bin Seva, the custom master. Inform him what the vessel has to sell and what she wishes to return cargo . . . He will propose at once to call the merchants together at my house; show them the samples of cotton and fix a price for them. Should the captain conclude to sell at the offer made, Jairam will be the person to whom you will deliver the goods and also charge them to, he being the only person you are to know in the business . . . Before you conclude the sale, you will talk to Jairam in regard to what you may want for return cargo.

Other American merchants were not happy with this partnership. Americans frequenting Zanzibar chafed at what they regarded as the monopolistic activities of Waters. They complained in vain to the State Department. Despite its monopolistic tone, it was arguably the partnership that helped quicken commerce between Zanzibar and the United States. Cotton sheeting, crockery, muskets, gunpowder, ship stores, clocks, shoes and specie were brought from America, and the return cargoes consisted of gum copal, copra, cloves and ivory.

In east Africa, prominent among the English firms was Newman Hunt and Christopher of London. The firm appointed Robert Norsworthy as its resident agent in the 1830s. Norsworthy was not comfortable trading with Jairam Shivji in Zanzibar. He lodged several complaints accusing Jairam of transferring business that was rightfully his to the American Waters. He charged Jairam with insisting that Norsworthy give up half of his commissions to Waters. Finally, Norsworthy made a financial claim on Jairam Sewji for $2232 for lost commissions. This was forwarded to the British Government. Though the Sultan disliked British interference, Atkins Hamerton, the British Consul at Zanzibar, referred the matter to London. Jairam, well supported by his business partner, explained his actions and refuted the charges of monopoly. Hamerton produced depositions of Norsworthy and Edgar Botsford (Norsworthy's American Partner) against Jairam. Norsworthy accused even the Imam of engaging in the practice of monopoly. Norsworthy strongly felt that there existed a 'monopolistic ring' of Jairam, the American consul and Seyyid Said, which he claimed hindered English trade. The Bombay government commented that if the charges of monopoly against Jairam were true, then it stood as a clear violation of Article 10 of the Treaty of 1839. Norsworthy also published a complaint about the

Salem monopoly in the *Bombay Times*. Waters heard of this from Cursejee Merwanjee, a Bombay merchant who acted as trading agent for Salem merchants. Waters describes the situation to his brother John G. Waters, calling it 'a laughable affair.' He also writes, 'Poor man [Norsworthy], he is quite done up. He makes Mr. Waters quite an important character. I wish I could persuade myself that it was true.' Meanwhile, Norsworthy came up with new complaints. Most of them were exaggerations. Independently, the British government was suspicious of the Americans' position in Zanzibar. Hamerton wrote in an assertive tone, 'Great preference is always given to the Americans.' Nevertheless, he concluded that matters had considerably improved for English merchants, and the monopoly that earlier existed was no longer in force. The British government decided to ask the Imam of Muscat to enforce Article 10 of the Treaty of 1839. Hamerton succeeded in partially restricting the Indo-American monopoly. The Sultan prevented Jairam from acting as agent for the American Consul. Hamerton and Norsworthy nibbled away at the Jairam-Waters partnership. The partnership disintegrated when Waters drifted off to manage his business independently. Waters diversified his local clientele and he competed in the market like any other local merchant. He even came to terms with Norsworthy. He endeavoured to use his own schooner to reduce dependency on local middlemen. He reduced his business ties with Jairam and established connections with at least nineteen Indian and Arab traders and plantation owners. In response, Jairam decided to forego the advantages of a single partner and encouraged numerous foreign traders, trying to turn the situation to his advantage. Salemites referred to Jairam as a 'hard grasping character'. Salemites were interested in becoming sole traders with Zanzibar. But by now, the Sultan and Jairam were interested in expanding trade with everyone. The firms of Pingree-West and Bertram-Shepard became fierce competitors. Jairam kept his business growing, especially with new entrants Boston, New York and Providence. His success resulted in his name being stamped on an American ship in the 1840s. During the 1840s and 1850s, Zanzibar witnessed healthy competition among at least nine important American, French and German firms, in addition to the many Indian merchants. Jairam was heavily involved in trade with India and had dhows regularly plying between Zanzibar and Bombay. After Waters' departure, Jairam worked with various American merchants and helped them when they were in need. During the Mexican War (1846–48), when American merchants had difficulty in obtaining specie, Jairam lent them what they required to stay in business.

Jairam and Waters remained friends. When there was an attempt to assassinate Jairam, Waters wrote with concern in July 1843: 'Four weeks since some person got in Jeram bin Seva's house in the night and stabbed Jeram in seven different places and came very near taking his life.' It is curious to note who Jairam called in this emergency: 'Jeram sent for me and also Capt. Hamerton & Capt. Webb and we dressed the wounds as well as we could.' Sewji (Jairam) even appointed Waters and Hamerton as executors of his will! An extremely concerned Sultan visited Sewji every day for two weeks. While the perpetrator was never found, Sewji did eventually recover his health.

By 1839, it was stated that Jairam was making an annual profit of about MT$100,000 from his various activities. In 1842, the assets of his firm stood at MT$4 million; this rose to MT$5.5 million by 1846. In the mid-1860s, 'his profits in Zanzibar alone during the past four or five years were over $1 million.' Broquant reported that Jairam had '30 million in a Bombay bank', perhaps francs.

Jairam, Friend to all Kachchhis

Jairam Shivji helped his fellow Kachchhis freely transfer their money from Zanzibar to Kachchh. He provided visiting Kachchhis board and lodging. To serve them food, his firm opened a big community kitchen. There were many Kachchhi merchants grateful to Jairam Shivji because they had started as apprentices in Jairam's firm and then moved on to establish their own businesses. One notable apprentice was Thariya Topan, who was known for his neat handwriting and who was employed in the firm as a scribe to Laddha Damji. The ultimate tribute to the quality of training he received came through when Thariya Topan became a big-enough businessman in the 1870s to challenge the firm of Jairam Shivji for its customs contracts.

A *Panjrapole*, which still stands just before the entrance to his hometown Mundra, received its first donation from Jairam. According to Jairam's descendants, he built two lakes in Mundra. When cholera broke out in Zanzibar in 1870, Laddha Damji (from Jairam's firm) and Seyyid Hamood, a relative of the Sultan's and a large landowner in the island, immediately came up with a proposal to supply the town with water through pipes. To Bartle Frere, Laksmidas Laddha (also from Jairam's firm) in 1873 professed his willingness to give the land and 7000 dollars for the purpose of a hospital or for some other purpose beneficial to the community at large.

Moving the Firm from Owner to Manager

Jairam Shivji retired in 1853 to live in Kachchh and in order to make various pilgrimages. Laddha Damji, a veteran employee of the firm, was handed over responsibility for its managerial decisions. Laddha Damji Babla, a Bhatia born in Mundra, Kachchh, was a self-made person and a dynamic manager of the firm of Jairam Shivji. Overcoming his poverty, Laddha, through his business acumen, rose to the prominent position of *munim* or manager of the firm. Burton regarded Laddha as 'a man of highest respectability.' Still standing, the magnificent and ornate Navlakho Bungalow at Mundra was built by his son Laxmidas Laddha. Under Laddha Damji, the firm maintained sound relations with the British authorities in Zanzibar. In 1857, when the British Consul Atkins Hamerton died, Laddha Damji took care of the consulate for a year. Christopher Rigby, British Political Consul, commented on Laddha's role as customs master as follows: '. . . he (the Sultan) is surrounded by a greedy and unprincipled set of people. With the exception of the Customs master, there is not a single honest or trustworthy person about him, or any one whose word, on with could be trusted.'

In 1865, the new lease for the customs house went, as usual, in favour of the firm of Jairam Shivji for the annual sum of $310,000 for five years. A competing Bombay firm, according to the French representative Jablonski, offered Sultan Majid, successor to Seyyid Said, the sum of $400,000 for the contract. But Majid refused because of his outstanding debt and his good relations with Laddha Damji. When Ladha died, all of Zanzibar grieved. John Kirk, the British Consul, who was very close to Laddha, flew the flag at the British Consulate at half-mast as a tribute.

The Twilight Years

In 1876, under the new Sultan Barghash, the firm of Jairam Shivji lost the customs contract in Zanzibar after having held it for forty-one years. Thariya Topan won the bid. A bitter dissension that divided the house of Jairam in two was the stated reason for the loss. The firm was unable to meet the Sultan's demand for a proportionate raise. John Kirk believed the firm boasted that the Sultan would in the end need to borrow from them and would have to favour them. This assumption proved to be wrong; the contract was transferred to Thariya Topan for $450,000. Jairam Shivji claimed $300,000 from the Sultan in balance payment, but things were not that simple. The Sultan too had counter-claims. Clearly, the death of Laddha Damji in 1872 had weakened the firm. Despite his close relations with Sultan Barghash, Thariya Topan found the customs collection role a bit more troublesome than he had bargained for, and in 1880, after just four years of winning it, he gave up the contract. The firm of Jairam Shivji stepped right back in with an offer of $100,000 more than the previous amount.

Meanwhile, other plots were brewing. The firm of William Mackinnon made a proposal along with several other wealthy and influential men represented by Walters, to take over and administer Zanzibar in the Sultan's name for a period of seventy years. They proposed to administer Zanzibar and all its dominions on the African mainland and farm the customs revenue after the expiry of Thariya Topan's lease. Mackinnon's 1877 was a calculated move. Western firms in Zanzibar were prohibited from trading on the nearby mainland. The proposed company would have hurt Kachchhi intermediaries. But the British government declined to provide any support to Mackinnon. Jairam Shivji held the customs contract for five years till 1886 when Sultan Barghash finally discontinued the system of accepting private tenders. Over the years, the British tried to marginalize Ratansi Purshottam in Muscat and Jairam Shivji in Zanzibar by trying to dismantle their customs contracts. But the British themselves were not clear about their objectives.

For more than fifty years, from 1835 to 1886, the firm of Jairam Shivji dominated Zanzibar. John Kirk held that the firm ruled the Sultan and the traders of the kingdom alike. According to a Zanzibar newspaper, the citizens of Zanzibar town regarded the estate of Jairam Shivji as 'Nyumba Serikali' or the prime minister's residence. A Kachchhi Bhatia, Jairam Narayanji, who visited Zanzibar in the 1880s, found the office of the firm of Jairam Shivji served by many servants inside and guarded by African soldiers on the outside. He found the building formidably impressive—from the large hall where agents worked, to the treasury room, the kitchen, the entertainment room and even the bedroom. He remarked that it looked like the palace of a king. On New Year's Day, Sultan Seyyid Said customarily visited Jairam Shivji's house with an entourage of followers. A grand celebration would then follow in the presence of all the prominent merchants of Zanzibar. The Swahili trade ended up resulting in a change in Jairam's family name. The family assumed the surname 'Swali'. At Mundra, a small lane near Jairam Shivji's house is known as 'Swali Sheri' (Swali lane).

Details of the transactions of the firm of Jairam Shivji were, according to Bartle Frere, subjected to judicial investigation in the Consular Court in 1872. These details reveal a firm that had capital invested and credit extended to the Sultan and his family, to Arabs in Zanzibar, to Arabs on the east African coast and in the interiors of Africa. Most of the borrowers were slave owners and slave dealers. The securities included mortgages on property and trade goods. A large quantum of loans had also been made to Europeans and Americans and, of course, to Kachchhis in Africa. The firm's own assets included businesses in Africa, Mandvi and Bombay, in addition to inventories and investments in firms promoted by family members. Bartle Frere estimated the capital employed in African trade and banking by the family to be a million sterling. This information tallies with that from Jairam Shivji's family papers and other papers filed in court in 1872, which contain the valuations of precious jewels, property and other assets of the firm. Jairam Shivji and other Banias were akin to ruling powers.

Jairam Shivji died on 25 August 1866. His will, last updated in 1865, divided his wealth between his two sons Damodar Jairam and Khimji Jairam, who were born to his first and second wives, respectively. Both turned out to be disappointments in running the firm's business. Khimji Jairam squandered the family wealth and had the reputation of being an excessive pleasure-seeker. He committed suicide when he was only thirty-nine. Jairam's brother Ibji Shivji, on the other hand, made attempts to revive the fortunes of the firm. But he was not able to keep pace with the demands of the changing times. Jivandas Ibji continued the business tradition on a lesser scale. He ran a ginning factory. The business, which had been strong from 1785 to 1885, fell on bad times as a result of internal dissension and litigation. Today, the descendents of Ibji Shivji Swali are settled in Mumbai and in different parts of the world. Jairam Shivji's own descendants lead a modest life in Mundra.

Thariya Topan

Thariya Topan's journey from an apprentice to a tycoon who competed with the firm that trained him is a fascinating and inspiring one. He was born in 1821 in Lakhpat in Kachchh, and was the son of a small vegetable seller. In his hometown, he received four years of basic schooling, which was quite considerable for the time. He moved to Zanzibar when he was only twelve years old. Initially, he worked with Jairam Shivji and was employed as a scribe by Laddha Damji. There was clearly no issue with respect to religious background as far as the pragmatic Kachchhis were concerned. Thariya, a Muslim, may have been from a different religion, but for Laddha he was a good apprentice scribe to have. Contrariwise, Laddha was a Hindu but to Thariya Topan, he was probably the best teacher that could be found. It is said that as an apprentice, Topan started in the traditional way—cleaning floors. His first business was started with borrowed money. He bought a donkey-cart, which he used for transporting cloves and coconuts. His business flourished and he was able to repay his loan. He established contacts with plantation owners in the hinterland and made sure that he had access to regular supplies of cloves. Having made sure of his supplies, he then tackled the demand side of the business. He visited India and made agreements with Ismaili firms for the sale of cloves. Soon he was no longer just a transporter but a bulk trader. He opened a warehouse and developed a reputation for selling at very competitive prices.

The next business move was an ambitious one. He reached out to the contacts he had made while working for Jairam Shivji—mainly American traders. In the 1860s, he developed a cordial relationship with the American Consul, and using his contacts, established a commanding position for himself in the market for American goods. He bought whole cargoes or batons of some merchandise, which helped him dominate those particular markets. In Zanzibar, next to Jairam Shivji, Thariya Topan emerged as the principal partner for the Americans. A six hundred and thirty-one tonner owned by the firm of John Bertram bore the name of Thariya, attesting to Topan's importance. Business relations with Americans had its challenges. Thariya Topan advanced a large amount of money to the firm of Edward Ropes, who was an attorney in Zanzibar. Ropes's son became the agent for Topan's firm in Mozambique, which unfortunately lost Rs 1 lakh in the course of two-and-a-half years. Topan was extremely angry and wrote a strong letter to Ropes about the limited abilities of his son. Thariya Topan was a venture capitalist of his time. He financed and managed his supply line from the coast to the interiors. He was the chief backer of Tipu Tib, the Caravan King. Tipu Tib acknowledges this in his memoirs. This is corroborated by a message from Sultan Seyyid Bargash to Tipu Tib about a gunpowder shipment: 'The powder which you wanted to buy has been given to your patron Thariya Topan, 2000 pounds.'

There is evidence to suggest that Thariya Topan also advanced money to some travellers who were purely into discovery expeditions, with the hope that some high-return business opportunities may emerge from them. His business operations extended to Kachchh, Bombay, Zanzibar, Muscat, Aden, China, Mozambique, Quillimane and the Bender Coast. His firm had business relations with Maclean, Moris of London, Clarke and Smith of London, T.P. Charlesworth of

London, Arnold Hines of New York, Ropes, Emmerton of Salem, W. Birch Jun of Manchester and F. Ottens of Hamburg.

He was a close associate of influential persons in Zanzibar—the Sultan, Laddha Damji and John Kirk. He was the first Indian to be chosen by Sultan Barghash as his companion for a state visit to London. He also enjoyed close relations with the British Consul Euan Smith, to whom he presented a diamond ring. His cordial relations with the Sultan enabled him to bid for the highly remunerative and prestigious customs contract. The first such proposal came in 1871, directly from Sultan Barghash, who wished to change the customs authority. John Kirk found Thariya the only merchant capable of entering into competition with Jairam Shivji. Due to the indebtedness of Sultan Barghash, Thariya did not secure the contract in 1871. In 1875, he finally got the contract, ending the long monopoly of Jairam Shivji. From 1875 to 1880 he farmed the customs for Barghash at the rate of $350,000 per year. In 1880, he again lost the customs contract to Jairam Shivji's firm, who offered more for the franchise.

Thariya's rivalry with Jairam Shivji was limited to business. At the personal level, Thariya Topan had friendly and cordial relations with Laddha Damji. In fact, Laddha Damji nominated him, along with John Kirk, as caretaker trustee of the wealth of the firm of Jairam Shivji. Thariya Topan himself wrote Laddha

Damji's will. This is one more example of the solidarity and cooperation between Hindu-Bhatia Kachchhis and Muslim-Khoja Kachchhis.

Thariya settled down in Bombay in 1885, leaving his Zanzibar business in the custody of his sons Musa and Jaffarbhoy. He completed his customary pilgrimage to Mecca. In his later years, Thariya used his African fortunes to finance the China trade in tea and possibly opium.

Thariya Topan was the leading member of the Khoja community at Zanzibar. He lobbied with the British Consul on matters affecting his community's interests. Along with twenty-eight other merchants, both Hindu and Muslim, he petitioned for steps to improve security in the town. He was nominated as a *mukhi* or treasurer of the Khoja community. He also acted as guardian to the young Aga Khan in Bombay. He donated the princely sum of 150,000 for a hospital founded in Zanzibar in 1887. Thariya Topan's charities were extensive. He offered a sum of 200,000 for building a school, even though his first preference was construction of a hospital. But John Kirk wished to utilize the funds for 'the school, as he observed lack of education among the Khojas'. Thariya Topan's son Jafar Thariya provided Rs 10,000. The Aga Khan gave Rs 3500. With this, a school was opened in 1891. The British knighted him in 1890 for his services in the promotion of their anti-slavery mission. He was now known as Sir Thariya Topan.

His son Jafar Thariya succeeded him and acted as
agent for many Arab and Zanzibari caravan owners in
Africa. Like his father, he continued to act as an agent
for Tipu Tib. Of Thariya Topan, who died in 1891, his
contemporary H.M. Stanley remarked:

> One of the honestest among men, white or black,
> red or yellow, is a Mohammedan Hindi called 'Tarya
> Topan.' Among the Europeans at Zanzibar he has
> become a proverb for honesty, and strict business
> integrity. He is enormously wealthy, owns several
> ships and dhows and is a prominent man in the
> councils of Syed Burghash.

Sewa Haji Paroo

The earliest move into the interior of east Africa was
by Sewa Haji Paroo, who operated from Bagamoyo
in German east Africa. Haji Paroo Pradhan and his
brother Jaffer Paroo migrated from Bhuj to Zanzibar
in 1850. There, Haji established a small general store
in 1852. Haji progressed steadily, and in 1860 opened
a branch of his store at Bagamoyo. His son Sewa Haji
was born in 1851. Sewa joined his father in his business
at an early age. In 1869, when his business lessons
were still in progress, tragedy struck. Sewa's two older
brothers died and Sewa was obliged to take charge of
the firm of Haji Kanji. Sewa found Zanzibar to be an
overcrowded market. He decided to enter the riskier

but less crowded space of caravan financing. Through the 1860s, he supplied caravans with goods such as cloth, beads, copper wire and brass pots. In return, he purchased ivory. In exchange for supplies, he agreed to deposit his stockpiles of ivory, rhinoceros horns and hippopotamus teeth in the warehouses of Haji Kanji. He broadened the scope of his business by supplying labour (porters) and provisions for the caravans themselves. He established an important position for himself in Bagamoyo, which endured till his death in 1897. Henry Stanley recollects in his work how he trusted Sewa to equip him with the required material and porters for his expedition, calling him the best man to procure *pagazi* (porters) in Bagamoyo. Similarly, Sewa entered into a contract with Dr Hans Meyer around 1890, to launch a caravan to Kilimanjaro. Caravan investments by their very nature were long-term. Over time, Sewa's clients included not just the traditional Arab-Swahili merchants, but also Euro-American traders, Christian missionaries and explorers. From financing caravans to starting his own caravan company was a logical step. He also increased the range of goods for exchange to include textile products and firearms. His company, now well expanded and consolidated, sent its own caravans carrying goods. Bagamoyo served as a major funnel for arms and ammunition sent into the interior. Sewa transported around ten thousand guns to Unanyembe. Individually, and in partnership with Europeans, Sewa's was the largest share in the arms market. Even after German firms established their own branches in Bagamayo, Sewa Haji continued to be a major arms importer. The secret of his success was the solid caravan business he had built.

The division of east Africa between Germany and Britain led to Sewa appointing agents operating from German Tanganyika and British Uganda. He was the first Indian to receive the honour of a title from the German government. Henry Stanley, in his reports, made some disparaging remarks about him. However, when Henry Stanley again launched an expedition to Congo, he sought Sewa Haji's assistance, indicating that Sewa's services were indispensable! Continuing with the tradition set by Jairam Shivji and Thariya Topan, Sewa Haji acted as a principal creditor to Sultan Sayed Hamid bin Thwain.

He willed all his houses located in Dar-es-Salaam and Bagamoyo to the German colonial government, with the condition that the income was to be used partly to provide food to leprosy patients and partly to sustain the Bagamoyo hospital. In early 1880, he purchased a few stone houses for the express purpose of erecting a hospital for the destitute and orphans. The Sewa Haji Hospital in Dar-es-Salaam stands tall as a symbol to his philanthropy. The Sewa Haji Hospital is now an annex of the Princess Margaret Hospital. Sewa offered a multi-storeyed building and funds to missionaries to start a multi-racial school in Bagamoyo. Christian missionaries at Bagamoyo fondly referred to the Muslim Sewa as 'our generous friend'. Eight days after his death, an entry was placed in the mission journal: 'This devoted friend of the mission will not forget (us) in his last wishes.'

Sewa Haji secured his name in the list of the three uncrowned kings of east Africa along with Sir Thariya Topan in Zanzibar and Alidina Visram. Sewa Haji died in 1897 at the young age of forty-six. After his death, his cousin managed the firm.

Alidina Visram

Alidina Visram, known as one of the founders of modern east Africa, is credited with having opened up much of Uganda by setting up a series of trading stations there in the 1880s. His career in east Africa was typical of Kachchhi merchants of the time. He arrived in Zanzibar as a young apprentice of an established firm. He then moved to Bagamoyo in 1877 as an assistant to Sewa Haji. In late 1885, Alidina Vishram worked with Nasser Virji. Having acquired enough experience, Alidina started his own enterprise in the 1890s. He supplied goods to the inland markets of central-east Africa, Tabora and Ujiji. His goods were considered valuable and were exchanged for ivory and skins. Alidina won a contract to operate as the sole provider of packaged foods to hunters. In 1897, after Sewa's death, he entered the caravan trade with vigour, expanding it as far as Uganda, Kenya, parts of Congo Free State and southern Sudan. He was known as 'King of Ivory' in Africa. He controlled the entire supply chain from Africa to Zanzibar without any external dependencies. His firm branched out to Dar-es-Salaam and Sadani, and to Kalima and Tindo in the Belgian Congo. He established a chain of shops known as 'Dukas' in Kampala, Jinja and Kisumu much before the introduction of the Uganda railway line. His next stop was Mombasa. He was both a risk-taker and one who shared profits with his partners. In the Congo alone, he invested $130,000, and shared his profits with seventeen agents. By 1901, the age of the caravan was over as the Uganda railway line connected the hinterlands. Alidina used this as an opportunity to grow his empire. He successfully straddled the British and German colonial possessions in east Africa. Alidina was way ahead of his times in the areas of financial innovation and inclusion. He converted his 'Dukas' into bank branches. His clients, who included colonial civil servants and traders, purchased supplies against cheques issued by his company. These cheques were cashed in Mombasa. Thus, Europeans in Kampala could pay for goods or services with monthly or quarterly cheques. Alidina expanded his firm into a business conglomerate, going way beyond ivory. He diversified into sesame, wax, peanuts and cotton, among other goods. He became known as a business mogul with a footprint in more than thirty locations in east Africa, covering Kenya, Uganda, eastern Congo (present day

Zaire) and southern Sudan. His main offices were at Bombay, Mombasa and Bagamoyo. He owned several dhows and also had a small steamer on Lake Victoria. He operated a well-organized transport service between Mombasa and Uganda. His company had a telegraphic address—*pagazi*—meaning transporters or porters. He owned seven large sugarcane and rubber plantations. In east Africa, he experimented with crops, introducing grams, fruits, flowers, tea, and cotton. He employed over three thousand workers for his projects. His entry into manufacturing started with a factory to supply furniture to his retail outlets in Kampala and Entebbe (both in Uganda). He then started a factory to extract oil from sesame seeds later in Kisumu (western Kenya). He started a soap factory in Mombasa (Tanganyika) and sawmills in Uganda and at Nyeri near Mount Kenya. He reversed the direction of the cotton trade by setting up ginning factories in Uganda. He purchased raw cotton in Uganda, processed it in his ginning factories, transported the cotton to Mombasa by railway, and then shipped it to Bombay. For this pioneering move, if for nothing else, he deserves to be called one of the founders of modern Uganda.

He made regular annual visits to every important branch of his vast business empire. On one of his routine trips to a branch in the Belgian Congo, he was very upset at being unable to recover a small outstanding amount from a merchant. The story goes that after this shock he contracted a fever. It is said that when he died he was worth more than Rs 3 million. Though his son Abdul Rasul Alidina Visram attempted to carry forth his father's business, life betrayed him in 1923.

Alidina served the anti-slavery movement with good judgement. In the 1870s, he was counted as an influential leader of the Indian community. He had forty-eight retail stores and several branch offices all over east Africa. He was known as the uncrowned king of Uganda. He donated a considerable sum for construction of the first *jamatkhana* in Kisumu. This was inaugurated by the Imam in 1905. The title *Varas* was bestowed on him for his invaluable services.

Alidina assisted new immigrant Ismailis in settling down in Kisumu and other parts of Kenya. He established for them small provision stores. Immigrant Ismailis settled in Homa Bay, Mumias, Sio Port and other small towns. It is said that many Ismailis who became prosperous in Kenya and Uganda owe much to Alidina. Many came as his employees and later established their own businesses.

Cyril Ehrlich writes in 'The Uganda Economy 1903–1945' as follows: 'Perhaps the most important individual in the early history in east Africa, Sheth Alidina Visram was responsible for laying the firm foundation not only of trade in Uganda but of such industries as cotton, sugar, rubber, tea and various other agricultural products as well as of shipping across Lake Victoria.' *Oriental Nairobi* noted, 'An interesting point is that the Khoja community was in

East Africa even before the foundation of Nairobi, the merchant, Prince Alidina Visram, also known as the Uncrowned King of Uganda, extended his activities on the mainland from Mombasa to the lower reaches of the Nile.'

Ali Mulla Jeevanjee

Ali Mulla Jeevanjee's firm A.M. Jeevanjee and Co. were known all down the east African coast as contractors, shipowners and general merchants. Jeevanjee was a Kachchhi Bohra whose family had earlier moved to Karachi in Sind. His ambitions were truly global. In 1886, he established an import business in Adelaide, Australia. In 1896, his firm was hired by Uganda Railway to recruit Indian construction workers. At one time, thirty-two thousand coolies were involved in constructing the railway. Jivanjee quickly moved from the recruitment business to the construction business. Jivanjee's firm took contracts for building government offices and railway stations between Nairobi and Mombasa. He amassed a great fortune, which he invested in properties in and around the Indian bazaar of Nairobi. A descendant of the family claimed that in 1913, one-third of Nairobi's revenue from municipal rates was paid by Jivanjee. The family donated land to the Kenyan government for building the municipal market. The Jivanjee public gardens are still enjoyed by the citizens of Kenya. Jivanjee played a leading role in the politics of Kenya until his death in 1932. He was known as the 'grand old man' of Kenya.

Adamji Alibhoy

Several Kachchhis ventured into the interiors of Kenya. Adamji Alibhoy first moved from Zanzibar to Mombasa in 1862. In Mombasa, he prospered as a contractor working with the British authorities and with Christian missions. He recruited porters for many explorers and travellers visiting east Africa. In the 1890s, Adamji Alibhoy left Mombasa and opened a shop about two hundred and fifty miles west of Mombasa at Machakos. Alibhoy was responsible for making the Indian rupee the popular currency in the interior. He made sure that his services were valuable to the Imperial British East Africa Company (chartered in 1888).

The Jivanjees and Karimjis

Jivanjee Budhabhai was the son of a Bohra Muslim Budhabhai Noor Muhammed, who had a hardware business in Mandvi. Jairam Shivji advised Budhabhai to send his son to Zanzibar. Once again, we note the easy cordiality in relations across religious denominations. As a result, Jivanjee travelled by dhow to Zanzibar in 1818. Here he opened a hardware business. When the business prospered, Jivanjee brought over his three sons to help him. Pirabhai, the son of his first wife, and Karimjee and Ismailee of the second, thus came to Zanzibar. In 1860–61, the brothers separated their business interests. Karimjee established a separate business, and Pirabhai and Ismailjee carried on their father's business. After the death of Pirabhai, Ismailjee gave his name to the firm. Pirabhai Jivanjee had extensive dealings with American firms, especially with John Bertram of Salem and Arnold Hines of New York. The old firm of the Karimjees became major importers of grain and also owned the agency of kerosene in east Africa. In the late nineteenth century, the firm exported ivory, copra, groundnuts, cereals, beeswax and cloves from Zanzibar and the east African mainland to India. Karimjee proved to be a resilient entrepreneur through ups and downs. In the 1860s, Karimjee wished to arrange the marriage of his only son Alibhai. For that purpose he visited Mandvi. There, he spotted a business opportunity and bought a lot of goods, which he shipped to Zanzibar. Unfortunately, the cargo ship encountered a violent storm and Karimjee lost all his goods. When Karimjee reached Zanzibar, he was in an impecunious state. Karimjee started all over again, regaining his lost fortune and going on to build a trading empire. Karimjee managed the business of his firm till 1898. Since his only son died early, his grandsons, who were encouraged to join the business, carried it forward. By the 1900s, the firm of Karimjee traded in a wide range of agricultural products and textiles. Shipments were brought from England, Germany, India and the Far East for the Zanzibar market. Return cargoes went to the same countries as well as to Mauritius, the Seychelles, and Ceylon. The firm's coastal trade covered Pemba, Tanga, Dar-es-Salaam, Bagamoyo, Kilwa, Lindi, Mikindani, Mombasa and Lamu. The firm operated its own dhows.

> Their principal imports are Manchester cotton goods; sugar from Austria, Germany and Russia; rice from India; tea and coffee, beads (Bohemian and Viennese); metal-especially galvanised iron from Birmingham; oil, paints, nails, and all kinds of merchandise except hams and bacon which are prohibited owing to their religion. Exports . . . local produce, such as cloves, copra, hides, beeswax, rubber, chilies, all kinds of merit for cloves awarded at the Zanzibar exhibition of 1905.

For instance, Yusufali, one of the grandsons of Karimjee, travelled to Europe to learn about the European market. He managed to pick up about fifty contracts from different European and American companies. Yusufali Karimjee was regarded as a born trader and an expert in dealing with new markets and new partners. The Karimjee family diversified into coffee, tea and sisal plantations. Sisal became very rewarding for the firm. The Karimjees also started an agency business for the import of cars. They started a properties' division to manage the growing number of offices, stores and other buildings. Even today, the Karimjees are leading agents for Toyota in the region. James Christi, a British medical officer, must have had people like the Karimjees in mind when he said that the Kachchhi Banias were the ruling power in Zanzibar.

CONCLUSION

This book portrayed the dynamic role Kachchhi entrepreneurs played in the Indian Ocean trading network, connecting Kachchh, Muscat and Zanzibar. The study, in that context, endeavoured to identify in what ways, and to what extent, Kachchhis set out the distinctive entrepreneurial standards in Muscat and Zanzibar. At home, a variety of factors pushed them towards the foreign littorals. In a changed milieu then commenced a longstanding adaptation process. Overcoming the dichotomies of known and unknown societies, a significant placing of the Indians was carved out. In many eyes, the dream of securing better standards of life was invoked by the pioneering merchant groups. The success of these pioneering entrepreneurs is noteworthy in the sense that other than bringing business opportunities for the country, they charted out newer horizons of settlement and interaction. The study figured out the equation between the polity and the trade and its impact on the existing sailing tradition, the development of the port towns and seaborne trade. I have argued that though Kachchh experienced a major political change in the early nineteenth century, which resulted in the formation of the semi-feudal political order, the mercantile activities withstood the turbulent times and instead of losing momentum, they picked up a greater pace of expansion. The merchants of Kachchh profitably explored a distinct trajectory of the east African littoral than their counterparts, namely the Marwaris and the Parsis. This distinction was empowered with remarkable historical continuity over a long period.

In Kachchh, merchants formed a strong mercantile society and enjoyed a high status. Very often, the merchant capital generated funds in the running of the state and in supporting the drought-stricken populace. The Mahajan of such merchants also wielded greater power and greater influence in the durbar. They not only mediated the disputes between the merchants but also kept an ethical watch over the mercantile activities. Since they emerged as a dominant group, the states often negotiated with them in balancing the status quo. The land of Kachchh, in a true sense, was the land of entrepreneurs, who belonged to a range of energetic mercantile communities. It was the culture and ethos of these communities to which the merchants owe their support and success. The land of Kachchh was fortunate in having energetic commercial port towns, which were home to different types of networks engaged in international trade and finance. The study of the history of those networks can throw new light on the question of the commercial and cultural relationship between networks and empires, which is seen by many as one of importance to an understanding of our present. One such dynamic port town of Kachchh was Mandvi, which being connected with several deep seas, coastal and regional trajectories, emerged as the significant town of the merchant groups, banking houses, shipbuilding culture and marine insurance systems. These attributes widely and profitably contributed in winning the status of maritime state. Kachchh's economy was, thus, dynamically oriented towards deep-sea commerce, and its commercial energy banked much on enterprise of the merchants, artisans and the sailing class. Merchants, when they approached newer horizons, were equipped with their effective language of business, remarkable accountancy and financial skills, practical apprenticeship tradition, sailing technologies, individual and partnered enterprises, family firm-based trading networks and many more conventional local customs.

With such apparatus, when they made their commercial inroads to Arabia, the Arabs were more than happy to welcome them. The Muscat economy, undoubtedly, absorbed the Kachchhi capital in the running of state affairs and in raising the maritime status. This was more so towards the end of the eighteenth century as the Sultans, in their quest for money to finance their military apparatus, which were directed to consolidate the Omani position in east Africa, increasingly came to depend on advances and loans extended by the Bhatia merchants. Most interestingly, some of these money providers were also nominated as the custodians of customs collections. The unsettled affairs with the other political groups of the Persian Gulf and east Africa compelled Omani rulers to make use of the available Kachchhi capital. Undoubtedly, this financial dependency provided the required leverage to the merchants to exert considerable influence on the economy of Muscat and Zanzibar.

Having made their successful entry into Muscat, the merchants of Kachchh vigorously invested their finances in the commodity-exchange trade. They became the most powerful players in not only procuring high-value articles such as pearl, but also distributing it to various domestic and foreign markets. This type of detailed control over the commodities and their circulation converted Muscat and Bombay into truly international ports of exchange. The merchants also became instrumental in enriching existing consumer culture. They also dealt in key plantation products. In dealing in dates especially, through their American contacts, they kept pace with the changing character of bulk packaging and mass-scale export in pleasing American clients and consumers. Besides dealing in marine and farm products of numerous varieties, they bravely plunged into the arms trade which was fraught with high risk. While the world order was marching on a fragile balance triggered by the tense relations between the Western powers, which were loudly echoed in the Asian continent, Kachchhi merchants used their commercial foresight in making quick money out of the increasing demand for arms. By doing so, they kept the importance of Muscat alive, which experienced reverses in its established hegemony after the death of dynamic Sultan Seyyid Said—the diminishing shipbuilding industry in the wake of steam navigation and the surges of 'tribal' political disputes.

At Zanzibar, the introduction of Kachchhi enterprise brought manifold changes. Compared to Muscat, the Zanzibar island had multiple high-value resources to offer, including human beings. After the departure of the Portuguese, the Omani Sultans gradually sculpted a progressive economic policy to fruitfully exploit the natural wealth of the island. Sultan Seyyid Said opened the doors of east Africa for many Western powers to trade. In all the Sultan's endeavours, the first beneficiaries were Kachchhis as not only did they capture the control of customs management, but they also built up mercantile capital through inviting foreign trade. The Kachchhis formed some kind of socio-economic relationships with their customers which kept both buyers and sellers together during this era of competition. With the help of direct and indirect support of the local Swahili and Arab merchants, producers, caravan leaders, porters and planters, Kachchhis could firmly root their trading settlements. These factors ensured that the Kachchhis would dominate the trading network throughout the nineteenth century, despite the beginning of competition from their Western counterparts. The commodities, namely ivory and gum copal, connected the African interior and mainland with the industries of America and Europe and manufacturing units of the Bombay Presidency and Rajputana. The ivory trade assessed the impacts of certain imperatives of the cultures of consumption of the West and India, as commodities were sold and traded in a variety of social and cultural settings. This single article, supplied chiefly through the Kachchhi ivory merchants, was utilized variously in the oriental and occidental spaces which represented distinct consumer culture. The industrially-advanced West could accrue greater benefits by leading the mass-scale manufacturing of the piano and billiard balls, while the Indian units could transform this highly-prized substance into mere bangles, combs, toiletries, boxes and toys without large-scale production, in the absence of machinery plants. On the one hand, ivory industries in Connecticut and Ivoryton generated greater employment opportunities, while on the other, Indian ivory workers struggled for daily requirements. Irrespective of the huge contrast in the making and use of the dental substance, both spaces contributed in making the ivory merchants rich and in disturbing the ecological balance of Africa. The study of commodity consumption and the historical context behind the developed tastes of consumers as materially-, socially- and culturally-engrafted processes, have offered binding insight into how societies, communities and people create and maintain status and identities.

In sum, this study remained primarily concerned with the local trade of items produced and consumed in varied coastal and hinterland regions. Although there were some subtle transformations in the structure and operation of this internationally-oriented trade, for the most part the links within the regional economy remained fairly consistent throughout the nineteenth century. Essentially it was the existence of these local trading networks which integrated the different peoples and ecological zones of the coast into a regional unit, and facilitated the existence of long-distance trade. By focusing on the trade in some of these items, which were consumed extensively throughout the coastal region—such as ivory, cloth, gum copal, and pearl— one can illustrate how merchants were empowered to enjoy the wide range of commodities that were at their disposal through the complex trading network. By examining the social links created by these cultural ties, in tandem with the economic links provided by local trade, we do gain a clear picture of the institutional connections which foster the cohesion of regional socio-economic units.

Pre-industrial trade networks in the Gulf of Kachchh were able to cling to a viable economic system as they confronted droughts and swarms of locusts, 'tribal' raids in the coastal societies of Muscat and east Africa that fleeced them of capital, or royal monopolies of scarce resources such as ivory and copal. Even so, they sustained such adversaries or had no choice but to continue. Unquestionably, irregularities at sea and military invasions incurred huge costs for merchants in terms of lost capital, commodities or labour. The flexibility of trade of that age can be judged in the creation of diverse routes of trade, or secondary markets. The merchants of Euro-American lands and Kachchh and Gujarat earned profit only after meeting the several challenges which the land and coast of east Africa offered at several stages of trading endeavours. Other than geographic difficulty, the most challenging undertaking was pleasing the choosy African consumers. This particular rigidity on the consumers' side inundated the African bazaar with a variety of piece-goods, brass wire, beads and other trinkets. It made the market increasingly and fiercely competitive, especially for the American *merikani* and Kachchhi *kaniki*. The trade in cotton textile also triggered Anglo-American rivalry which could pace down only at the start of the civil war in America. Another obstruction the merchants encountered was of time management during the monsoon-wind-governed trading season. The merchants also handled and balanced an equation with the 'tribal' chiefs and their taxation system. Thus, the whole of maritime trade was attributed to varieties of constructs which, especially, underscored entrepreneurial spirit.

Even though the African land was difficult to trade and settle in, the Euro-American mercantile firms geared up in situating their branch houses all around strategic trading points of the Zanzibar dominion. The Salemites, who were among the earliest from the West to explore the potentiality of Zanzibar trade, had many competitors from England, Marseille and Hamburg. They also had their own compatriots from Providence and New York to compete with. In this interesting commercial competition, though Salemites managed to secure the upper hand, it was not achieved without Indian support. The Indian merchants were the ones who remained consistent in the changing global order to move the trading wheels. Considerable knowledge of the foreign terrain, sources of supply and market conditions were key in building their wider market relations. Through their agency network they were constantly involved in relaying the information regarding the evolution of African and Arabian demand and Indian supply. Their inbuilt capacity to adapt to the prevailing conditions and crisis situation by morphing into new commercial circuits indeed afforded long-standing hold over the business enterprise. The fundamental to success remained their years of experience which passed down from one merchant to the other. Their proficiency in business matters, their knowledge of bookkeeping and their working systems equipped them to compete and negotiate with their foreign counterparts. The study of arms trade, especially, proves that they were persistent in negotiating profitable trade deals and had bigger stomachs for commercial risk. Kachchhis generally attracted immediate attention because of their expertise in commodity circulation. The British administrative reports in a singular way credit them with complete control of the trade. Yet, this much-vaunted ability was visibly accompanied by a habitual criticism of foreign partners. This was a customary way of exhibiting status and performing the duty. For them, there were multiple merchant associations, partnerships and agents, and local associates working for the network. Thanks to their mobility and knowledge of languages and customs, Kachchhi merchants managed to penetrate the local milieu and find the necessary auxiliaries for their business. They were encouraged to settle because they were not proselytizers, did not vie for political positions at least in the early stages, nor tried to challenge the rules. In performing multiple roles a merchant was the agent and diplomat in service of local sovereigns and European companies. This capacity of adaption, allied with unequivocal solidarity, constituted an important asset of the risk and uncertainties inherent in trade. But they were more than simple compradors, associates of capitalism's expansion into the preindustrial regions of the world in the late nineteenth century. Their relation to capital and political authorities was too ambivalent as the state loomed as a threat for many merchants, chiefly when its governors confiscated merchant fortunes or fleeced money or over taxed them; and it also sometimes partnered their enterprise and facilitated their commercial operations. The trading transactions upon which their livelihoods depended relied on the creation of a transversal trading network. These key participants in the business of commodities were no passive actors of imperial designs who just floated the moving ridge of a globalization determined by the powers of the West; they followed their own course of action, claiming the spaces of the shore and the port, the custom-house and the warehouses as their own. More than that, they themselves threaded spatial relations, carving out new landscapes of acquaintance, and pulling together dispersed localities in unforeseen and novel ways, as from straightforward date dealers they could morph into powerful arms dealers. In this way, they can be called the Black Swan, who kept shifting the trade games all through the dynamic mercantile societies of Kachchh at Muscat and Zanzibar in the eighteenth and nineteenth centuries—and yet, very few noticed them or now know them. These black swans carry the message that to be really successful one needs to start realizing what one does not know and stop dwelling upon what one knows.

This book helps one to see the western Indian Ocean world with a different perspective, which is somewhat different than those records which talk about Indian or Asian diaspora in east Africa since the building of the Uganda Railway. Travelling through history and the economy of Zanzibar, one comes across Kachchhi entrepreneurs who laid the strong foundation of long-standing trade settlements during the last quarter of the eighteenth century, which was eventually shaped in the broad trade triangle between Mandvi, Muscat and Zanzibar. The complex trading triangle is an excellent example of the emerging links between the global economy in the nineteenth century, which not only involved closer contacts between Europe and Asia, but also with Africa and America. Kachchhi merchants introduced retail trading practices by the means of *Duka* in the interior of east Africa. They advanced capital for commodity trade and reaped the lion's share of the profits. In the conduct of trade, Arab and Euro-American merchants depended on the services provided by Bhatia, Khoja and Bohra brokers and bankers. On the other hand, the presence of Euro-American firms and their business interests in east Africa brought in global flair of trade and interdependency—wherein, though the Indians had visibly captured the markets, they were also equally dependent on foreign trade and traders. The foreign capital in circulation enabled Indian and Arab middle managers of limited capital to collect the commodities from the mainland, without investments from their short pockets, to finance caravan trade and the plantation products. Thus, the interaction among the Indian, Arab, Swahili, European and American merchant groups was of mutual interdependence—reciprocal and dynamically fruitful. Explanations for why Kachchhi business has been excessively important in Arabia and Africa typically stress cultural influences, including the role of family, dialect groups and the business value system. With respect to the latter, it is often argued that social trust—the social obligations that bind family and lineage—is strengthened by community affinity, and that had provided the bedrock of commercial networking. The story of Indian presence in Arabia and east Africa over the *longue durée*, stresses on burgeoning pre-colonial Indian Ocean trading nexuses and emphasizes the fact that both Euro-American enterprises could not ignore the importance of Indian mercantile actors in the Indian Ocean world.

Of course, other than trading, there was much more to a trader's life in the Gulf or Africa than making money. Their sojourns to the Gulf or Africa were not all that rosy. The sea became a meaningful space of experience to which the merchants and mariners contributed by charting new terra firma and by adding new stories which amalgamate fortune, misfortune and hope. It did represent a period when most of the Hindu merchants, without their families, went through the difficult life of living alone as the man out there toiled to adjust and adapt to unfamiliar ties, customs, climate and culture. One can only imagine the anguish they experienced during their stay miles and miles away from home. Living in old Muscat and Muttrah towns, rather than the clean and spacious modern Muscat, or living in the filthy 'Stinkibar' of the yesteryears, as compared to the developed Zanzibar stone town, was indeed altogether a distinct experience. Those who decided to stay there permanently, most of whom were Ismailis, also had their similar experience, but the only difference was that they were accompanied by their families. Each mercantile community struggled to preserve or retain their existing identities. What is imperative to emphasize here in the concluding notes is the fact that in spite of the increasing Indian diaspora overseas after the second half of the nineteenth century, which unfolds the whole interesting paradigm of Indian presence and experience, at the early years it remained exclusively, along with the commercial settlement, a merchant's struggle to sow the seeds of newer roots. These pioneers, especially the transients, lived a very low-profile life in an unfamiliar environment, where they also struggled with some of the basic issues such as: Whether to drink water from the pipe or fetch water directly from the well? Which type of sugar to eat, crystallized or un-crystallized? Which quarter to live in? Where to bury the dead? How far to intermingle or maintain distance from the locals? They solved these preliminary dilemmas by basing upon their personal and religious convictions, in a way, to smoothen out the process for future generations. To a large extent, the early Indian presence in Oman and east Africa was shaped by notions of recreating a similar environ rather than feelings of remoteness and twinge in the distant countries. The initial, impermanent stay within the host countries frames the Indian diaspora in an inimitably favoured status, spread across the three spaces without conceding or eliminating either. Their initial way of living had a greater impact and continuity throughout the nineteenth century settlements as most of the second-generation settlers remained apolitical and highly identity conscious. In the foreign lands, the trade-centric approach and absence of any desire to dominate was attributive to their characteristics. Once the new era set with the births of South Asians in Arabia and Africa, with a growing detachment towards origins and roots, a new flair and dimension added up in the South-Asian experience. They were developed into a distinct group of people with more complex experiences, including emotional ones. As Asha Iyer expresses in her Omani diaspora novel, *Sand, Storm and Summer Rain,* 'the kaleidoscope of their lives presents endless patterns'. Even M.G. Vassanji's *The Gunny Sack* produces stories of Asians caught up in the intriguing dilemmas during their migratory sojourns to Africa and onward.

GLOSSARY

Gujarati terms

Aadatiya: An agent

Aakhar mausam: The closing season for oceanic trade

Aavadat: Skill

Aavang: A type of insurance

Ashadh: July

Ashadhi Sud Bij: The second day of the full-moon month (usually falls in the month of July)

Aval aakhar mausam: The last leg of the closing season

Avaro: Journal; income; an account-book in which the total monthly receipts and expenditure are recorded

Batila or *Batela*: A sort of boat used in western India, Sindh and Bengal, which invariably had a square stern and a long grab-like head

Bhalamaniya: A recommender, through whom the trader sought to sell and purchase goods

Bhantar: Learning; education

Chandraus: Copal tree

Cheelo: A Gujarati word for the transit duties on grain or custom; practice

Chheli ghos: The closing season

Chopdi: A book

Darbari lagat: State tax

Dariyayi vimo: Marine insurance

Darshani: A type of *hundi* where money is paid at sight

Daryayi Navu Varsh: Maritime era at Mandvi

Dasondh: A religious tithe

Derasar: A Jain temple

Dharmashalas: Rest houses

Dharmau lagat: Religious tax

Dhung: A vessel

Endhanjog hundi: A *hundi* with the description of the receiver

Feria vepari: A peddler

Gantar: Calculation; counting

Ghos: A trip or voyage

Gupt Bhagidar: The anonymous or hidden partner

Haksi: The share of the recommender

Hathavahi: A handwritten notebook

Hundi: Bill of exchange; a credit note

Hundini Nondh: The bill register

Hundiyaman: Foreign exchange

Jahajwado: A shipyard

Jakat: Customs tax; toll-tax; octroi-duty

Jangbar: Zanzibar in Gujarati

Jokhami: Insurer

Jokhmi: A *hundi* with an element of risk

Kagar: A letter

Kaja: Hazards; a problem

Kaskazi: The fair season

Khalas bhata: Crew allowances

Kharwa: Carrier of salt

Khatavahi: Ledger

Kusi: The closing season

Mahajan: A corporate merchant body; term also used for social organization of Hindu merchants like Bhatia Mahajan

Mahant: The chief of the monastery

Malam: A navigator

Malami hisab: Textual collection of charts and diagrams used during the sea voyage

Mandvi or *Madai*: A mart

Math: Monastery

Mathadhish or *Mathadhikari*: The head of the monastery

Mora: The stem of the ship

Mudati hundi: Durational *hundi*; periodic; after a fixed period

Munim: A manager

Nagarsheth : Chief or leading person in city; sheriff; an honorific title given to a prominent Indian merchant, meaning 'the (chief) city merchant'; Head of the Hindu community

Nakhwa: The captain of the ship

Namjog hundi: A *hundi* payable only to the person named

Namu: An art of accountancy or bookkeeping

Naroj: From a particular day; duration

Nava Naroj: The traders' festivals that were conducted down to the sea or Kunbi new year, also denoting the maritime era

Nava naroj: The 'trade new year'; literally meaning 'from the new day'

Nichatia vepari: A retailer

Noori: A rented ship

Nukh: The exogamous division of the caste

Panjari: Lookout men were known as *khalasi*

Pantiada: Trading partnership

Pathan Salamat: Insuring the keel of the ship

Pedhi: A firm

Penth: A copy of *hundi*; letter of advice (in trade)

Per Penth: If *Penth* is lost, the second copy of *hundi* or issued

Petradio or *Petbalio:* Assistant, galley hand. *Petbalio* as the name indicates was an apprentice who was not paid but was given meals to foster his food needs of the stomach i.e. *Pet*

Prassidh: The known partner

Rash: Capital

Rojmel: The cash book; a day-book maintained to note daily transactions

Rokadvahi: The book in which all the ready paid items are recorded

Roznamas: Recorded guidelines for the *Malam*

Saji mausam: The fair season or the open season for doing business

Sarang: Foreman; the trainer of *petbalio*; Second in command in the crew, who also mediated conflicts and organized the division of labour among the *Khalasis*

Satmi: The register which made entries of goods and was used by the insurer and broker

Shahjog hundi: A *hundi* with the word Shah; honest; fit to be accepted, valid, legal; *hundi* payable

Suthar: A carpenter

Tarat hundi: A type of *hundi* wherein immediate payment is made—at once, immediately, presently—to bearer or holder

Tryat: The third person or a party, used especially in the partnership business

Vahi: A book, used by both the merchant and the broker

Vakhar: A warehouse

Vakharwala vepari: A wholesale merchant

Vamani: Damage, with reference to goods on the ship

Vanki: The sample of goods for the sale

Vepari: A merchant

Veparni aanti guti: Twists and turns of the trade

Vijavahi: The separate interest book

Vimo: Insurance

Viradh: Insurance premium

Vohorvu or *vyavahar*: A Gujarati word meaning trade; to transact practically

Arabic, Persian and Swahili terms

al-Qasimi: The singular and adjective of al-Qawasim (pronounced al-Jawasim in Gulf Arabic), who were one of the two principal maritime Arab-ruling families of the Gulf. (The British called them the 'Joasmees')

Amuldari: A council of five elders

'Bab' (babu) Gujarati: A type of ivory meant for the Gujaratis

'Bab Wilaiti': A type of ivory sorted out for foreign merchants

Bawaur or *bahavir*: Those who do *bypar* or *bybashahi* (business)

Chardaghs: Temporary woven reed huts

Qaum-e-Bawahas: An Arabic term which means a business community

Baweer: An Arabic word which means trade

Gendai: A form of ivory kept for the western markets

Ismailias: The Aga Khani Khojas

Ithnashri Khoja: The Twelvers

Jackass or *chakazi*: Raw copal

Jamat Khana: The House of Assembly of the Khojas

Jumbe: A Swahili word for local headman

Kadri: An Arabic word which signifies social status

Kashshi: A Swahili word which means a type of ivory especially meant for the Kachchhis

Kaure: An Arabic word that means cowries

Khalasis: Groups of men working in shipyards as labourers and sailors; the word etymology was derived from the tradition of paying sailors for the season's work in grain with a lump sum known as '*khalas*'

Khete: A Swahili word used for cowries

Khwajah: A Persian word which refers to a rich and respectable man

Masandru: Copal tree in Swahili

Maumins: The believers

Merkani: A Swahili word for American cloth

Mrima: An African term for Mainland

Mtepes: A Zanzibar rafter

Mukhtiyar: The trustee

Musaygum: An Arabic term used to refer to Bania

Muttowas or *Mutawas*: Compellers of obedience; morality police

Nakhoda or *Nakhuda Nakhava*: An Indo-Islamic word used for a ship's captain or owner; the master captain of the ship, shipmate; person in charge of ship's cargo; pilot

Pagazi: A Swahili word used for the porter

Sabins or Ismailias: The Seveners

Salifeh-ul-Ghous (British Spelling): The member of a marine court

Sandrusi: Ripe copal

Sebundy or *Sirbundhi*: The Arab soldiers recruited in the service of the Rao of Kachchh

Shajar El Sandarus: Copal tree

Shamba: Plantation

Sumat: An assembly of elders

Takashima: An Arabic word signifying generosity of the Arabs

Tambun: Pan

Ushru: Government tax

Wahindi: Indian-Muslim merchant

Wahabi: Members of the Muwahhidum (Unitarian and Puritarian) sect of Sunni Islam, founded by Shaikh Muhammed bin 'Abd al-Wahab (1703–92) in Najd; the common term for the Al Saud and their followers who belong to this sect

Wali: The Governor, spelt *vali* in Ottoman-Turkish and Farsi

LIST OF ABBREVIATIONS

1. MSA: Maharashtra State Archives.
2. NA: National Archives
3. SPD: Secret and Political Department
4. PSD: Political and Secret Department
5. PD: Political Department
6. RD: Revenue Department
7. FD: Foreign Department
8. PC: Political Consultation
9. SC: Secret Consultation
10. Vol.: Volume
11. np.: No page number or no publication/place
12. nd.: No date

BIBLIOGRAPHY

A) Primary sources (The Maharashtra State Archives, Mumbai)

Political and Secret Department Diaries from 1800–19.
Political Department Volumes on Kutch 1820–90.
Political Department Volumes on Muscat 1820–90.
Political Department Volumes on Persian Gulf 1820–90.
Political Department Volumes on Zanzibar 1820–90.
Revenue Department Volumes 1820–90.
Administration Reports of the Bombay Presidency from 1860–99.
The Bombay Calendar from 1802–68.

B) Primary sources (The National Archives, New Delhi)

Foreign Department Records on Kutch 1820–90.
Foreign Department Records on Muscat 1820–90.

Foreign Department Records on Persian Gulf 1820–90.
Foreign Department Records on Zanzibar 1820–90.

Most of the ideas and information on the dates and arms trade in chapter two, and on Ratansi Purshottam's trading firm in chapter four, have been derived from the original business and family papers of Ratansi Purshottam. These records are in the form of invoices, private correspondences, cables and bills of lading. William Hills Jr. was a New York-based importer who collaborated with Ratansi Purshottam to trade in Omani dates. His available letters, written to Ratansi, are mainly of the years 1906 and 1907. The letters concerning the arms trade cover the years 1906 to 1908. These letters were posted by London-based arms firm Schwarte and Hammer, Auguste Francotte & Co. of Liege, Belgium, Moritz Magnus Jr. of Hamburg, Germany and B.D. Zisman of Bucharest, Romania, to the Muscat-based firm of Ratansi Purshottam. I have consulted all the letters chronologically to develop a more nuanced understanding of both the dates and arms trade from a global perspective. This archive of private papers of Ratansi Purshottam was developed by Dr Allen Calvin. These records are preserved by Vimal Purecha. He is the direct descendent (great-grandson) of Ratansi. I had interviewed him on three occasions to get a knack of his family's business history.

Similarly, the material on the trading and banking activities of the Goswamis of Mandvi in chapter one is gathered from the original papers of the Dnyangiri, Nirmalgiri Math (monastery) of Mandvi. These untapped records were given to me for consultation by one of the trustees of the *math*, Rajeshgiri Goswami.

Scholars wishing to pursue serious research are welcome to contact the author for details on the endnotes at chhayagoswami@hotmail.com.

Private collection

Records of Dnyangiri Nirmalgiri Math, Mandvi, 1866–68.

Business letters of Ratansi Purshottam.

Documents of Dates Trade: 1905–25.

Documents of Arms Trade: 1906–08.

Gazetteers

'Gujarat Population. Musalmans'. In *Gazetteer of Bombay Presidency,* Vol. IX, Part II. Bombay: Government Central Press, 1899.

'Gujarat Population, Hindus'. In *Gazetteer of Bombay Presidency,* Vol. IX, Part I. Bombay: Government Central Press, 1901.

Campbell, James. *Gazetteer of the Bombay Presidency*, Vol. V. Bombay: Government Central Press, 1880.

Lorimer, J.G. *Gazetteer of the Persian Gulf, Oman and Central Arabia*, Vol. I (Historical), Part I&II. Oxford: G.B. Archives Edition, 1986.

Patel, G.D. *Gujarat State Gazetteer: Kutch District*. Ahmedabad: Government Printing Press, 1971.

Government publications

Burnes, Alexander. 'Report on Architectural and Archeological Remain in the Province of Kachh'. 18 February 1827. Dalpatram Pranjivan Khakhar, issued under the direction of J. Burgees, Archeological Survey of India. Bombay: Government Central Press, 1879.

Burns, Cecil L. *A Monograph on Ivory Carving*. Publication N10262, c.1900, MSA.

Captain Durand, E.L. First Assistant Political Resident, Persian Gulf. 'Notes on the Pearl Fisheries of the Persian Gulf'. In Lieutenant Colonel Ross, E.C. Political Resident Persian Gulf, *Report on the Administration of the Persian Gulf, Selections from the Records of the Government of India*, Publication 14284, MSA. Calcutta: Foreign Department Press, 1878.

Captain Smee, T. and Lt Hardy. 'Observations during a Voyage of Research on the East Coast of Africa from Cape Guadrafui South to the Island of Zanzibar in the H.C. Cruiser Ternate'. In *Transactions of the Bombay Geographical Society*, the secretary (ed.), Vol. VI, (September 1841–May 1844). Bombay: Times Press.

Digest of Local Customs in the Province of Cutch Relating to Trade and Giras. Published under the order of Maharao Shri Khengarjee, Rao of Kutch. Bombay: Education Society's Press, 1885.

LeGrand, G. 'Extract from a Journal Kept during a Tour Made in 1851 through Kutch, Giving Some Account of the Alum Mines of Murrh, and of Changes Effected in 1844 by a Series of Earthquakes, that Appear Hitherto to Have Escaped Notice.' In *Transactions of the Bombay Geographical Society*, Vol. XVI, (June 1860–December 1862). Bombay: Education Society Press, 1863.

Lieutenant Colonel Pelly, Lewis. 'Remarks on the Port of Lingah, the Island of Kishim and the Port of Bunder Abass and its Neighbourhood'. In *Transactions of the Bombay Geographic Society*, Vol. XVII, (January 1863–December 1864). Bombay: Education Society Press.

Lieutenant Postans, T. 'Some Account of the Present State of the Trade, between the Port of Mandvie in Cutch, and the Eastern Coast of Africa'. In *Transactions of the Bombay Geographical Society*, Vol. III, (June 1839–February 1840). Bombay, 1840.

MacAdam, J. 'A Report on a Disease which Prevailed in Parts of Kutch and Kattyawar in the Years 1815 and 1816, Addressed to the Secretary of the Medical Board'. 6 November 1816. In *Anjar*, Publication 383, 1836, MSA.

Pengelley, W.M. 'Remarks on a Portion of Eastern Coast of Arabia between Muscat and Sohar'. In *Transactions of the Bombay Geographical Society*, *Selections from the Records of the Bombay Government*, R. Hughes Thomas (ed.), Vol. 16, XXIV, XXIV–3306,

1856, MSA. Bombay: Bombay Education Society's Press, 1860–62.

Hughes, Thomas R. (ed.). 'Historical, Geographical, and Statistical Memoirs on the Province of Kattywar' In *Selections from the Records of the Bombay Government*, XXXVII. Bombay: Bombay Education Society's Press, 1856.

Raikes, S.N. (ed.). 'Miscellaneous Information, Connected with the Province of Kutch'. In *Selections from the Records of the Bombay Government*, New Series, XV:3315, MSA. Bombay: Bombay Education Society's Press, 1856.

Speke, J.H. 'On the Commerce of Central Africa'.19 January 1860. In *Transactions of the Bombay Geographical Society*, Vol. XV, (May 1858–1860). Bombay: Smith Taylor & Co., 1862.

The Kutch Bhayad Papers, Being a Compilation of the Official Correspondence Relating to the Status of the Bhayads and the Extent and Scope of the British Guarantee Held by Them. Publication 9587A, 1877, MSA.

Published primary sources

Johnston, Alexander Keith. *A Dictionary of Geography, Descriptive, Physical, Statistical and Historical Forming a Complete Gazetteer of the World*. London: Longman, 1864.

Badger, George Percy. *History of the Imams and Seyyids of Oman by Salil Ibn Razik*. London: Hakluyt Society, 1871.

Beardall, William. 'Exploration of the Rufiji River under the Orders of the Sultan of Zanzibar'. In *Proceedings of the Royal Geographical Society and Monthly Record of Geography*, New Monthly Series, 3:11, November 1881.

Buckingham, J. S. *Travels in Assyria, Media and Persia*. 2 vols. London: Henry Colburn, 1829.

Burns, Cecil L. *A Monograph on Ivory Carving*. Publication N10262, c.1900, MSA.

Burton, Richard. *The Lake Regions of Central Africa: A Picture of Exploration*, Volume II. London: Longman, Green, Longman, Roberts, 1860.

Burton, Richard. *Zanzibar City, Island and Coast*. London: Tinsley Brothers, 1872.

Charles, New. *Life, Wanderings, and Labours in Eastern Africa: With an Account of the First Successful Ascent of the Equatorial Snow Mountain, Kilima Njaro: And Remarks upon East African Slavery*. Hodder and Stoughton, 1873.

Elton, Frederic J. *Travels and Researches among the Lake and Mountains of Eastern and Central Africa*. London: John Murray, 1879.

Fraser, James A. *Narrative of a Journey into Khorasan, in the Years 1821 and 1822*. London: Longman & Co., 1825.

Frere, Bartle. *East Africa as a Field for Missionary Labour*. London: John Murray, 1874.

Heude, William. *A Voyage of the Persian Gulf and a Journey Overland from India to England in 1817*. London: Longman, Hurst, Rees, and Orme, 1819.

Jones, Griff. *British in Nyasaland*. London: George Allen and Unwin, 1964.

Lieutenant Colonel Johnson, John. *A Journey from India to England, Persia, Georgia Russia, Poland and Prussia in the Year* 1817. London: Longman Hurst, Rees, Orme, and Brown Paternoster Row, 1818.

Lumsden, Thomas. *A Journey from Merut in India to London, during 1819–20*. London: Black, Kingsbury, Parbury & Allen, 1822.

MacMurdo, James. 'An Account of the Province of Kutch, and of the Countries Lying between Guzerat and the River Indus'. In *Transactions of the Literary Society of Bombay*, Vol. II. London: Richard and Arthur, 1828.

Nathaniel, Isaacs. In *Travels and Adventures in Eastern Africa*. 2 vols. London: Edward Churton, 1836.

Osgood, Joseph. *Notes on Travels or Recollections of Majunga, Zanzibar, Muscat, Aden, Mocha, and Other Easter Ports*. Salem: George Creamer, 1854.

Owen, W. F. W. *Narrative of Voyages to Explore the Shores of Africa, Arabia, and Madagascar*, Vol. II. London: Richard Bentley, 1833.

Palgrave, William Gifford. *Narrative of a Year's Journey through Central and Eastern Arabia, 1862–63*, Vol. II. London & Cambridge: Macmillan & Co., 1865.

Parsons, Abraham. *Travels in Asia and Africa*. London: Longman, Hurst, Rees and Orme, 1808.

Pelly, Lewis. *Journal of a Journey from Persia to India*. Bombay: Education Society Press, 1866.

Raikes, S.N. *Memoir on the Thurr and Parkur Districts of Sindh*. Bombay: Education Society Press, 1859.

Raikes, S.N. *Memoirs and Brief Notes Relative to the Kutch State*. Bombay: Bombay Education Society, 1855.

Ruschenberger, W.S.W. *Narrative of a Voyage Round the World During the Years 1835–36–37, Including a Narrative of an Embassy to the Sultan of Muscat and the King of Siam*, Vol. I. London: Richard Bentley, 1838.

Sadlier, Forster. *Diary of a Journey Across Arabia, 1819*. Bombay: Education Society Press, 1866.

Sheikh, Mansur. *History of Seyyid Said Sultan of Muscat, Together with an Account of the Countries and People of the Shores of the Persian Gulf, Particularly of Wahabees*. London: John Booth, 1819.

Speke, J.H. *Journal of the Discovery of the Source of the Nile*. London, 1863.

Stanley, Henry M. *How I Found Livingstone: Travels Adventures and Discoveries in Central Africa*. London: William Clares and Sons, 1872.

Stanley, Henry M. *In Darkest Africa*. London: Sampson Low, 1890.

Wellsted, J.R.F.R.S. *Travels in Arabia*, Vol. I. London: John Murray, c.1837.

Secondary sources (English)

Aitchison, C.U. *A Collection of Treaties Engagements and Sanad*, Vol. XII, (Part II Kutch). Calcutta: Superintendent Government Printing India, 1909.

Al–Khudari, Mohammed Sulaiman. 'The Sultanate of Muscat and the United States'. Ph.D. diss. University of Essex, 1989.

Allen, Calvin H. Jr. 'Sayyids, Shets and Sultans: Politics and Trade in Masqat under the Al Bu Said, 1785–1914'. Ph.D. diss. University of Washington, 1978.

Alpers, Edward A. *Ivory and Slaves: Changing Pattern of International Trade in East Central Africa in the Late Nineteenth Century*. Berkeley: University of California Press, 1975.

Arnold, Wilson T. *The Persian Gulf*. Oxford: Clarendon Press, 1928.

Arnold, Wright (ed.). *The Bombay Presidency, the United provinces, Punjab etc.* London: The Foreign and Colonial Compiling and Publishing Co., 1917–1920.

Loesser, Arthur. *Men, Women and Pianos: A Social History*. New York: Simon and Schuster, 1954.

Barendse, R.J. *Arabian Sea in 1700–1763: The Western Indian Ocean in the Eighteenth Century*. Netherlands: Brill, 2009.

Bennett, Norman R. *A History of the Arab State of Zanzibar*. London: Methuen, 1978.

Bhacker, Reda M. *Trade and Empire in Muscat and Zanzibar*. London: Routledge, 1992.

Bosworth, Clifford Edmund. *Historic Cities of the Islamic World*. Leiden: Koninklijke Brill NV, 2007.

Braudel, Fernand. *Civilization and Capitalism 15th –18th Century: The Wheels of Commerce*. Los Angeles, California: University of California Press, 1992.

Busch, Briton Cooper. *Britain and the Persian Gulf*. University of California Press, 1967.

Caser-Vine, Pamela. *Oman in History*. London: Immel Publishing, 1995.

Coupland, R. *The Exploitation of East Africa, 1856–1890*. London: Faber and Faber, 1939.

Coupland, R. *East Africa and its Invaders*. Oxford: Clarendon Press, 1938.

Craig, Roell. *The Piano in America, 1890–1940*. Chapel Hill: University of North Carolina Press, 1989.

Craster, J.E.E. *Pemba, the Spice Island of Zanzibar*. London: T. Fisher Unwin, 1913.

Curtin, Philip, Feierman, Thompson, and Jan Vansina. *African History*. London: Longman, 1978.

Cynthia, Moss. *Elephant Memories: Thirteen Years in the Life of an Elephant Family*. New York: William Morrow, 1988.

Das Gupta, Ashin and M. N. Pearson (eds.). *India and the Indian Ocean 1500–1800*. New Delhi: Oxford University Press, 1999.

Das Gupta, Ashin. *Indian Merchants and the Decline of Surat c. 1700–1750*. New Delhi: Manohar, 1994.

Das, Gurucharan. *India Unbound*. New Delhi: Penguin India, 2000.

Duignan, Peter, and Lewis H. Gann. *United States and Africa: A History*. New York: Cambridge University Press, 1987.

Dumper, Michael and Bruce E. Stanley. *Cities of the Middle East and North Africa: A Historical Encyclopedia*. ABC-CLIO, 2007.

Emerson, Ralph Waldo. *The Topical Notebooks of Ralph Waldo Emerson*, Vol. I. University of Missouri Press, 1990.

Engineer, Asghar Ali. *The Muslim Communities of Gujarat: An Exploratory Study of Bohras, Khojas and Memons*. Delhi: Ajanta Publications, 1988.

Enthoven, R.E. *The Tribes and Castes of Bombay*. 3 vols. New Delhi: Asian Educational Services, 1990.

Esposito, John. *Bohras*. In *The Oxford Encyclopedia of the Modern Islamic World*, 1995.

Fattah, Hala. *The Politics of Regional Trade in Iraq, Arabia, and the Gulf*. New York: SUNY Press, 1997.

Freeman, Grenville. *The East African Coast*. Oxford: Clarendon Press, 1962.

Gerhard, Emmanuel Lenski. *Power and Privilege: A Theory of Social Stratifications*. UNC Press Books, 1966.

Gijsbert, Oonk. *The Karimjee Jivanjee Family Merchant Princes of East Erica 1800–2000*. Amsterdam: Pallas Publications, 2009.

Gregory, Robert G. *Quest for Equality: Asian Politics in East Africa, 1900–1967*. New Delhi: Orient Longman, 1993.

Hooda, V.N. *Khoja Gnanti'nu Gorav*. Bombay, 1927.

Ingham, Kenneth. *A History of East Africa*. London: Longmans, Green and Co., 1965.

Ingram, W.H. *Zanzibar: Its History and Its People*. London: H. F. and G. Witherby, 1931.

Kinney, Thomas A. *The Carriage Trade: Making Horse-Drawn Vehicles in America*. Baltimore, 2004.

Landen, Robert G. *Oman since 1856: Disruptive Modernization in a Traditional Arab Society*. Princeton, New Jersey: Princeton University Press, 1967.

Langer, William L. *An Encyclopedia of World History*. London: George G. Harrap, n. d.

Lenski, Gerhard. *Power and Privilege*. New York: McGraw Hill, 1966.

Lodhi, Abdul Aziz Y. *A Small Book on Zanzibar*. Sweden: Annette Rydstrom for Fattares Bokmaskin, 1979.

Lombard, Denys and Jean Aubin (eds.). *Asian Merchants and Businessmen in the Indian Ocean and the China Sea*. New Delhi: Oxford University Press, 2000.

Louis, Elson. *History of American Music in 1904*. Reprinted by Kissinger Publishing, 2005.

Mangat, J.S. *Asians in East Africa c.1886–1945*. Oxford: Clarendon Press, 1969.

Marsh, Zoë and Kingsnorth. *An Introduction to the History of East Africa*. Cambridge University Press, 1957.

Martineau, John. *The Life and Correspondence of Sir Bartle Frere*, Vol. II. London: John Murray, 1895.

Maxwell, Marius. *Stalking Big Game with a Camera in Equatorial Africa with a Monograph on the African Elephant*. London: William Heinemann, 1925.

Miles, S.B. *The Countries and Tribes of the Persian Gulf*. 2 vols. London: Harrison & Sons, 1919.

Mohammed, Amir A. *A Short History of Zanzibar*. Zanzibar: Al Khariya Press, 1991.

Nadri, G.A. *Eighteenth Century Gujarat: The Dynamics of its Political Economy, 1750–1800*. Leiden: Brill, 2009.

Nair, P.R. *Bills (A Reference Book)*. Malad–Mumbai: Development Co–Operative Bank Training Centre, n.d.

Nightingale, Pamela. *Trade and Empire in Western India 1784–1806*. Cambridge: Cambridge University Press, 1970.

Pearce, F.B. *Zanzibar: the Island Metropolis of Eastern Africa*. London: T. Fisher Unwin, 1920.

Prestholdt, Jeremy. *Domesticating the World: African Consumerism and the Genealogies of Globalization*. University of California Press, 2008.

Risso, Patricia. *Oman and Muscat an Early Modern History*. London: Croom Helm, 1986.

Roberts, Edmund. *Embassy to the Eastern Courts of Cochin–China, Siam, and Muscat in the U.S. Sloop of war Peacock, during the Years 1832–34*. Delaware: SR Scholarly Resources, 1972.

Ruete, Emily. *Memories of an Arabian Princess from Zanzibar*. Zanzibar: Gallery Publications, 1998.

Saldanha, J.A. *The Persian Gulf Precis*, Vol. III. Buckinghamshire, England: Archives Edition, 1986.

Salvadori, Cynthia. *We Came in Dhows*. 3 vols. Kenya: Paperchase, 1996.

Seidenberg, Dana April. *Mercantile Adventures: The World of East African Asians 1750–1985*. New Delhi: New Age International History, 1996.

Sheikh, Abdalla Saleh Fars. *Seyyid Said Bin Sultan, the Joint Ruler of Oman and Zanzibar*, 1804–1856. 1986.

Sheriff, Abdul. *Slaves, Spices & Ivory in Zanzibar*. Oxford: James Currey, 1987.

Sheriff, Abdul. *The History and Conservation of Zanzibar Stone Town*. London: James Curry, 1995.

Sheriff, Abdul. *Zanzibar under Colonial Rule*. London: James Currey, 1991.

Simpson, Edward. *Merchants, 'Saints' and Sailors: the Social Production of Islamic Reform in a Port Town of Western India*. Ph.D. diss. University of London, 2001.

Skeet, Ian. *Muscat and Oman: The End of an Era*. London: Faber and Faber, 1974.

Standish, John F. *Persia and the Gulf: Retrospect and Prospect*. New York: St. Martin's Press, 1998.

Subramanian, Lakshmi. *Indigenous Capital and European Expansion: Bombay, Surat and the West Coast*. USA: Oxford University Press, 1996.

Tajddin, Mumtaz Ali. *101 Ismaili Heroes*, Vol. I. Karachi: Islamic Book Publisher, 2003.

Thacker, V.R. *Cutch: Its Coin and Heritage*. Bhuj, Kutch: Alpa Arts, 1985.

Tod, James. *Travels in Western India*. Delhi: Oriental Publishers, 1971.

Wendell, Phillips. *Oman: A History*. Beirut: Librairie Du Liban, 1971.

Wesley Gilbert. 'Our Man in Zanzibar: Richard Waters, American Consul (1837–1845)'. Unpublished thesis for the Degree of Bachelor of Arts, Wesleyan University. Middletown, Connecticut, April 2011.

Whitely, W.H. (trans.). *Maisha Ya Hamed Bin Muhammed El Murjebi Yanni Tippu Tib*. Dar-es-Salaam, 1974.

Wilkinson, John. *The Imamate Tradition of Oman*. Cambridge: Cambridge University Press.

Williams, Rushbrook. *The Black Hills: Kutch in History and Legend*. London: Weidenfeld and Nicolson, 1958.

Ylvisaker, Marguerite. *Lamu in the Nineteenth Century*. Boston University: African Research Studies Center, 1979.

Zahlan, Rosemarie Said. *The Making of the Modern Gulf States*. Oman: Unwin Hyman, 1989.

Secondary Sources (Gujarati)

Acharya, Gunvantrai. *Dariyalal*. Ahmedabad: Gurjar Publication, 1956.

Dholakia, Bachubhai and Chandrakant Chothani. *Omanma Gujaratio Ni Asmita*. Ghatkoper, Mumbai: Kalyan Printing Press, 1991.

Joshi, Narendrakumar. *Bhatigar Bhomka Kutch*. Ahmedabad: Nirav Prakashan, 1977.

Karani, Dulerai. *Kutch Kaladhar*, Part II. Mumbai: Suman Prakashan, 1987.

Karani, Dulerai. *Kachchhno Cromwell Jamadar Fatehmohammed*. np., nd.

Naygandhi, Jairamdas Jethabhai. *Kutchno Brihad Itihas*. Ahmedabad: Aditya Mrudanalay, 1926.

Naygandhi, Jairamdas Jethabhai. *Kutchnu Arthshastra Chalan Ane Hundiyaman*, Part I. Ahmedabad: Aditya Mrudanalay, 1934.

Oza, Ishwarlal. *Mirja Maharao Raydhanji Bijana Samay nu Kutch, 1778–1813*. Ahmedabad: Swati Printing Press, 1986.

Patel, Bhailalbhai D. *Geography of Africa and India*. n. p.: Printer Jayantilal Patel, 1932.

Patel, Harjivan Meghji. *Kutchma Dustavej Tatha Namu Lakhvani Paddhati*, Part 1. Ahmedabad: Anglo Vernacular Printing Press, 1891.

Sampat, Dungarshi Dharamshi. *Kutchnu Vepartantra*. Karachi: 1945.

Sampat, Dungarshi Dharamshi. *Sagar Kathao*. Jamnagar: R.R. Shethni Company, 1947.

Thakkur, Jairam V. Naryanji. *Jangbar Bhatia Pravas*. Ahmedabad, 1893.

Vacha, Ratanji Faramji. *Mumbaino Bahar*, Book I. Bombay: Union Press, 1874.

Selected articles from books, journals and magazines

Alpers, Edward A. 'Gujarat and the Trade of East Africa, c. 1500–1800'. In *The International Journal of African Historical Studies*, 9:1. Boston University African Studies Center, 1976.

Amiji, Hatim. 'The Bohras of East Africa'. In *Journal of Religion in Africa*, 7:1. 1975.

Anderson, J.N.D. 'The Isma'ili Khojas of East Africa: A New Constitution and Law for the Community'. In *Middle Eastern Studies*, Vol. 1. 1964.

Arnold, Wilson. 'A Periplus of the Persian Gulf'. In *The Royal Geographical Society, The Geographical Journal*, 69:3. 1927.

Barendse, R.J. 'Trade and State in the Arabian Seas: A Survey from the Fifteenth to the Eighteenth Century'. In *Journal of World History*, 11:2. University of Hawaii Press, 2000.

Beachey, R.W. 'The East African Ivory Trade in the Nineteenth Century'. In *The Journal of African History*, 8:2. Cambridge University Press, 1967.

Benjamin, N. 'Trading Activities of Indians in East Africa (with Special Reference to Slavery) in the Nineteenth Century. In *The Indian Economic and Social History Review*, XXXV 4. New Delhi: Sage Publications, 1998.

Bennett, Bronson. 'Pearls Without Price: The Rise and Fall of a Sometimes Precious Gem'. Delivered to The Chicago Literary Club, 10 April 2000.

Bennett, Norman. *France and Zanzibar*, 1844–1860, Part II. In *The International Journal of the African Studies*, VII #1. 1974.

Bennett, Norman. *France and Zanzibar, 1844–1860*, Part I. In *The International Journal of the African Studies*, VI:4. 1973.

Bhinde, Aashish. Mumbai Panjarapole: Jivdayanu Dheyay Jyan Varshothi Jadvayu Che'. *Rangberangi, Mumbai Samachar*. Mumbai, 2002.

Bouchon, Genevieve and Denys Lombard. 'Indian Ocean in the Fifteenth Century'. In *India and the Indian Ocean*, Das Gupta, Ashin and M. N. Pearson (eds.). New Delhi: Oxford University Press, 1999.

Campbell , Rob. 'Tuskers, Trade, and Trypanosomes: The Ecologies of the Victorian Parlor'. In *Agrarian Studies Colloquium*. Yale, 2003.

Captain Dallons, P. 'Zanzibar in 1804'. In *The East African Coast*, G.S.P. Freeman (ed.). Grenville, Oxford: Clarendon Press, 1962.

Cariño, Micheline and Mario Monteforte. 'An Environmental History of Nacre and Pearls: Fisheries, Cultivation and Commerce'. *In Global Environment: A Journal of History and Natural and Social Sciences*, 2:3. 2009.

Das Gupta, Ashin. 'India and the Indian Ocean 1500–1800'. In *India and the Indian Ocean*, Das Gupta, Ashin and M. N. Pearson (eds.). New Delhi: Oxford University Press, 1997.

Das Gupta, Ashin. 'The Ship-owning Merchants of Surat, c. 1700.' In *Asian Merchants and Businessmen in the Indian Ocean and China Sea*, Lombard, Denys and Jean Aubin (eds.). Delhi: Oxford University Press, 2000.

Malcarne, Donald L. 'Ivoryton, Connecticut: The Ivory Industry and Voluntary and Involuntary Migration in the Late Nineteenth Century'. In *North American Archaeologist*, 22:3. 2001.

Dutia, Dwarkadas. 'Namankit Sahasik Kom Bhatiaoni Choriyasi Nukho, Bhattiona KulGor JasaBhate

Lakhelu Rasprad Bayan'. In *Kachchh Sata Deepotsavi Visheshank*. ed. Bhatia, Leena. Mumbai, 1991.

Egbert, Henrik. 'Entrepreneurial Advantages and Disadvantages of Belonging'. In *GeoJournal 46*. Netherlands: Kluwer Academic Publishers, 1998.

Eilts, Hermann F. 'Ahmad Bin Naamans Mission to the United States in 1840: The Voyage of Al-Sultanah to New York City'. In *Essex Institute Historical Collections*. XCVIII:4. Salem, Massachusetts, 1962.

Engineer, Asghar Ali. 'A Special Issue on Bohras, Khojas and Memons'. In *Islamic Perspective: A Biannual Journal*, Vol. I. Bombay: Institute of Islamic Studies, January 1988.

Esposito, John. 'Bohras'. In *The Oxford Encyclopedia of the Modern Islamic World*, 1995.

Gilbert, Erik. 'Coastal East Africa and the Western Indian Ocean: Long-Distance Trade, Empire, Migration, and Regional Unity, 1750–1970'. In *The History Teacher*, 36:1, 2002.

Goffman, Erving. 'Status Inconsistency and Preference for Change in Power'. In *American Sociological Review*, 22, 1957.

Gommans, Jos. 'The Horse Trade in Eighteenth-Century South Asia'. In *Journal of the Economic and Social History of the Orient*, 37:3, 1994.

Gundara, Jagdish S. 'Aspects of Indian Culture in Nineteenth Century Zanzibar'. In *Journal of South Asia, South Asian Studies*, Indian Ocean Issue, New Series, Vol. III, 1980.

History and Natural and Social Sciences, 2:3, 2009.

Ibrahim, Farhana. 'Narrating the Frontier: Perspective of Kachchh'. In *Frontier Scouts and Border Crossers, Sarai Reader,* 2007.

Kellenbenz, Hermann. 'German Trade Relations with the Indian Ocean from the End of the Eighteenth Century to 1870'. In *Journal of Southeast Asian Studies*, 13:1. Cambridge University Press, 1982.

Kellenbenz, Hermann. 'Shipping and Trade between Hamburg–Bremen and the Indian Ocean, 1870–1914'. In *Journal of Southeast Asian Studies*, 13:2. Cambridge University Press, 1982.

Kikambo, I.N. 'The East Africa Coast and Hinterland, 1845–80'. In *UNESCO General History of Africa VI*, J. F. Adeajayi (ed.). California: University of California Press, 1989.

Lam, Helen B. 'The Indian Merchant'. In *Traditional India: Structure and Change, The Journal of American Folklore*, 71:281, (July–September, 1958).

Machado, Pedro. 'Cloths of a New Fashion: Indian Ocean Networks of Exchange and Cloth Zones of Contact in Africa and India in the Eighteenth and Nineteenth Centuries'. In *How India Clothed the World: The World of South Asian Textiles, 1500–1850*. Riello, Giorgio and Tirthankar Roy (eds.). The Hague: Brill Publishers, 2009.

Machado, Pedro. 'A Regional Market in a Globalised Economy: East Central and South Eastern Africans, Gujarati Merchants and the Indian Textile Industry in the Eighteenth and Nineteenth Centuries'. In a Conference on Cotton Textiles. Pune, (18–20 December, 2005).

Markovits, Claude. 'Indian Merchant Networks Outside India in the Nineteenth and Twentieth Centuries: A Preliminary Survey'. In *Modern Asian Studie*, Gordon Johnson (ed.), 33:4. UK: Cambridge University Press, 1999.

Martin, Peter J. 'The Zanzibar Clove Industry'. In *Economic Botany*, 45:4. (October–December, 1991).

Moreman, Tim. 'The Arms Trade and the North–West Frontier Pathan Tribes, 1890–1914'. In *Journal of Imperial and Commonwealth History*, 22:2, 1994.

Munro, Forbes. 'Shipping Subsidies and Railway Guarantees: William Mackinnon, Eastern Africa and the Indian Ocean, 1860–93'. In *The Journal of African History*, 28:2. Cambridge University Press, 1987.

Nanji, Azim and Farhad Daftary. 'Ismaili Sects—South Asia'. In *Encyclopedia of Modern Asia*, Levinson, David and Karen Christensen (eds.), Vol. 3. New York, 2002.

Newitt, M.D.D. 'East Africa and Indian Ocean Trade, 1500–1800'. In *India and the Indian* Ocean, Das Gupta, Ashin and M. N. Pearson (eds.). New Delhi: Oxford University Press, 1999.

Oonk, Gijsbert. 'Gujarati Business Communities in East Africa Success and Failure Stories'. In *Economic and Political Weekly,* Vol. 20, 14 May 2005.

Oonk, Gijsbert. 'Negotiating Hinduism in East Africa, 1860–1960'. In *Transforming Cultures eJournal*, 3:2, 2008.

Pandhi Manubhai. 'Kachchhnu Vahanvatu'. In *Art, Culture and Natural History of Kutch*. Vadodara, Museum and Picture Gallery, 1976–77.

Penard, Jean Claude. 'The Ismaili Presence in East Africa: A Note on its Commercial History and Community Organization'. In *Asian Merchants and Businessmen in the Indian Ocean and the China Sea*, Lombard, Denys and Jean Aubin (eds.). New Delhi: Oxford University Press, 2000.

Peterson, J.E. 'Oman Diverse Society'. In *Middle East Journal*, 58:1, p.39.

Philip Curtain. *Cross–cultural Trade in World History*, pp. 26–32, 57–60. New York: Cambridge University Press, 1984, 2004.

Prakash, Om. 'The Indian Maritime Merchant, 1500–1800'. In *Between the Flux and Facts of Indian History: Papers in Honor of Dirk Kolff, Journal of the Economic and Social History of the Orient*, 47:3. Leiden: Brill, 2004.

Ramaiya, K.L., Swai, A.B., McLarty, D.G., Bhopal, R.S., and K. G Alberti. 'Prevalence of Diabetes and Cardiovascular Disease Risk Factors: Hindu Indian sub communities'. In *British Medical Journal*, 11:303. Dar-es-Salaam, Tanzania, August 1991.

Ray, Rajat Kanta. 'Asian Capital in the Age of European Domination: The Rise of the Bazaar, 1800–1914'.

In *Modern Asian Studies*, 29:3, pp. 547–590, July 1995.

Salim, A.I. 'The East Africa Coast and Hinterland, 1800–45'. In *UNESCO General History of Africa VI*, J. F. Adeajayi (ed.). California: University of California Press, 1989.

Schneider, Jane. 'The Anthropology of Cloth'. In *Annual Review of Anthropology*, Vol. 16, 1987.

Sharma, G.D. 'Vyapari and Mahajans in Western Rajasthan'. In *Essays in Medieval Indian Economic History*, Satish Chandra (ed.). New Delhi: Munshi Manoharlal, 1987.

Simpson, Edward. 'Apprenticeship in Western India'. In *Journal of the Royal Anthropological Institute*, New Series, Vol. 12, 2006.

Spear, Thomas. 'Early Swahili History Reconsidered'. In *International Journal of African Historical Studies*, Vol. 33, 2000.

Subramanian, Lakshmi. 'Banias and the British: The Role of Indigenous Credit in the Process of Imperial Expansion in Western India in the Second Half of the Eighteenth Century'. In *Modern Asian Studies,* 21:3. Cambridge University Press, 1987.

Sunseri, Thaddeus. 'The Political Ecology of the Copal Trade in the Tanzanian Coastal Hinterland c. 1820–1905'. In *The Journal of African History*, Vol. 48. Cambridge University Press, Colorado State University, 2007.

Sweet, L.E. 'Pirates or Polities? Arab Societies of the Persian or Arabian Gulf, 18th Century'. In *Ethno History*, 11:3. Duke University Press, 1964.

Tominaga, Chizuko. *Indian Immigrants and the East African Slave Trade*. Osaka, Japan: Shun Sato and Eisei Kurimoto, 1996.

Vardhrajan Lotika. 'Traditions of Indigenous Navigation in Gujarat'. In *Journal of South Asia, South Asian Studies*, Indian Ocean Issue, New Series, 3:1, 1980.

Webster and Unomah. 'East Africa the Expansion of Commerce'. In *Cambridge History of Africa*, Flint, John E (ed.). Cambridge: Cambridge University Press, 1980.

Wolcott, Susan. 'What Can Colonial Indian Sowcars Teach Us About Modern Microfinance?' JEL classification: O16; O17; N25, 2009.

Wright, Arnold (ed.). *The Bombay Presidency, the United Provinces, Punjab etc.* London: The Foreign and Colonial Compiling and Publishing Co., 1917–1920.